THE IMMIGRANTS' INFLUENCE
ON WILSON'S PEACE POLICIES

THE IMMIGRANTS' INFLUENCE ON WILSON'S PEACE POLICIES

EDITED BY

JOSEPH P. O'GRADY

UNIVERSITY OF KENTUCKY PRESS / 1967

To the
American Immigrant:
A Brave Man

ACKNOWLEDGMENTS

Portions of this book have been published previously as indicated below: A version of Chapter I appeared earlier as "German-Americans and Wilson's Peacemaking" in *Social Justice Review*, LVI (June-September, 1963), 93-96, 126-30, 166-71.

A shorter version of a portion of Chapter II appeared as "Irish-Americans, Woodrow Wilson, and Self-Determination; a Re-evaluation" in the *Records* of the American Catholic Historical Society of Philadelphia, LXXIV (September, 1963), 154-73.

Chapter III appeared as "The British-Americans and Wilson's Peacemaking," in the *Duquesne Review*, IX (Spring-Fall, 1964), 115-36.

Chapter IX originally appeared as "H. A. Miller and the Mid-European Union of 1918," in *Slavic Review*, XVI (1957), 472-88.

Professor George Bárány wishes to acknowledge grants from the American Philosophical Society and the University of Denver which enabled him to do research at the National Archives and the Hoover Institute of War, Revolution and Peace. Professor Bárány would also like to express appreciation to Professor Daniel M. Smith of the University of Colorado for the permission to use his photostats of Lansing's private memoranda from the manuscript division of the Library of Congress.

The editor wishes to acknowledge the aid of the history department and the administration of La Salle College in the initial lecture series from which this book developed; the assistance of Brother Daniel Bernian, the President of the college, in contributing to the cost of publication; the

viii ACKNOWLEDGMENTS

special encouragement and interest in the completed project shown by Professors Otakar Odlozilik and Victor Mamatey; the generous forebearance of the individual contributors; the La Salle College Secretarial Services under the direction of Mrs. Rita Kieffer; the contribution of Mrs. Helen Hartley, whose skill as a typist is overshadowed only by her patience as a reader of difficult manuscripts; and to my wife who lived the ordinary life of housewife and mother without the assistance of a husband who was thus able to linger many hours with his books.

CONTENTS

INTRODUCTION

JOSEPH P. O'GRADY

The intellectual historian is interested in many aspects of the past but he wishes, above all else, to discover ideas that have motivated and characterized mankind: to identify the "spirit of the times" that defines an age. In like manner the student of the diplomatic past can divide American diplomatic history into two periods: the nineteenth century, when realism was the "spirit" of America's foreign relations, and the twentieth century, when idealism took its place.

Throughout the nineteenth century, America experts on foreign affairs pursued a policy that balanced aims and means. They sought only what American power could guarantee, no more and no less. They believed that certain facts of geography determined what policy the United States would practice and that popular opinion had no great part to play in the formation or implementation of policy.

The successes of the nineteenth-century American policy were due to its recognition of certain facts of international life. In the first place, even if her leaders had desired it, America did not possess sufficient power to project her aims beyond her own immediate geographic vicinity. Second, the Monroe Doctrine precluded interference in European affairs. In addition, no need for interference developed; American interest in Europe—the maintenance of a relatively secure balance of power—was never really jeopardized from 1815 to 1914. At the same time, although technology progressed rapidly, especially during the latter part of the century, it remained sufficiently primitive to permit Americans to live without interference in their own world and to prevent them from attempting to include the world beyond their immediate boundaries within their field of interest. Finally, although Americans were easily aroused over questions of freedom throughout the globe, they found themselves, both before and after the Civil War, involved in enough domestic and internal questions to absorb most of their energies. In spite of their inherent idealism, the American people generally accepted the fact that they had not the time, technology, desire, energy, or need to follow any other foreign policy but that which proposed to defend their immediate frontiers, one that would tie aims to real or at least potential power.

The transitional years from 1890 to 1912 saw the end of this fortunate situation. The factors that had supported the old policy slowly disappeared. During the 1890s many Americans began to believe that their country possessed almost unlimited power, which, potentially at least, could project American interests to the four corners of the globe. At the same time powerful voices cried for American involvement in the world beyond the ocean. Strangely enough the great industrial development that had absorbed American energies for the thirty years following the Civil War now reinforced this new trend as the search for potential markets and sources of raw materials covered the earth. As the great west was conquered and settled, as technology rapidly compressed the earth, the old favorable European power balance slowly crumbled. America by 1907 no longer had the desire or the ability to remain uninterested in the outside world. She had emerged, for all practical purposes, as a world power.

At this crossroad the progressive spirit captured the American public imagination. In its philosophical foundations progressivism owed much to the populists and other reforming elements of the previous decade, especially in its emphasis upon social responsibilities and the need to moralize society. The moralism and idealism that characterized the progressive impact upon domestic American political, economic, social, and religious life also affected America's foreign policy. After years of fighting for legal devices which would drive the political bosses from power, and against the economic power of the new aristocracy of industrialists, it seemed only natural to apply the same sense of morality and Christian charity to the poor of the world. In this way Americans justified imperialism with the cloth of honor and humanitarianism. The psychological prescription was filled. Americans would enter the struggle of nations to extend their areas of influence; yet they would do so, not for realistic reasons, but for idealistic ones. The arrival of Wilson as a spokesman for both the progressives and the new idealists in foreign policy climaxed the new developments.

Some diplomatic historians contend that this shift from realism to idealism followed rapidly on the heels of the Spanish-American War and that John Hay's occupancy of the State Department marked the change. However, the battle actually continued throughout the administrations of Theodore Roosevelt and his handpicked successor, William Taft. Not until the election of 1912 and the victory of Woodrow Wilson did the idealistic approach emerge victorious, to mark the end of an era. The appointment of William J. Bryan, the personification of morality, to the State Department pointed the direction of the future, and Wilson's own speeches shortly after he assumed office clearly stated that henceforth morality would determine America's approach to foreign policy.

The election of 1912 marked the end of the transition from the nineteenth century to the twentieth, from the old diplomacy to the new, from the age when public opinion failed to influence policy formulation to one in which it seemed to be a dominant consideration. But, in truth, how much has public opinion influenced policy in the last fifty years? The evidence offered by the advocates of idealism in foreign policy is hardly conclusive. In an effort to provide a documented answer to this question, the editor undertook the direction of a cooperative comparative study of immigrant groups and their efforts to influence the peacemaking policies of Woodrow Wilson at the end of World War I.

A number of considerations prompted the cooperative and comparative approach. The problem of language alone would have made it impossible for any single person to undertake such a study. The study of an immigrant group is a highly specialized field; no one scholar could amass the knowledge necessary to analyze eleven such groups in depth. A comparative analysis seemed appropriate for two reasons. First, in both published and unpublished material, authors have for some time claimed for various immigrant groups a degree of influence upon Wilson that others have hotly contested. It was hoped that, by studying several groups together and comparing their successes and failures, a more accurate evaluation of just how much influence they had upon him could be obtained. Second, only by comparing methods used by the various groups and evaluating their effectiveness can one arrive at an adequate understanding of the relationship of public opinion to foreign policy.

Four major factors influenced our selection of this particular topic. First, President Wilson at least publicly welcomed pressure from the "people"; in fact, the concept that the "people" should rule was a cardinal principle of his political philosophy. It may be assumed that those groups attempting to influence policy would have greater effectiveness under a President who approved of such efforts. Second, by this time (1914–1918) immigrant groups were skilled in organizing their attempts to influence politicians. The more established groups had had long experience, and the newcomers learned the techniques rapidly. Third, events in Europe during the war dramatically strengthened the view that freedom was possible for a vast number of the world's peoples. Finally, the close balance of power among political leaders and parties made it necessary for political leaders to cater to the desires of groups that they thought might tip an election. This situation, forming an almost ideal historical basis for immigrant group influence on policy, can be studied as an example of the influence of public opinion on foreign affairs.

The study began as a lecture series, sponsored by the history department of La Salle College, in honor of Maurice Francis Egan, '74, during the academic year 1962–1963. Seven of the lectures (those concerning the Irish, the British, the Germans, the Czechs, the Slovaks and Ruthenians, the Poles, and the Jews) were subsequently rewritten for publication. To these were added studies on the Italians, Magyars, South Slavs, and the Mid-European Union. The findings of these studies become most dramatic when placed in their proper chronological framework.

The attempts to influence Wilson's peacemaking policies began shortly after the war opened in Europe, three years before America's entry. In fact one could claim that the beginning even preceded the war; many groups were organized years before 1914 (the Irish and Germans before the Civil War), and many old-country politicians had traveled through the United States to win immigrant support for this or that party in the old country. Such activities, however, were mere preparations, for the war overnight created undreamed-of opportunities that did not go undetected.

Almost upon the outbreak of the war in early August, 1914, the immigrants sensed the need for organization.

On August 30 the American Zionists met to select Louis Brandeis as their leader in the fight for a Jewish homeland. Before the year ended he had informed Wilson of his new position. In September the Slovaks, forced by Count Michael Károlyi's spring visit to examine their very existence, issued their "Memorandum of the Slovak League of America," which called for autonomy for their fellow countrymen in Europe. Interestingly enough at this early date they did not demand independence. Seven months later the Czechs formed the Bohemian National Alliance in Cleveland with the aid of Herbert A. Miller, an American citizen and old friend of the Czechs in America. Miller had traveled to Prague in 1912 to confer with Professor Thomas Masaryk, and upon his return published numerous articles about the need for change in Central Europe, which led to his participation in the creation of the organization that would eventually offer Masaryk indispensable aid. In the same month Franko Potočnjak, who had arrived in January specifically to organize the South Slavs, participated in a convention at the La Salle Hotel in Chicago. The delegates demanded the destruction of the Austro-Hungarian Empire and the creation of a democratic Serb-Croat-Slovene state in the Balkans. In the next month the South Slavs made a direct attempt to influence the peace settlements when they asked the Russian ambassador in Washington to inform his government that, since they considered Russia the protector of the Slavs, they wanted Russia to intervene in the negotiations then underway to bring Italy into the war, so that Slavs would not live under Italian rule. But the Treaty of London was signed without Russian action.

With this basic organizational work completed by the summer of 1915, the Central Europeans began their attempt to influence policy. The South Slavs met in Pittsburgh again in July and sent the resulting resolution to Wilson. At the same time they organized the Yugoslav National Council in Washington, which published numerous pamphlets and other items of propaganda. In October, 1915, the Slovaks and Czechs were able to organize a joint meeting and even produced the Cleveland Pact, which called for an independent Czech-Slovak state with full national autonomy for Slovakia. They also opened their propaganda machinery in New York, the Czech-Slav Press Bureau under Charles Pergler. In effect an American citizen, born in Bohemia, began to propagandize for a foreign state that did not exist. And all the while the Czechs, Slovaks, and South Slavs sent such large sums of money to their respective national committees in London and Paris that both the Czechoslovakia National Council and the Yugoslavia National Committee remained financially independent of the allied governments throughout the war.

Such activity was not limited to what may be termed allied groups; in the days before the American declaration of war those sympathetic to the Central Powers were also active. The German-Americans, well organized and ably led, fought a great propaganda war with the British government, while the Irish in America cheered for the German war machine, on which rested their hope for Irish freedom. Even the Hungarians supported the Central Powers against the traditional foe, Russia, but as early as January, 1916, they publicly avowed their loyalty to their adopted country in a meeting in Madison Square Garden. The Germans and Irish did likewise.

Both sides relied upon typical methods of influencing public policy in a democracy. But even in late 1915 and early 1916 it was becoming evident that such methods did not necessarily gain the desired results. The case of the Poles is significant. The first meeting between Ignace Jan Paderewski and Colonel Edward M. House on November 12,

1915, marked the beginning of a relationship in which the artist was able to convince the politician that Poland was a special case, that the great powers would have to make allowance for her, and that she must have her independence. Although the Poles in America held public demonstrations and used the other normal devices to influence policy, such measures accomplished little in comparison with Paderewski's influence on House.

This raises the question why Paderewski was so successful. It might be argued that the demonstrations won House to the belief that Poland deserved special handling; if so, it is strange that House gave such early recognition to the Poles and not to the others, since they all used the same methods. Some could argue that he accepted the Poles because of the history of American sympathy for their cause that stretched back to the American Revolution; but the Irish had at least as much sympathy, if not more, as the Polish issue had arisen only occasionally in American history while the Irish question was virtually constant after 1848. Nor can one claim that House acted to win the Polish vote. All the immigrant groups voted, and there were more Irish and Germans than Poles. One could dismiss these since the Germans voted Republican anyway, while the Irish would vote Democratic no matter what happened. But what about the others without such liabilities? It seems strange that House and Wilson would cultivate the Poles and ignore the Czechs, Slavs, and Jews. The South Slavs did not discover how important they were to the Wilson cause in the California election until it was over; and there is no indication that the administration accepted the Jewish position for political reasons. In addition, the argument that Wilson's October speech was a direct appeal to the Poles seems weak, since the speech itself contained appeals to all Europeans in

America and was not specifically tied to the American election.

Up to 1916 the Poles and the Jews were successful in reaching House and Wilson because both these men had inclinations to accept what Paderewski and Brandeis told them. Thus, the appeals to the public and the pressure created by politics failed greatly to influence the course of events, while the personal contact with people in positions of responsibility succeeded.

Although this must have been recognized in immigrant circles by the end of 1916, the knowledge did not discourage their public activities. The South Slavs held their congress on November 29 and hopefully sent Wilson their resolutions urging him to recognize the committee in London as the spokesman for all South Slavs.

Meanwhile, the Poles and the Jews were making the most of their opportunities. In early December Rabbi Stephen S. Wise spoke to House concerning the future plans of Zionism. A month later House asked Paderewski for a detailed memo on the Polish question, which he proposed to give to Wilson. Fifteen days later—three months before the declaration of war—Wilson publicly endorsed the concept of Polish freedom and even called for sovereignty based upon the consent of the people.

On April 2 Wilson asked Congress to declare war, and on April 6 Congress acted. Some immigrants immediately intensified their activities, while others were virtually at a standstill. The Irish suddenly had to shift their meager hopes from Germany to America, while the Germans found themselves in a dilemma. For three years they had worked against England and France, but now they faced the fatherland. Both groups quickly pledged their loyalty to America, but in the eyes of the government both were suspect. In fact, American reaction struck a blow at Germanism in America from which it never recovered.

Meanwhile, the Czechs, under Pergler's direction, convinced Senator William S. Kenyon and Congressman Adolph J. Sabath to introduce resolutions in their respective chambers in favor of an independent Bohemian Slovak state. Oddly enough, these never reached the floor of either the Senate or the House—an interesting point in view of the later success of the Irish in prompting congressional action.

The American entry also caused the French to encourage various allied nationalities to recruit American immigrants for their new armies, then emerging in France. The Polish plan received quick approval from Wilson's administration, mainly because of the strong backing of House. When Milan Štefánik arrived in Washington to complete the same arrangement for the Czechs, the leaders of the Bohemian National Alliance and the Slovak League informed Secretary of State Robert Lansing, who, however, failed to recognize the mission. Štefánik, as a major in the French Army, went to Ambassador Jean Jusserand, who finally secured approval for the mission on the condition that the recruiting be accomplished without publicity. Professor Mamatey claims that Štefánik's mission failed, when sponsored by the immigrants, because they could not move Wilson and American public opinion. The success of the Poles can only be attributed to their contact with House.

Much the same fate met a similar attempt on the part of the South Slavs. When the United States entered the war, the South Slavs in America cheered the news and continued to organize conventions. Such activity, however, could not hide the basic division between those who wanted a monarchy and those who wanted a republic. The Declaration of Corfu, which Dr. Ante Trumbić and Nikola Pašić signed on July 20, called for a monarchy; this so intensified the disagreement that Pašić sent an unofficial representative to heal the wounds. The United States permitted the representative to enter, but when in September he tried to send an official military mission, including members of the committee in London, the government refused because the London committee represented people hostile to a country with which it was not at war. Only after the American declaration of war on the Austro-Hungarian Empire in December was the mission allowed to enter and meet Wilson. It must be noted here that Washington permitted some recruiting by both Montenegro and Serbia during 1915, 1916, and 1917, but this also was before the American entry into the war.

Wilson's rigid position on this point conditioned relations with the Hungarians as well. Marcus Braun, the chairman of the executive committee of the Hungarian Republican Club in New York, working with Fiorello La Guardia, sent his memo to Lansing in May. He proposed to organize the Hungarian-Americans and use them to lead a revolution against the dual monarchy. Lansing, it seems, paid no attention to this plan; Professor Bárány claims it failed because the Hungarians in America were unable to organize on a nationwide basis, as the others had, because the Hungarian leaders at home would not have accepted such a solution, and because Braun had little stature either with Americans or Hungarian-Americans. It is more likely that it failed for the same reason that the Yugoslavs could not get permission to send their military mission in September: Wilson would do nothing to antagonize the Habsburgs.

Again the activity of the Jews throws much light on this subject. In the spring of 1917, Ambassador Henry Morgenthau set out for the Near East, where he hoped to convince the Turks to withdraw from the war and sign a separate peace. When he reached Gibraltar, however, the Zionists reached him. They did not want Turkey to break with the Central Powers, since a separate peace would have eliminated the possibility of dismembering the Ottoman Empire, which was essential to the establishment of Palestine. Morgenthau turned around and went home.

Meanwhile, the British were considering issuance of a declaration in favor of Zionism. In May Brandeis spoke to Arthur Balfour and advocated such a declaration. Then in June Rabbi Wise was told by the President, "I will be ready to act when you and Justice Brandeis" decide the time is ripe. By then Balfour, the British Foreign Secretary, had returned to England, and on September 4 the British asked House if Wilson would favor a declaration. House advised Wilson against it and on September 11 told the British the President did not think it was time for a "definite commitment." Within the week Brandeis knew about the exchange; he and Rabbi Wise went to House, read the proposed declaration, and received House's assurance that Wilson would accept it. The result was the famous Balfour Declaration of November 2, 1917.

Both instances are interesting because in the summer of 1917 the United States was not at war with Turkey; in fact, war was never declared. At that time the administration was anxious not to offend the Austrians (with whom war had not been declared), in the hope that Austria could be weaned away from Germany. Consequently, the Czechs could recruit only in secret, while the Yugoslavs were not even permitted to join an official military mission of a friendly ally, Serbia. And the Hungarians did not even get a hearing. But the Poles recruited in the open, and the Jews stopped the Morgenthau mission and encouraged the Balfour Declaration. The Jews knew Wilson; the Poles, House; but the Czechs had only the French ambassador, and the

Yugoslavs had no one. At least the Hungarians had La Guardia, but what was a lowly congressman?

The plight of the disunited and unlooked-after Hungarians is illuminated by the events of November and December, 1917. In November Count Károlyi made his peace plea to the United States, but again nothing came of it. The plan was basically weak: Károlyi planned to use control of the Hungarian government to force the Austrians to bring Germany into a peace conference. Although Professor Bárány claims that Károlyi's plan failed because he did not gain control of the government, even if he had accomplished the impossible, time had run out. The United States declared war in the following month. Furthermore six days after Károlyi met Hugh Wilson the Germans mounted their successful counterattack against the British penetrations near Cambrai. At that moment the German military did not think of peace, and Ludendorff did not lose his will to win until August, 1918. Károlyi's plan failed because it was impossible: even a powerful voice in American-Hungarian circles would not have changed its fate.

In the following month La Guardia made his proposal. He would start a revolution and create a separate republic— the old Braun plan. Although the Italians supported the proposal in the hope of relieving pressure on the northern front, Wilson refused to accept it. "There are too many irresponsible 'agents' at large and they are apt to do a great deal of harm." Lansing agreed, although at the time he privately believed in the dismemberment of the empire. In Hungary, however, he did not want La Guardia starting a revolution.

Professor Bárány's claim that immigrant support in America could have resulted in improved Hungarian-American relations seems unlikely. As even Professor Bárány admits, there were many obstacles to better Hungarian-American relations. One major obstacle lay in the fact that before January, 1918, neither Wilson nor House nor Lansing had accepted any foreign spokesman who did not have a strong immigrant force behind him; even some who had such support were refused. Immigrant pressures could, however, only open the door. Even the hated Irish were able to bring their case directly to Wilson. He did nothing, to be sure, but at least he listened. The failure of the Hungarians to organize on a national level or to produce a prominent leader in America or in Europe was fatal. Without the constant barrage that only an immigrant group could maintain, there was no hope; La Guardia's efforts were futile. Still more important was the fact that in January, 1918, although the United States was at war, Wilson did not want Austria destroyed. Consequently, any revolution that led to a separate Hungarian state was tabu.

This aspect of Wilson's policy can be seen clearly with respect to the South Slavs and the Fourteen Points. When House gave Dr. Milenko Vesnić the proposal concerning Serbia, he was shocked by the Serb's violent declaration that peace required the destruction of the empire. When House told Wilson of Vesnić's reaction, he recommended that he follow the original plan; the President asked only that autonomy be given to the many nationalities of Austria. Wilson used the same term—autonomy—with respect to the Jewish question. Although the Jews interpreted this to mean independence, it is hard to believe that Wilson, who was so precise in his language, could have meant one thing in one place and another at another point in the same speech. This may mean that in January, 1918, he had not accepted the destruction of Turkey, despite his Palestine policy. The discrepancy appeared not to trouble Wilson.

If he spoke at one point of maintaining the empire, he

was most explicit with regard to Poland. Paderewski got exactly what he wanted, more than the Inquiry was willing to give. His link with House resulted in Wilson's demand for complete Polish independence, a demand that meant the breakup of at least part of the empire. Again, this discrepancy did not trouble Wilson.

In Wilson's speech a number of scholars have found an indication that Wilson was a political realist, not an idealist. They claim that he wrote the points to raise the hopes of the Allies, while weakening the will of Austria to continue. Although this may be true, it can only be a side issue; Wilson firmly believed what he said. The specific points are not the important part of the speech: Wilson's true stamp appears at the end of the speech, in the summary demanding justice for all. Wilson was an idealist who believed that the United States would create a world of justice.

Reactions to the speech varied among and within the immigrant groups. The British-Americans applauded the continuation of Anglo-American solidarity. The Poles had no complaints, while the Jews interpreted "autonomy" to mean independence; their interpretation may have rested on a profound confidence that their man at the White House would prevail. The Irish were divided, while the Germans and Hungarians found in the speech a ray of hope for a just peace. But the rest were profoundly shocked. The Czechs and Slovaks told Senator William Stone of their forebodings, while the South Slavs remained virtually speechless when their hopes for the destruction of the empire did not materialize.

The question of autonomy or independence did not seem to trouble the Jews in the weeks following Wilson's address. They simply continued to exert their formidable power whenever necessary. In late February the Zionists asked

Lansing for permission to send representatives and a medical unit to Palestine. When Lansing refused on both counts, Wise went to House and Wilson. In March the State Department changed its position, and the Jews in addition received permission to recruit and form a military force that arrived in Palestine in July, to fight a country against which the United States had not declared war.

Meanwhile, the faint ray of hope they detected in Wilson's speech prompted the Irish to attempt once more to get Ireland on the list of states that were to receive their freedom. Delegations arrived at the White House; resolutions were introduced into both houses of Congress; mass meetings were organized across the country; and finally, in May, the Second Irish Race Convention met. Although Justice John Goff presented to Wilson the resolutions emanating from this gathering, his success in gaining an audience pointed to the eventual downfall of the Irish. Unfortunately for the Irish, one of their leaders had aroused Wilson's famous feelings. Wilson bitterly hated Judge Daniel Cohalan, who was originally selected to present the resolutions, and refused to meet a committee that included him. It would be unfair to Wilson, however, to accuse him of refusing to fight for Ireland's freedom for this reason; he made it clear, as Congressman Henry D. Flood had done the previous March, that he could not interfere in the internal affairs of an allied power. (Flood's language was more correct when he referred to England as a "co-belligerent," since no alliance had been signed.)

Wilson was also probably too preoccupied with the question of the Habsburgs to attend to a seemingly settled problem. He had finally, after months of "agonizing reappraisal," agreed to the dismemberment of the empire. Of course this was interference with the domestic affairs of another nation, but of an enemy nation. Why he reached this decision may not be easy to say, but at least one can be sure it was not because of the fanfare that followed Thomas Masaryk, the visits with Pergler, Sabath, King, and other prominent congressmen, the work of the Pittsburgh Convention, the contact with Crane in the State Department, or even Masaryk's visit with Wilson. Nor did the publicity surrounding the Czech army exploits in Siberia, which aroused American public opinion, have any effect upon Wilson. The decision rested upon other forces, especially Lansing's estimate of the situation. The real influence may have come from Albert Putney in the department, but in any case it did not derive from the immigrants. Even after the decision, in fact, Wilson remained cautious in his dealings with the immigrants. He did not recognize the Czech Council in Paris as a de facto government until September 3, after the other allies. It was not until February 6, 1919, that he did the same for the Yugoslavs, although in the previous June he had privately intimated to the Serbs that they would receive his support. Even the Hungarians received some recognition in June, 1919, when he remarked that they should be considered a separate nationality. Thus, it would seem that Professor Bárány may be wrong in his statement that Wilson would not have been deaf to justifiable Hungarian demands if only sufficient leadership in American-Hungarian circles had existed. Rather, it seems that they got what they wanted without that leadership, without applying any real pressures, because Wilson had made other decisions. It was a kind of bonus windfall. It must be remembered that only the Poles had got their demands before May, 1918. Although the Irish and Germans had both justifiable aims and adequate leadership, neither of them could influence Wilson. The Germans, in fact, lived in a "Halts-Maul" atmosphere and could only hope that Wilson would be true to his points. If the Germans failed, and the Irish also, it does not seem correct to assume that the Hungarians would have succeeded, except of course, if they had been able to find another Paderewski, or a Brandeis.

Although the announcement of the change in American policy inspired many reactions, that of the Carpatho-Ruthenians was unique. On July 23, 1918, this virtually unknown nationality organized a most important meeting at Homestead, Pennsylvania, during which they created the American National Council of Uhro-Rusins. The aims of the new body included first an independent state (even the Ruthenians at home had discovered just before the war that they constituted a separate nationality); if this proved impossible, they desired union with fellow Ukrainians from Galicia and Bukovinia; failing this, they wanted, as a final demand, autonomy. Fortunately, they failed to name the country they would join under an autonomous arrangement, and this gave their leader, Gregory Zatkovich, room to maneuver in his later negotiations. The American policy change thus virtually created a new immigrant pressure group.

If Wilson needed anything in the summer and early fall of 1918, it was not another pressure group; for every group, sensing the end rapidly approaching, intensified its efforts to influence the administration. The Irish refused to relax their activities throughout the summer and fall, but Wilson maintained, properly, that it would be most unwise for him to intrude in British affairs. As he continued to expound the ideals upon which he hoped the peace would be based, however, he produced at least a kind of smoothing effect while also giving the Irish hope.

Wilson's speeches of July and September, in fact, raised the hopes of all the immigrants; they were so general and all-inclusive that every group thought he was talking directly to it. In August the Montenegrin Committee for National

Unification asked Wilson to recognize the Montenegro National Committee in Paris as the de facto government in place of King Nicholas. Then the South Slavs broke with Pašić's concept of a great Serbia. At this point Lansing intervened and on September 21 proposed the formation of a Yugoslavia that would include the territories of Dalmatia, Bosnia, Herzegovina, and Montenegro, in addition to the Serbs, Croats, and Slovenes. Professor George Prpić implies that this internal dissension was the cause of the United States' failure to give the Yugoslav Committee in London the status conferred upon the Czechs in Paris. By late September, however, the forces of history were moving too rapidly for either the United States government or the immigrants to control them. By then the advantage that the Central European leaders had gained by being on the scene began to overshadow the advantage of having the ear of Woodrow Wilson.

Before the control of events fell from American hands, however, one last great attempt was made to shape Central Europe from the safety of America. Miller had indicated his interest in the breakup of the Austro-Hungarian Empire as early as 1913; when Wilson officially endorsed its dismemberment, he revived his dream of a loose union of independent democratic states as a bulwark against Russian pressure. The Creel Committee endorsed this idea, and on September 15, after an active summer, Miller proposed to Masaryk the creation of an organization of European nationals. At the mass demonstration of oppressed nationalities that Masaryk and Miller were attending the idea gained rapid acceptance, and on the following day the Mid-European Union was born. Paderewski nominated Masaryk to the position of chairman, and the Czech leader immediately offered Miller the role of executive director. Since both House and Lansing viewed the organization as a method by which various boundary disputes might be solved before the end of the war, House urged Miller to accept the position; when the CPI promised to pay his salary, he agreed. He immediately called for a meeting of the new organization and invited a number of prominent men from the administration and the diplomatic corps. The Italian Ambassador, calling it a Slav trick to deprive Italy of earned territory, refused to attend; this forced the CPI to withdraw its support, while William A. Phillips, the original contact in the State Department, also failed to attend. Richard Crane took his place along with other prominent congressmen. Undisturbed by this obvious sign of future trouble and without any guarantee of ever receiving a salary, Miller organized a meeting at Independence Hall for October 23-26. This merely permitted a public airing of the vast differences, and the Union virtually disappeared with the end of the meeting.

Although Miller's idea failed to materialize, at least one good came from it. With the aid of Representative Guy E. Campbell, Zatkovich met Wilson on October 21 and gave him the resolutions of the Homestead meeting. Wilson felt that the first two alternatives were not possible and encouraged Zatkovich to work for autonomy. He also suggested that he attend the meeting of the Mid-European Union that was to open on the 23rd. Thus, on October 25 Zatkovich arrived in Philadelphia, spoke to Masaryk, and proposed the incorporation of Carpathian Ruthenia in the new Czechoslovakian state. Masaryk agreed and on November 12 the National Council approved the plan in Scranton. Wilson, Lansing, Masaryk, and others were informed of this decision; interestingly enough, when Putney received the information through Lansing he gave his approval, since at that time he stood strongly in favor of Masaryk. In spite of this seemingly universal approval Zatkovich struck upon a unique method of gaining additional leverage with world leaders.

He submitted the plan to a plebiscite of all Ruthenians in America. When 60 percent approved, he felt that he could argue from a position of real strength at Paris. In this way he implemented Wilson's concept of selfdetermination. Up to that point he had not even troubled himself to ask the people who lived there what they wanted.

The formation of the Mid-European Union and the work of Zatkovich point to an important fact. Except for the Poles, Wilson granted the Central Europeans nothing until he had made the decision to break up the empire. Only after this did he permit, and publicly encourage, the immigrants to organize efforts to control events in Central Europe. It would not be wise to accuse them of influencing him; after June, 1918, it was rather Wilson who attempted to influence them to solve their problems as quickly as possible, because he knew that the advantage would be with those present on the scene once Austria fell, and he obviously feared what certain agents would produce.

This was not true, of course, of the Poles and the Jews. In September, Paderewski learned that the Inquiry had not gathered information on the Polish corridor and immediately applied pressure to have a study made. At the same time Brandeis and Wise wrote out a policy statement on the Palestine question which Wilson issued on August 31, 1918.

By the late summer it seemed as if only the Irish and Germans had failed to influence events. The Germans, who still feared to make any public efforts to reach Wilson, condemned such attempts by other immigrant groups. They simply hoped that Wilson would fulfill the promise of his public and private statements to the effect that America would be just to friend and foe alike.

If the Germans feared public activity, the Irish reveled in it. They tried to make the Irish question an issue in the elections of 1918 and called for huge mass meetings across the country during Self-Determination Week, December 8-15. These reached their culmination in a great rally held in Madison Square Garden. William Cardinal O'Connell gave the principal address, and resolutions were sent to Wilson as he sailed for Paris. Meanwhile the pressure from the politicians increased; a letter from Senator Thomas Walsh elicited from Wilson, in December, a promise to work for a just and satisfactory solution to the delicate problem. For all their work this was the best the Irish gained. In the final analysis, their hope rested in Wilson's ability to fulfill his own dreams.

When Wilson arrived in Paris he may have hoped for some relief from the constant pressure from the immigrants, but he was not to find it there. In December the Jews gathered in Philadelphia and sent Wise and Frankfurter to Paris. Zatkovich arrived on February 3, while the Third Irish Race Convention sent a delegation of prominent Irish-Americans to represent their interests. Meanwhile the Yugoslavs and Italians opened their propaganda war over the question of Fiume. The Italians held their meetings and sent their resolutions, and La Guardia arrived in Paris. It seemed that only the Germans and Hungarians remained at home.

At the conference itself Wilson had few problems with the Central European groups, since the destruction of the Empire either fulfilled their dreams or at least made fulfillment possible. The question of whether the Ruthenians in Ruthenia would accept the American immigrant solution of autonomy with Czechoslovakia was solved when Zatkovich convinced them to join Masaryk. Although Wilson also lost some of his enthusiasm for the Poles, the Inquiry's increasing warmth offset the loss. Outside Central Europe Wilson had his problems. The mistake of Fiume led not only to Premier

Vittorio Orlando's withdrawal from the conference but also to repercussions in American politics. Republicans attached themselves to the Italian-Americans' grievance; when Wilson in turn became more convinced of the correctness of his position, compromise proved impossible.

The case of the Jews, however, produced a number of interesting developments. Although on March 2 Wilson exceeded the provisions of the Balfour Declaration when he asked for a Jewish commonwealth, yet at the end of the month he proposed that a commission study the question of Palestine on the spot. He saw this as the "only scientific basis possible for a settlement" and implied that the commission would apply the principle of selfdetermination. The mere thought of such action aroused Wise and Frankfurter. It meant the end of the Jewish homeland dream, since the Arabs would not vote for such a settlement. The commission left on May 15, and on the next day Frankfurter met Wilson to discuss the implications. When the President assured him that he would support the Balfour statement, he undermined the work of the commission. Then, in late June, Brandeis told Balfour that when the time came Wilson would reconcile his concepts of selfdetermination to his Palestine policy, leaving no doubt that Wilson would violate that principle if it were necessary in order to give the Jews what they wanted.

While the Jews continued their success, the Irish failed to move Wilson. Although they were able to meet him privately, Wilson would do nothing in spite of the pressure from Congress, from individual politicians, from state political organizations and legislatures, from numerous prominent churchmen, and from other sources. The work of Senator William Borah in particular aroused Irish feelings, and the debates in the Senate on his resolution only intensified them. Yet even Borah could not get the Senate to pass a strongly worded resolution that would have embarrassed Wilson.

By the time Borah stepped in, however, the time to influence the treaty had passed. On May 7 it was released to the press and the immigrants in America learned about the future. The Jews received the treaty with great joy, since it gave them their cherished homeland and minority rights as well. The British-Americans remained loyal to Wilson and the treaty since it meant continued Anglo-American cooperation. The Poles and other Central Europeans were relatively happy except for the majority of the South Slavs. The Germans, of course, were shocked but there seems to be little evidence that they mounted an immediate offensive! Although they created some opposition, it could not be compared to that generated by the Italians and the Irish. All three, however, received praise from the opposition when the Senate rejected the treaty in November and again in March. Even the passage of the famous Irish reservation could not save the treaty.

What effect all this had upon the election of 1920 is difficult to say. The Germans voted as Republicans anyway, and the treaty only helped them follow time-honored practice. Most observers have said that the Irish abandoned the Democratic party en masse in 1920, as did the Italians. In spite of this, the victory of Republicanism can hardly be attributed to the immigrants. Many factors converged to produce a Republican year.

What then can be said about the impact of public opinion upon American foreign policy during this period? That the immigrants indicated an interest in American policy goes without saying, and this interest was probably greater than at any other time in history. They attempted to express this interest and to influence policies with the various means at their disposal, which may be conveniently divided into five categories: appeals 1) to the general public; 2) to the "establishment" of leadership in journalism, business, education, and religion; 3) to politicians both local and national; 4) to various departments and agencies in the government; and 5) to Wilson himself or to his immediate staff.

Although all groups made attempts to arouse the general public and used much the same tools, their attempts varied in degree. Even the quiet Germans and slightly more active Hungarians attempted to convince their fellow citizens in America that they were loyal to their country of adoption. Neither made any great attempt to arouse public opinion in favor of a more lenient peace or to encourage acceptance or rejection of the peace settlement, activities which were virtually precluded by their positions before America's entry into the war. The Jews made certain attempts to influence the general public, but they did not concentrate on this approach. The Poles had a certain backlog of good will upon which they could base their public appeals, but again they did not overwork it. On the other hand, the Central Europeans took such an interest in this approach that they even established propaganda agencies in the United States—something the Irish did not do until the battle of the treaty's acceptance arrived. Yet none made as serious an effort as the Irish. All organized parades, called national conventions, passed resolutions, and issued reports that filled the pages of both the immigrant and the American press. The results of these activities remain impossible to gauge. It would appear that for all their efforts the immigrants merely galvanized their own followers, both immigrant and American, and publicized their grievances. Even the Central Europeans had little success until late in the war. In most cases such activities helped to attract the attentive public, but the politicians had little effect on the administration and none whatsoever on Wilson. The limits of such work must have been obvious to the immigrants, since they used other methods to gain their ends.

The second stage in the process was to gain the sympathy of those who controlled important aspects of American life. Here the British excelled, as they gathered into their fold men prominent in journalism, education, religion, business, and other fields. They also had their public gatherings, but these were more often private and obviously more select than such shows offered by the Irish and others. It was the private conversation, the friendly dinner party, that worked for the solidification of Anglo-American unity. The advantage of the British was their ability to enter the "establishment," whereas only a few of the others could produce men of such stature as to permit this. Paderewski and Masaryk were somewhat successful, while the Jew, Brandeis, not only could enter it but was part of it. The Irish, Italians, and Hungarians could not break the barriers, while the Germans who did belong most probably avoided the issues of the war for fear of accusations of disloyalty. But again the results of such activities are most difficult to assess. In all probability these prominent Americans had an inclination to accept the British propaganda. It fell upon fertile ground; one could even say it was clearly within American self-interest. The British effort consequently added strength to an existing connection. It was much harder for Paderewski and Masaryk to convince the Americans—until their interests coincided with American interests.

Regardless of their success at these levels, the immigrants did not forget their need of political power, and they pushed their efforts with both local and national politicians. Here the Irish were most successful; state party conventions, state legislatures, governors, and various local political figures called for Irish selfdetermination. Resolutions appeared in both houses of Congress, and the Irish even succeeded in forcing Congress—both Democratic and Republican ones—to pass them. Yet even the Irish could not get the national politicians to agree to hard and specific resolutions; the two that were passed had suffered under the watering of congressional maneuver. However, they did force the Senate to accept the Irish reservation, and the House held meetings on the Mason Bill. Congressman Mason eventually accepted a substitute for his bill, but even this failed to make the floor of the House—and this was in June, 1919, just months before the national election. If the Republicans had really wanted the Irish vote, they could have won it by passing this bill. Others had limited success with this approach. The Italians and Hungarians reached La Guardia, while the Czechs and Slovaks had Sabath and Kenyon. Even the Carpatho-Ruthenians found Campbell at the last minute. But the Czechoslovakian resolutions introduced by Sabath and Kenyon never reached the floor of Congress, and the others succeeded only in arranging meetings with prominent officials, including Wilson. The Central Europeans gained little from such meetings until the interests of the immigrants coincided with those of the United States, and then Wilson did more than listen. He attempted to wield the influence.

Their inability to gain results with these methods caused the immigrants to search for friends in the administration—the Creel Committee, the Inquiry, and the State Department. Here the Irish failed completely, while the Central Europeans were somewhat more successful. The Creel Committee became interested in the Mid-European Union, but only after Wilson had made his decision. The Czechs had Richard Crane in the State Department, who must have had some influence, but the real influence seems to have come from Putney. Phillips also showed some interest in the Mid-European Union but seems to have lost it as soon as he saw the problems inherent in solving boundaries. Again, the influence of the immigrants upon these men is difficult to gauge.

The crux of the problem seems to lie with Wilson and his advisors. The Poles were most successful in getting to them because Paderewski was able to reach House as early as November, 1915. As a result the United States agreed to fight for Polish freedom months before entering the war and years before Wilson decided on the breakup of the empire. For all their work the other Central Europeans could not influence Wilson before he made that decision; even after it, he insisted on moving slowly. His interest in the Mid-European Union can be seen as his attempt to influence the immigrant. For instance, his interest in Zatkovich, which arose only after the recognition of Czechoslovakia, can clearly be interpreted as his attempt to influence the settlement in Europe. Neither the Irish nor the Italians could convince Wilson that their needs demanded such help. The Germans of course never even attempted to reach him, while the Hungarians were at least able to get him to accept the fact that they were a different nationality.

The chaos of Central Europe was not created by Wilson or the immigrants or the Versailles settlement. It was created by the national groups there and their leaders. Wilson did not even permit these developments; except in Poland, he merely recognized them. But even here, although Wilson took the lead, the inspiration came from House. Finally, Brandeis was so close to Wilson that he could virtually write the American program on Palestine. Thus, only two of the immigrant groups studied really influenced Wilson, and in neither case was the principal means the operation of public opinion.

There are those who hold that diplomacy in the twentieth century is controlled by the people and not by the realities of power and geography, that it is free from the influence of the whims of individuals. Yet in the case of Wilson it would seem that geography did influence diplomacy, that power played its role, and that the whim of the individual had not been eliminated. The whole story is told in the following pages.

THE GERMANS

Austin J. App

In 1914 German-Americans formed one of the most influential, respected, and best organized minority groups in the United States, which was consequently able to engage in an extensive propaganda program second only to that of the British government. Between these two factions there ensued a bitter struggle over America's intervention in the European war. With the declaration of war on Germany on April 6, 1917, the German-Americans lost in their bid for public opinion, and so great was the reaction against all things German that they were virtually eliminated as a political and social force—a decline that may be traced in the fate of German-language publications.[1]

At the time of the war the German-Americans were divided into three major groups. The largest of these was predominantly Protestant, liberal, and republican. Germans with this persuasion found their organized expression in the National German-American Alliance. The next largest group was the Catholics, who supported a number of publications and whose activities were largely channeled through the Central Verein, a federation of many state and parish societies with its headquarters in St. Louis. The third distinctive group was made up of German socialists, whose press had a total circulation of 126,900 in 1914.[2] All three groups, sympathetic toward the Central Powers, devoted their full energies from 1914 to 1917 to support of American neutrality. Although their point of view was in accord with official government policy, it was the German-Americans rather than the more extreme supporters of the Allies who were harassed and discredited for wanting America to live up to Wilson's neutrality proclamations.

The National German-American Alliance, "by far the largest organization of any racial group in American history,"[3] was a loose federation of some ten thousand clubs and possibly two million members that provided a powerful organized voice against intervention. The Alliance was incorporated on February 27, 1907, as an "Educational and Patriotic" society that supported representative government, the maintenance of civil and political rights, the protection and naturalization of German immigrants, the study of U.S. history and institutions, the cultivation of the German language and literature, and the perpetuation of the memory of German-American pioneers.

A key to American resentment of the Alliance is provided by the *National Hibernian,* which reported that at a conference in Philadelphia on January 22, 1907, the Ancient Order of Hibernians of America and the National German-American Alliance resolved to oppose "an alliance of any kind, secret or otherwise, with any foreign power on the part of the government of the United States."[4] It was thus both natural and necessary for German-Americans before 1917 to oppose American intervention, and in 1919 to oppose the special provision of the League draft guaranteeing France's security.

The determination of the interventionists and the administration to destroy the German-American Alliance is under-

[1] Compare the statistics in the *N. W. Ayer Directory* for the appropriate years. In 1914, for instance, 532 German-language publications appeared regularly in the United States; by 1920 only 251 remained.

[2] Carl Wittke, *The German Language Press in America* (1957), 174.

[3] Clifton James Childs, *The German-Americans in Politics* (1939), 176.

[4] U.S. Senate, Subcommittee of the Committee on the Judiciary, "National German-American Alliance," *Hearings on Senate Bill 3529,* 65th Cong., 2nd Sess., Feb. 23–April 13, 1918, 645. Hereafter referred to as *Hearings.*

standable. To the very last, the Alliance strove to keep
America out of the war. As late as February 5, 1917, the
German-American Chamber of Commerce of New York
issued a statement that "he is the most loyal citizen who up
to the last minute strives for peace with all his strength,"
and Mr. Charles J. Hexamer, president of the Alliance, telegraphed all his state presidents to "arrange peace meetings,
adopt resolutions requesting Congress to submit the question
of declaring war to a referendum, and send the resolutions
to members of Congress by wire and letter."[5] Almost simul-
taneously, on February 7, the officials of the Alliance drew
up a pledge of loyalty in the event of war: "Under President
Wilson, as our Commander-in-chief, we will fight no less
loyally than the German-Americans fought under Lincoln in
the Civil War for preservation of the Union." And with
the declaration of war, the Alliance, in its April issue of
Mitteilungen, reaffirmed its loyalty: "Everything must be
avoided which is not in accordance with the highest duty of
a citizen of this country. No German-American will forget
the duty which he owes the country of his choice, the country
to which he has given his best, and he will unite all utter-
ances and his deeds only with its best interest."[6]

With the outbreak of hostilities between the United
States and the Central Powers, the position of the German-
Americans deteriorated rapidly. Their propaganda efforts
in favor of the Central Powers obviously had to cease; more
tellingly, they were ultimately reduced to passive bystanders
of the conflict and the succeeding negotiations. The fight
for and against intervention had been a long and bitter one.
The less justified they were, the more selfrighteously vin-
dictive the winners became. The successful interventionists

[5] Childs, *German-Americans in Politics,* 157.
[6] *Ibid.,* 162.

were not disposed to consider William Randolph Hearst's reasoning "that 'previous to the month of April, 1917, we were at peace with Germany,' and until our entry into the war 'it was the undoubted lawful right of every free American to sympathize with any one or with none of the European belligerents.'"[7] Americans harassed their fellow German-American citizens everywhere, outlawed the German languages from the schools and required public kissing of the flag; mobs beset former noninterventionists and lynched at least one. Legislators passed laws to bedevil the German-language press and restrain German-American institutions and organizations. "German music and literature, German church services, the German language, the activities of all German societies . . . came under the ban of superpatriots. . . . German societies postponed their conventions, and some never resumed their annual gatherings. . . . The 'Hun' language was banished from the curriculum. . . . German books were thrown out of libraries, sold as trash, . . . or burned in the public square with patriotic ceremonies."[8]

The triumphant interventionists were out to destroy any German-American public affairs organization that might incline the peacemakers toward conciliation. Senator William H. King of Utah, who introduced a bill to repeal the German-American Alliance's charter, held hearings between February 23 and April 13, 1918. During the cross examination the recently elected president of the Alliance, Pastor Siegmund George von Bosse, asserted that if the Alliance had acted enthusiastically upon America's entry into the war it would have been accounted hypocritical, and if it had protested it would have been considered disloyal; its only recourse, therefore, was to pledge its loyalty formally and otherwise

[7] *Literary Digest,* December 28, 1918.
[8] Wittke, *German Press,* 268-69.

to urge "in a notice sent to all our societies, 'Halts Maul'—
that is 'Keep your mouth shut' . . . to say nothing and not to
arouse any misconstruction."[9]

Although as Pastor von Bosse said, "No act of disloyalty
has been proved against the National German-American
Alliance," it felt its usefulness ended and on April 11, 1918,
dissolved itself, allotting the $30,000 in the treasury to the
American Red Cross.[10] In doing so, it anticipated the congressional action on Senator King's bill, which on July 2,
1918, repealed the charter of the Alliance granted in 1907.
Essentially the charter was withdrawn because, in the words
of one witness, the Alliance's enthusiasm for America's participation in the war was "not commensurate in any degree
with the enthusiasm that was manifested in behalf of Germany . . . in 1914."[11] The one German-American organization
that could have influenced the spirit of the treaty and its
ratification was thus destroyed.

The psychological effect of this suppression was deep and
lasting. German-Americans, demoralized, maintained a Halts
Maul attitude in matters of foreign policy for the duration of
the war. "The year 1918 concluded the history of a great
many German-American clubs, organizations, newspapers,
and churches. . . . German-Americanism was never to rise
again. The era of the hyphen was past. The German-
Americans as a group did not survive the year 1918."[12] The
superpatriots were so anxious to see that this happened they
often caused German records to be destroyed. As a recent
student of German-American publications expressed it:
"Through the tragic confusion of the first World War
Americans had often, in a falsely conceived display of

[9] *Hearings,* 351.
[10] *The American Weekly,* April 24, 1918.
[11] *Hearings,* 350.
[12] Dieter Cunz, *The Maryland Germans* (1948), 401-402.

patriotism, destroyed German-American records without giving any thought to the fact that these records frequently contained the only available day-to-day record of local history."[13] One quickly appreciates the extent of the loss when doing research on German-Americans from 1918 to 1920. Again and again bound volumes of newspapers or magazines end with 1917.

The first stage in making the peace treaty may be said to have begun with Wilson's proclamation of the Fourteen Points on January 8, 1918. In general these provided for "open covenants, openly arrived at," "equality of trade conditions," sovereignty based on "the interests of the populations concerned," frontiers "along clearly recognizable lines of nationality," and "territorial integrity to great and small states alike"—all of which was to be guaranteed by a league of virtually all nations, victors and vanquished alike. The peoples of the world, the Allied governments on November 5, 1918, and the German and Austrian governments in accepting the armistice on November 11, 1918, endorsed Wilson's program as the basis for the peace that was to end all war and make the world safe for democracy. The armistice as it was accepted included Wilson's amplifications of July 4, stressing selfdetermination in all territorial changes, and of September 27, calling for "impartial justice" both to "those to whom we wish to be just and those to whom we do not wish to be just."

The Germans, having surrendered with the hope that Wilson's Fourteen Points would serve as the basis for the peace settlement, were defenseless before the drafters of the peace, with nothing to protect them except the victors' sense of justice and no one to intercede for them except people of natural good will or special sympathy, among

[13] Karl J. R. Arndt and May E. Olsen, *German-American Newspapers and Periodicals, 1732–1955* (1961), 8.

whom should have been counted the millions of Americans of German descent. How did these Americans, a minority naturally sympathetic toward the idealism in Wilson's Fourteen Points and their envisaged justice to the vanquished, influence Wilson's peacemaking at Versailles and the consequent Senate rejection of the treaty?

The first stage of the peacemaking lasted until the German acceptance of the armistice conditions on November 11, 1918. During this time German-Americans were too anxious to prove their loyalty and too disorganized to do more than fan indirectly, if earnestly, every hope for a negotiated peace, fair to both sides. George Viereck, possibly the most brilliant and literate spokesman German-Americans ever had, wrote, "It is true we opposed the war to the last moment. We still hope that peace will come before much American blood is shed. We desire peace soon, but with honor."[14] In that fateful last stage of the war, however, all those, German-Americans most particularly, who welcomed what were denounced as German or Austrian "peace offensives" were vilified and their motives impugned. Senator La Follette, seeing this, "stated that it was a strange doctrine 'that the mass of the people who pay in money, misery, and blood all the costs of the war, out of which a favorite few profit so largely, may not freely and publicly discuss the terms of peace.'" An editorial in *Exhibitor's Trade Review* denounced "the German peace offensives—more fatal than their military offensives and a hundred times more ingratiating." When one Frank J. Klingberg, suspected of pro-German sympathies, was scheduled to lecture at a California university on May 23, 1918, on what the American Protective League thought would be a proposal for peace, the league forced the university to cancel the lecture.[15]

---

[14] *The American Weekly*, October 17, 1918.
[15] James R. Mocks, *Censorship 1917* (1941), 187, 193.

German-Americans, in spite of the fact that some of the Fourteen Points could not be considered favorable to Germany, welcomed Wilson's program. None was inclined nor would have dared to denounce Wilson, as ex-president Theodore Roosevelt did when he said, "In the cloak rooms of Congress it is a bitter jest to speak of the President thus: 'Here's to our Czar, last in war, first toward peace, long may he waver.' "[16] In fact one German-language paper on January 10, 1918, gave a summary of Wilson's Fourteen Points the front page lead. Its next issue again prominently carried excerpts from Wilson's message of December 4 to the effect that the U.S. did not want to ruin Austria-Hungary or interfere in its internal affairs, nor did it contemplate wrong to Germany. During this pre-armistice period the German press featured eagerly any "peace feelers" by statesmen of both sides and any suggestion of an acceptable and just policy. The basis of a just position, the German-Americans seemed to agree, was the Fourteen Points.

This eagerness for a negotiated peace that would be just and honorable for both sides was of course not shared by the former interventionists. As late as September 1918, in an item entitled "The Great Debate in the Senate," one German weekly reported: "Senator Lewis made a startling speech warning of the German 'Peace Offensive.' Senator Sherman voiced the conviction that we must continue the war until we have produced a decisive victory out of which shall come a permanent peace." In May the Pope urged prayers for peace and the reestablishment of justice, and on June 29 he directed all priests to celebrate a Mass for justice and peace; the response from the superpatriots was abuse. Auguste C. Barbize, in a pamphlet entitled "Pope Benedict, The Hun, and Peace Propaganda," attacked the Pope for urging a negotiated peace: "While he has often and fluently talked

[16] *Ibid.*, 113.

about peace, he has never raised his mighty voice or one finger to check or to condemn the barbarous atrocities committed by the Huns in all the lands they invaded."[17] These attacks not only weakened the Pope's influence for a conciliatory peace but touched German-Americans on a sensitive point: all their American patriotism could not keep them from feeling personally insulted when Germans were called "Huns" and when unbelievable atrocities (later disproven) were attributed to them. "The German-Americans were less German than American, except when their relatives in the Reich were called 'Huns.' Then sentiment and tradition welled up within them."[18] The truth is that a few propaganda manipulators had created in the minds of many Americans a desire not for Wilson's "peace without victory," not for a negotiated settlement honorable and fair to both sides, but for victory first and peace second. If even the Pope was subject to vitriolic abuse for wanting an honorable negotiated peace, then it was understandable that German-Americans dared do no more in their publications than to report all peace talk prominently without editorial comment. The spiritual adviser for *Nord-Amerika* in his weekly message entitled "German Catholics in Grave Times" informed his readers on September 5, 1918:

> We are attacked, suspected, and slandered. . . . They want us to condemn our native speech, our laboriously created societies, and even our own flesh and blood. . . . At the same time they expect from us exactly the same sacrifices for country as from any other American. To everything we should say Yes and *Amen,* but otherwise stay mum. . . . If we openly do our duty, the ones consider us hypocrites,

[17] Qoted in Philadelphia *Nord-Amerika,* August 12, 1918. All translations are by the author.

[18] Harold Lanine and James Wechsler, *War Propaganda and the United States* (1940), 15.

the others cowards. If we do it conscientiously but
secretly, they suspect our patriotic loyalty. It seems
almost unbearable that even our fellow Catholics
do not comprehend our difficult position and sometimes even exceed others in hysterical attacks upon
us and what is dear to us.

In short, German-Americans between January 8 and
November 11, 1918, prayed for a quick peace in harmony
with Wilson's Fourteen Points. Although they gave publicity
to all hopeful peace statements, they did not propose terms,
pass resolutions, or send delegations. Whereas their papers
carried such headlines as "Home Rule Committee Appeals
to Wilson, for Justice to Ireland" (April 10, 1918), no such
activity on behalf of German-Americans is reported.[19] They
were first of all afraid to take up the cause. Second, they
probably felt no critical urgency to do so, since until the
armistice they considered the Central Powers adroit enough
to obtain a Wilsonian peace from the victors.

The second and critical stage of the peacemaking occurred during the actual drafting of the peace settlement in
Paris, between the armistice and the enforced German
acceptance of the final treaty on June 26, 1919. That was the
fateful time when, if Wilson's cause had been more strongly
supported at home, and if he had been better informed, the
Fourteen Points might have come closer to realization. Other
minorities used these months to get a hearing from the peace
delegation. The German-American papers published many
sympathetic reports of Irish-American demonstrations, and
even of an Italian demonstration for Fiume, but not a single
report of a German-American rally or delegation. At that
critical moment in history when their voice might have

[19] Philadelphia *Tageblatt*, April 10, 1918. The *Congressional Record*
fails to disclose one such resolution, and none is mentioned in the German-
American papers; it is reasonable to conclude then that none was sent.

influenced Wilson, German-Americans were too demoralized
and intimidated to raise it.

From November 1918 to June 1919 German-Americans
exhibited a pathetic confidence that Wilson, acclaimed by
victor and vanquished as a messiah, would win the peace as
he had won the war. While they were suspicious of the
European Allies, they implicitly trusted Wilson's Thanksgiving proclamation that complete victory was to bring not
only peace but the hope of a new era, in which justice was to
replace might and intrigues among nations.[20] When Wilson's
plan to leave the country and participate personally in the
peace conference met with criticism, German-Americans
applauded his decision. "Every right-thinking person ought
to recognize that since the peace negotiations are to be con-
ducted upon the principles he laid down, the president is
right in attending. In any case President Wilson is the best
interpreter of his views, so that his presence at least at the
beginning of the conference can only be promising for its
success."[21] Then, as events suggested that some Allies had
only given lip service to the Fourteen Points, one German-
American columnist called for prayers for Wilson's effort:
"For according to all reports, which trickle through from
Europe, our President will virtually have to prove super-
human in order to redeem his pledge to give the world a
just and lasting peace."[22]

German-Americans, however, did not feel entitled to
intercede with Wilson directly, and some even viewed such
pressures with disapproval. "Not a day has gone by in the

[20] Philadelphia *Nord-Amerika*, November 14, 1918. In this post-armistice
edition the spiritual adviser wrote, "One may not writing in German
express oneself as plainly as one wishes," but "we the United States have
solemnly obligated ourselves to full justice, and we may under no circumstances violate our pledge. If it be necessary, we must enforce justice in
the face of all. Otherwise the enormous sacrifice would have been in vain."

[21] *Ibid.*, November 21, 1918.

[22] *Ibid.*, December 26, 1918.

last month in which some class of hyphenated Americans did not draw up some lengthy resolutions to put pressure on the President at the peace conference to espouse their special pretensions and to champion claims which are often contradictory. . . . It is a true blessing under the circumstances that the President knows exactly what he wants; otherwise all the unsolicited requests floating in on him daily would turn his mind into chaos." Asserting that Wilson was fortunately immune to such pressures, the editorial ended with the bold statement that "no citizen has the right, on his own, to engage in foreign policy."

Two interesting sidelights of the German-American condemnation of this political interference should be mentioned at this point. In the first place Germans in America felt aggrieved when the "super-patriotic press," which had so religiously attacked them for sympathizing with Germany, now failed to attack these activities of the hyphenated. One editor stated that "with very few exceptions, Americans of German descent never made the attempt to exert any political influence on Germany; their efforts were confined to lessen want and misery and were exclusively a matter of feeling. Yet even this was reckoned as treason in them, though they offered their goods and their lives for America in the war and do not even now move a finger to do any special pleading for Germany."[23]

Oddly enough, while denying Americans and German-Americans the right to try to influence Wilson, the German press did not attack the Irish. On January 12, 1919, the Philadelphia *Tageblatt* sympathetically quoted William Cardinal O'Connell of Boston as declaring that peace was possible only if those deciding the fate of nations were ruled by principles and regard for the welfare of all mankind and not by expediency and favoritism to special groups. Other-

[23] Philadelphia *Tageblatt,* January 9, 1919.

wise, O'Connell maintained, there was in prospect "only a longer and more terrifying war. Everything lies in the hands of those who confer in Paris and Versailles. Unless their decisions correspond to the real rights of all peoples and are founded on eternal justice, infinitely more harm than good will come from their discussions." In the following months, the same paper approvingly described "A Mass Meeting of Friends of Ireland," which called for a free Ireland and raised a million and a half dollars to promote it. It quoted James Cardinal Gibbons' declaration that Ireland has the same rights as other nations.[24]

Two months later the New York *Sun* reported that some Italian-Americans in Philadelphia had organized a boycott against Liberty Bonds in order to protest Wilson's stand on Fiume and commended them for idealistically denying themselves the advantage of profitable investment in order to promote their political wishes. The editor of the Philadelphia *Tageblatt*, under the heading "Two Moral Standards," asked what the *Sun* would call German-Americans were they to refuse to buy Liberty Bonds in order to support Germany in a controversy with the United States.[25] Such actions would obviously have been unthinkable.

The third and final stage in the making of the treaty occurred between the publication of the draft on May 7, 1919, and its rejection by the U.S. Senate on March 20, 1920. When the terms of the treaty became known, shock and disillusionment overwhelmed German-Americans. "Anyone who has hitherto indulged the delusion that the personal influence of President Wilson on the peace conference would have a moderating effect and result in tolerable relations between both sides of the war, will now, after having read the summary of the treaty terms, have grave doubts. More

[24] *Ibid.*, February 24, 1919.
[25] *Ibid.*, May 2, 1919.

harsh, one would think, the terms could not in any circumstances have been for Germany."[26] Some even felt that, were it not for the inhuman blockade directed against German children, Germany might find it preferable to accept total occupation rather than sign such a treaty. But most German-Americans favored a policy of wait and see. Although they were still too shocked by the earlier imputations of their hyphenism and intimidated by espionage legislation to organize protest rallies, the profound disillusionment brought forth a few clear voices of protest, which added to the more vocal disillusionment of many other minorities helped to influence the Senate. That may explain why administration spokesmen like George Creel and Joseph P. Tumulty angrily number the German-Americans among the minorities that contributed to the treaty's rejection.

According to Joseph P. Tumulty, Wilson's private secretary, Wilson believed that those Senators who insisted on reservations to the treaty were motivated either by party politics or by propaganda. "Before the war pro-German agitation had sought to keep us out of the conflict, and after the war it sought to separate us in interest and purpose from other governments with which we were associated."[27] Tumulty approvingly quoted George Creel, the director of public information, who wrote in February, 1919: "The draft of the League Constitution was denounced even before its contents were known or explained. The bare facts that the document proved acceptable to the British Empire aroused the instant antagonism of the 'professional' Irish-Americans, the 'professional' German-Americans, the 'professional' Italian-Americans, and all those others whose political fortunes depended upon the persistence and accentuation of racial prejudices. Where *one* hyphen was scourged

[26] *Ibid.*, May 8, 1919.
[27] Joseph P. Tumulty, *Woodrow Wilson As I Knew Him* (1921), 453.

the year before a *score* of hyphens was now encouraged and approved."[28]

Creel gave German-American sentiment and action considerable responsibility for the Senate's rejection: "Naturally enough, the great mass of Americans of German blood and descent are still possessed of their former sympathies, and the cry that comes to them from their kindred strikes down to their old affections. This fact, unfortunately, has been seized upon by politicians with keen appreciation of the strength of the German vote, and no attempt has been spared to convince every citizen of Teutonic extraction that savage revenge has been inflicted upon the Fatherland." He also complained that Will H. Hays, chairman of the Republican National Committee, who once feared that Wilson "meant to let 'the accursed Hun escape,'" and Senator Philander Chase Knox, who was "most clamant for a 'hard peace,'" raised their voices "only to attack the harshness of the terms inflicted upon Germany. To justify their position they now assert that the Germans did not surrender unconditionally, but laid down their arms under an agreement that peace terms should be based upon the Fourteen Points of President Wilson, and that this agreement was 'repudiated.'"[29] Even more bitterly, Creel accused the Republican Party of "babbling about 'poor Germany' where a year before it had hurled obscene hatred at the 'accursed Hun,' . . . yelling Americanism and indefatigably fanning the angers of Italians and Greeks and Germans."[30] Specifically he charged: "The forces of hyphenation were boldly called into being—Professional Germans, silent throughout the war for fear of treason charges, emerged from retirement, Charles Nagel going so far as to issue a pamphlet attacking the League of

[28] *Ibid.*, 345.
[29] George Creel, *The War, The World And Wilson* (1920), 300.
[30] *Ibid.*, 368.

Nations and arguing against the return of Alsace-Lorraine to France. Delegations of Irish, Italians, Egyptians, Hindus, and other races were brought to Washington and given elaborate hearings. . . . Irish, Hindus, and Egyptians deserted the sanities of judgment and joined in the attack upon the League in which lay their only hope."[31]

Creel's broadside is curious and significant in several ways. First, the director of public information for the war to make the world safe for democracy implied that it was a heinous offense for hyphenated Americans to express themselves against so American a problem as joining the League of Nations. Second, he resentfully and gratuitously attributed great influence to the German-Americans in the Senate's rejection of the treaty. Third, by denouncing delegations to Washington of other nationalities while making no reference to German-American delegations he implied that there were no such delegations by German-Americans to influence the treaty making. What influence there was must have been from individuals and from isolated protests. Yet there is the possibility that many midwestern senators strongly opposed the treaty because they knew many German-Americans would vote against it.

The only individual opposition from what Creel calls a "professional German" was that of Charles Nagel. Nagel's German-born father, a doctor, had left Houston in 1863 for St. Louis because of his sympathy with the Union cause. Charles Nagel, born in Texas, educated as a lawyer in St. Louis, rose to be Secretary of Commerce and Labor in President Taft's cabinet. During the war his frequent theme was that "in this land of ours there is no room for the hyphen. There are no German-Americans, Irish-Americans, or Anglo-Americans. We are all, and must always be, Americans."[32]

[31] *Ibid.*, 331.
[32] Charles Nagel, *Speeches and Writings* (1931), I, 16.

Creel would seem to be no more justified in calling him a "professional German" than in calling H. L. Mencken one.

The pamphlet to which Creel resentfully refers seems to have appeared first as an article in *The Nation* (July 23, 1919), under the title "The League of Nations—With a Letter on 'Moral Objections to the Treaty.'" Nagel calmly reasons that America's "all-absorbing commitment . . . to the League of Nations as now proposed" would be dangerous and ill-advised, and insists that the question has nothing to do with "whether Germany is treated too mildly, or the Allies are advantaged too much."[33] He does, however, point out that joining the League would commit America to use its army to enforce the Versailles treaty even where it was clearly unjust and in violation of the Fourteen Points. "The fourteen points are ours and not the President's to interpret and do with as he pleases. They were announced in our name and by our consent. . . . Apart from that, those fourteen points constitute the basis of the armistice and of the promised peace terms."[34] Demonstrating the issues on which the treaty draft violated the Fourteen Points, he asks, "What has become of self-determination?" In this connection he makes the comment on Alsace-Lorraine to which Creel refers: "We did not say that Alsace and Lorraine must be returned. We said that wrong committed must be righted . . . all people reasonably identified as French and taken over distinctly against their will should be reunited to France. We did not say that essentially German people, inhabiting large and contiguous sections of either Alsace or Lorraine, must be returned to France against their will. Indeed, we precisely said the contrary."[35] Although in his pamphlet the German problem receives a minimum of space,

[33] *Ibid.*, II, 189.
[34] *Ibid.*, 214.
[35] *Ibid.*

the whole range of topics covered by the treaty is discussed. He asks, for example, "If Poland can stand alone, what of Ireland?"[36] Considering that, with the possible exception of H. L. Mencken, Nagel was the most prominent American of German descent of the time (important enough for Creel to cite him by name), we may well assume that his considered disapproval of the treaty and the League may have added to the Senate opposition.

Creel complained of Americans of German descent that "the cry that comes to them from their kindred strikes down to their old affections."[37] There he struck the right key. For what really galvanized the German-Americans into action, defying the aspersions of pro-Germanism, was "the cry" that came from abroad that their kindred, that German women and children, were exposed to imminent starvation by the British hunger blockade. Their mounting determination to relieve this situation received decisive encouragement from no less a personage than Pope Benedict XV.

The Central Verein, founded by German-Americans in 1855 with headquarters in St. Louis, was described by the *Franciscan Almanac* for 1939 as "really the first national rural organization of Catholics as well as the first National Social Organization of Catholics in this country." When it held its sixty-third national convention in Chicago, September 14-16, 1919, a greeting from the Holy Father electrified the assembly. Archbishop George William Mundelein of Chicago read a special message dated at the Vatican, July 18, 1919, and signed by Peter Cardinal Gasparri, which the press headlined "Pope Praises Loyalty of German-Americans and Pleads for Blotting Out Hatred." In this remarkable message the Holy Father declared that German-Americans, although retaining a love for their fatherland, had not been hindered in "doing

[36] *Ibid.*, 206.
[37] Creel, *The War, The World*, 300.

their full duty toward their adopted country."[38] He deplored the "trail of hatred among nations," which must be "entirely blotted out" and the nations brought back to Christian brotherhood.

> In the struggle to accomplish this, the work of the German Catholics in the United States, who are united by the closest ties to both lately warring races, ought to be particularly successful. . . . Moreover, knowing the dreadful conditions under which brethren in Germany are now living the Sovereign Pontiff implores you most fervently to lend them every assistance, material as well as moral, and in the quickest and most effective way. . . . To this invitation the Holy Father feels certain that not only you will gladly respond but all the children of your generous country . . . for surely they will be mindful of the great services their fellow-citizens of German birth and descent have rendered their country during this war.[38]

Both Catholic and non-Catholic German-Americans responded to this papal call for German and Austrian relief with reawakened courage and heartwarming generosity. In virtually every issue German-American papers carried something on "Heimathilfe—Help for the homelands," including "Money Gifts to all Parts of Germany, Austria, and Hungary." Where no rallies were risked on the peace treaty, some were now organized for relief. Yet even these met with intimidating criticism from superpatriots. The Philadelphia *Tageblatt* of August 28, 1919, for example, advertised on its front page in a box about four by six inches a "Hilfsfond: Grosse Massenversamlung—Relief Fund. Big Mass Rally," in the Philadelphia *Turngemeinde*. Its printed tenpoint program included the "Star Spangled Banner," five other musical selections, the invocation by the Catholic

[38] Philadelphia *Nord-Amerika*, September 18, 1919.

Father Theodore Hammeke, the benediction by the Lutheran Pastor S. G. von Bosse, and two talks presumably on the need for relief. Although it was obviously a nonpolitical program devoted solely to charity, on the next day, August 29, another big box, about five by six inches, was headed "An Answer to Malicious Attack upon the Philadelphia Relief Society." It reported how the Philadelphia *Public Ledger* had delivered itself of an attack on the relief rally of the preceding night. Its attack was headlined "Mass-Meeting Called to Prove Loyalty to Fatherland. No Empty Phrase." The *Tageblatt* plaintively answered: "Fairminded Americans have sent out calls to ameliorate the suffering of women and children of the Central powers. . . . What is more natural for a brother, sister or friend than to come to the rescue of the suffering kinsfolk across the sea? . . . And who can have any respect for a paper, which slurs such humanitarian efforts?" This episode to some extent illustrates why German-Americans from 1918 to 1920 had less constructive influence on the peacemaking than their numbers and special interests warranted.

There were indeed pitifully few published protests. In the national convention of the Catholic Central Verein of September 14–16, 1919, in which the Holy Father's call for German and Austrian relief was read, the president, Michael F. Gerten, devoted only one short paragraph of his annual report to the "Peace Treaty." "Because as Americans we love our country and therefore hold its honor high, we may and should protest against the unjust peace treaty which the Allies have forced upon the Central Powers, and we should entreat our government to safeguard America's good name by insisting on a modification of the peace treaty before ratifying it."[39] One will note the apologetic tone! While other nationalities took for

[39] *Ibid.*

granted the right to urge on the government what seemed a
proper course of foreign policy, German-Americans spent
more energy justifying than daring to do. As a consequence,
the convention of the Central Verein did not introduce
among its many resolutions a single one protesting the harsh
peace terms that made necessary the relief the Holy Father
had urged. Instead it contented itself with bare hints of
dissatisfaction: "Statesmen and diplomats understandably
find it difficult to give the world peace because they rely on
human knowledge instead of the divine wisdom which
Christ and his Vicar could give them." And it thanks the
Holy Father for "his continued efforts to bring about a just
peace."

In a similar vein, but somewhat more directly, the Pennsylvania state branch of the Central Verein at Allentown,
August 30–31, 1919, devoted one full resolution to the treaty.

> The 25th Annual Convention of the German Roman
> Catholic State Society of Pennsylvania with thank-
> ful eyes to heaven greets the end of the terrible
> world war and the drafting of treaties for peace and
> a league of nations. But as Christians we cannot but
> express our deepest regret that no place at the peace
> table was found for the God of Peace and Mercy
> and for his Vicar on Earth, the Holy Father of
> Christendom. We also concur in the feeling of the
> most sympathetic observers in all countries that the
> accomplishments so far of the Paris peace confer-
> ence will only then lead to a lasting peace and a
> true league of nations if the final treaties and the
> constitution of the so-called league of nations will
> realize the eternal principles of natural law and of
> Christian ethics in a spirit of conciliation and in
> accordance with the Fourteen Points of our Presi-
> dent. We regret in the interest of all mankind that
> the conditions of the peace treaty and for mem-
> bership in the league have not been so formulated
> as also to be open to and be acceptable to the

vanquished nations and we affirm that the sooner
and the more completely this is done the sooner will
the world be normal and mankind secured against
the onrush of Bolshevism and anarchy. We also
consider it to be in the interest of world peace that
then too the millions of Germans in Central Europe
who by the treaties were placed under foreign
domination and the noble people of Ireland will be
accorded their right of self-determination.[40]

This resolution sums up pretty well the universal feeling
of German-Americans. Even more daringly critical of the
postarmistice treatment of Germany was a paragraph in the
address of Dr. Francis M. Schirp of New York at the twenty-
fifth annual convention of the New Jersey state branch of
the Central Verein held August 3–September 1, 1919, in
Elizabeth, New Jersey. After his main address he added a
few words on "what lies heavy on all our hearts. I mean
the terrible plight of our racial brothers (Stammesbrueder)
in the old country. The German people are suffering un-
speakably much. The reports seeping through of malnutri-
tion, more accurately, the slow starvation of our folkrelatives
is hair-raising. A conscienceless, brutal policy is bent on the
total extermination of the German people and the method
for this diabolical design is hunger."[41] The speaker declared
it a duty of German-Americans to do everything possible
to preserve their kinspeople from annihilation. He concluded: "As American Citizens who in the last few years
had to make greater sacrifices than citizens of non-German
origin, let us renew our protest against the illegal and inhuman hunger-blockade, which outrages all principles of
true humanity and international law and is not equalled in
the annals of human history."
     It is significant, however, that this assembly, whose

40 *Ibid.*, September 4, 1919.
41 *Ibid.*, September 17, 1919.

members were so deeply disturbed about the suffering in Germany, while passing seven resolutions on such varied topics as loyalty to the Constitution, parochial schools, suffragettes, and prohibition, did not risk one on the most important matter of all, the peace treaty then before Congress.

Nor did the German-American papers record any protest meetings or resolutions on the treaty and the League of Nations. The crying need of relief for Central Europe made every German-American keenly aware of the treaty's violations of the spirit and letter of the Fourteen Points, whose adoption they had naively trusted Wilson to secure. Although their fear of persecutions prevented them from gathering in mass rallies of protest, their disappointment in the treaty was so obvious that not only Wilson and George Creel but all the senators must have been keenly aware of it. The most influential of German-American papers, the New York *Staatszeitung,* in a lead editorial entitled "Faith in the American People" (December 9, 1919), accurately reflected the German-American disillusionment with Wilson's peacemaking. "The German people distinguished between the President and the American people. From the man whom they once greeted enthusiastically as a saviour, whom they revered as a new Messiah, they no longer hope for anything. Their trust, which was able to survive even the harshness of the armistice, was destroyed to the very roots by the Versailles treaty. . . . They have coffined and buried their trust in Wilson. . . . But they put their trust in the sense of right and justice of the American people."

The German-American attitude on the question of whether the Senate should ratify the imperfect treaty and league draft cannot, however, easily be determined. While Charles Nagel's negative view was probably representative, the German-language papers consulted—the New York *Staats-*

zeitung, the Philadelphia *Tageblatt,* the Philadelphia *Nord-Amerika*—made no active attempt to urge rejection of the treaty. Their attitude seemed to suggest that nothing much could be salvaged either way. Four days after the first Senate rejection (November 24, 1919), for example, the New York *Staatszeitung* carried a front-page dispatch to the effect that the German people welcomed it, but its editorial paradoxically suggested that the Germans were apprehensive that the rejection would provoke France to harsher guarantees against Germany. Although the editorial referred to the German people, it seems more a reflection of the paper's own German-American attitude.

After the final rejection, the Philadelphia *Tageblatt* on March 21, 1920, editorialized on Wilson's phrase about the world's broken heart. A careful reading was necessary to discover whether it approved or disapproved of the action. Asking whether Wilson's stubborn insistence on all or nothing might not mean that Wilson secretly wanted the treaty rejected so that the Republicans could be blamed for the world's broken heart, it concluded: "But in truth the boundless misery of mankind on the old continent is only the legitimate product of the blind hatred and the brutal peace of Versailles, whose revision must be the mission of an enlightened statesmanship during the next years. For this cure of the aching heart of the world probably nothing would have been gained by a ratification of the treaty by the United States either with or without reservation."

This expresses the prevailing attitude of German-Americans toward the Senate's rejection of the Wilsonian peacemaking, from which they and the world expected democracy, justice, and lasting peace but got instead what many German-Americans, then and now, see as the miscarriage of Versailles and Saint-Germain.

Only a few months after the rejection of the treaty, when

another national election was approaching, German-Americans were ready to register their feelings. One leading magazine reported an attempt at "Organizing the German-American Vote." Reflecting wartime prejudices, it declared: "Whether a brazen attempt by pro-German forces to dominate American politics, as its critics warn us, or a movement actuated by purely American aspirations and ideals, as its friends insist, the attempt of the German-American Citizens' League . . . to prevent the election of Governor Cox . . . is arousing lively interest. . . ." In a convention in Chicago in August the league, before unreservedly endorsing Harding, waited for him to express himself "in unequivocal terms on other subjects involving the honor of our country, such as the pernicious peace pacts of Versailles and St. Germain, which turned the fourteen pledges, so solemnly enunciated by the President of the United States, into fourteen scraps of paper."[42] That probably was, and still is, the sentiment with which all Americans of German descent who concern themselves with foreign policy regard Wilson's peacemaking and the ill-fated Fourteen Points, forerunners of the still more ill-fated seven-point Atlantic Charter of Roosevelt and Churchill.

From January 8, 1918, until March 20, 1920, there were three distinct stages of active, or more often passive, German-American activities whose purpose was to influence Wilson. During the first stage, between January 8 and the armistice on November 11, they strained to prove their loyalty, bought bonds, responded to the draft, and hoped for a speedy peace. They welcomed all "peace offensives," stressing the need for a just and conciliatory peace according to Wilson's pronouncements. During the second stage, between the armistice and the publication on May 7, 1919, of the treaty provisions, they reposed an almost childlike trust in Wilson's

[42] *Literary Digest,* September 18, 1920.

will and ability to secure from the Allies a draft honestly
grounded in the Fourteen Points, and tensely but passively
awaited it. In the third stage, they first reacted with a numb
shock, then relieved their worst frustration and despair by
plunging into massive relief work to alleviate the blockade-
induced starvation in the vanquished countries. Finally, a
few dared to voice restrained but desperate protests. But
for the most part the German-American, whether organized
or not, exuded enough disillusionment with the treaty to
have in some way influenced the Senate's rejection of it.

Unfortunately, however, precisely in the second stage,
when their conciliatory influence was most needed to
strengthen Wilson's hand in Paris, German-Americans were
too frightened, too persecuted, too wishfully trustful, to
agitate for an honest application of the Fourteen Points to
Germany. When finally in the third stage they roused
themselves, in desperation, after the Germans had been
forced to sign the treaty and our Senate had little choice
other than ratifying or rejecting it, its unjust provisions
could hardly be moderated. During the critical period in
1919, when the treaty was being drafted, German-Americans
should have spoken, and Wilson should have been eager to
consider their suggestions. But they had been eliminated as
a force in public opinion—they were not even allowed to use
the hyphen in their name. In general, one must conclude
that, in contrast to some other minorities, the German-Americans had little, if any, influence on the treaty, had no contacts
with Wilson or his cabinet, and, though intensely concerned,
were more passive than active.[43]

[43] These negative findings are confirmed by a letter from Dr. Charles
Callan Tansill, Professor Emeritus of Georgetown University.

THE IRISH

Joseph P. O'Grady

The story of the Irish-American attempt to influence Woodrow Wilson in the twentieth century must begin in the middle of the nineteenth, when the Irish in America acquired the tools necessary to create political pressure—numbers, leaders, and organization. During the late 1840s three events in Ireland shifted the force of Irish nationalism to the United States. Daniel O'Connell's failure to use force in the Repeal Association's agitation in 1844 (the first event) led the young bloods of Irish politics to seek the solution to their dream in open rebellion, the revolution of 1848. When the British smashed this attempt (the second event), the leaders of the revolt fled to the four corners of the world, then regained their courage and made their way to the United States, where they discovered the results of the Great Famine (the third event). During the late forties potato crop after potato crop failed and millions of Irishmen faced starvation. Hundreds of thousands refused to accept this certain death and fled to the safety of the United States. Thus, by 1850 the Irish in America possessed the basic materials for political action, the leaders and the led. What was needed was organization, which came in 1858 with the founding of the American branch of the Irish Revolutionary Brotherhood, commonly referred to as the Fenians. This organization had as its stated purpose use of Irish power in America to bring war to England and peace to Ireland. As the Civil War came to an end, the brotherhood geared for its first attempt to influence foreign policy; for the Irish in America were ready to test the belief that public opinion determines that policy.

From the end of the Civil War to the final battle in the

long Anglo-Irish struggle, Irish-Americans used their voice in American politics to force the government of the United States to aid in this struggle. The first attempt, following fast on the heels of the Union's defeat of the South, centered on a plan that called for action in both Ireland and America. The Irish at home were to revolt, while the Irish in America were to attack Canada, which then was to be traded with England for Irish freedom. The success of the American phase depended ultimately upon unofficial sympathy at least of the administration in Washington. To gain this support, the brotherhood relied upon two forces: the threat of a solid Irish vote, and the strained relations between England and the United States; and their hopes did not go completely unrewarded. Whether the mild success resulted from his inherent political power or the condition of Anglo-American relations, or both, did not really concern the Irish-American. He simply felt that what happened once could happen again. Consequently, as his economic and political influence in American affairs grew, he made further attempts to shape American foreign policy and to enlist support for Ireland's cause—during the Parnell era in the 1880s, at the turn of the century, and finally during World War I. In the early stages of that war he abandoned this traditional means of action and turned to the Germans for aid. He even organized a number of joint Irish-German plots to overthrow British rule; but when the United States entered the war in April, 1917, this avenue of hope for Irish freedom disappeared. Americans of Irish descent, because they were more American than Irish, no longer could support a German victory. Thus, the Irish returned to the old device of using the United States to champion Ireland's cause, but they had little hope of success until Wilson gave them a faint ray on January 8, 1918.

In an address before a joint session of Congress, Wilson announced to the world America's war aims. "What we demand in this war, therefore, is nothing peculiar to ourselves. It is that the world be made fit and safe to live in; and particularly that it be made safe for every peace-loving nation which, like our own, wishes to live its own life, determine its own institutions, be assured of justice and fair dealing by the other peoples of the world as against force and selfish aggression." He went on to enumerate his Fourteen Points and concluded by summarizing the principle that ran through the whole program. "It's the principle of justice to all peoples of all nationalities, and their right to live on equal terms of liberty and safety with one another whether they be strong or weak."[1]

Literally millions received these words as a sign of the bright new world that was to emerge from the ashes of war. The Irish in America, however, accepted them with mixed emotions. Some felt they indicated that Wilson would champion Ireland's claim to determine her own destiny; others urged caution. John Devoy, a veteran of fifty years of Irish revolutionary movements, emphasized what he called the "one fatal defect in Wilson's points, [they apply] only to a portion of the world—that controlled by Germany and her allies—and utterly ignore the rest."[2] Devoy asked "What about English Imperialism?" and thus raised the question of Ireland. But Devoy was not the only one who recognized the limitation. Representative Atkins J. McLemore of Texas took a similar position declaring, "Since we propose to enter into the internal affairs of Europe, many will regret that the President did not include Ireland among those oppressed countries that are to be given liberty and autonomy."[3]

[1] *The Messages and Papers of Woodrow Wilson*, 2 vols. (1924), I, 467, 471.
[2] New York *Gaelic-American*, January 12, 1918. Devoy served as the editor and publisher.
[3] *Ibid.*, January 19, 1918.

In this way, Irish-American opinion chose a line of attack that continued until the signing of the peace treaty—applause for the concept of selfdetermination and condemnation for any program that did not include Ireland in the list of countries to receive the right. As a result, from January, 1918, to June, 1919, the Irish in America worked with ferocious vigor to force the administration to include Ireland under the umbrella of American war aims.

The pressure began almost immediately after Wilson's address. On January 11 he received Mrs. Hanah Sheehy-Skiffington, the widow of one of the leaders of the Easter Rebellion, who presented him with an urgent plea from the Irish Women's Council of Dublin that the United States recognize the Irish Republic.[4] On the same day, a delegation of Irish-Americans led by Senator James D. Phelan of California, a close political associate of Wilson and one of his staunch defenders in the Senate, presented him with a statue of Robert Emmett, the nineteenth-century Irish revolutionary martyr. Phelan's prepared statement implored Wilson actively to support Irish freedom. A week later, in Ireland, Eamon De Valera, the future president of the Irish Republic, demanded that the great powers recognize the existence of an independent Irish state, speaking directly to Wilson. "We say that if those who go about mouthing of an independent Irish state do not take that interpretation of it, they are hypocrites, and we tell President Wilson, in view of the statements he has made, if he does not take that view of it, he is as big a hypocrite as Lloyd George."[5] Direct pressure on Wilson was supplemented by the more indirect method of pressuring Congress. By February, a number of repre-

[4] *Ibid.* Representatives McLemore, Mason of Illinois, and Champ Clark (in Devoy's words "a friend of Ireland") met Mrs. Skiffington and served as her guide through political Washington.

[5] Charles C. Tansill, *America and the Fight for Irish Freedom* (1957), 241.

sentatives had offered various resolutions asking for American support of Ireland's claim to freedom. When the chairman of the House Foreign Affairs Committee, Henry D. Flood of Virginia, did not indicate any willingness to push these resolutions to the floor of the House, the leaders of sixteen Irish-American organizations sent a joint letter to Flood asking that his Committee act upon these resolutions immediately.[6] Two weeks later the papers reported Flood's answer. "It would not be for the public interest, at the present time, to grant your request for such a (public) hearing. The serious consideration by the Committee on Foreign Affairs of these resolutions might well be considered as constituting an interference in the internal affairs of another nation, and that nation one of our cobelligerents, and could scarcely fail to prove a source of serious embarrassment to a nation associated with the United States in the war."[7] In early March, a similar resolution appeared in the Senate when Jacob H. Gallinger of New Hampshire, the Republican leader, pleaded for Ireland's cause. Within two months after the Fourteen Points address, the Irish in America had applied pressure to Wilson and to both houses of Congress.

At the same time, the Friends of Irish Freedom, the dominant Irish-American organization of the time, and other organizations began to generate public support through mass meetings. Irish-American newspapers were filled with notices of such meetings. During Easter week of 1918, these meetings were held in towns across the country, each one passing a resolution demanding that the United States support Ireland. The culmination occurred on May 18, when Irishmen from the corners of the world gathered in New York for the Second Irish Race Convention. At this gathering, Justice John Goff presented a resolution which called for

[6] Philadelphia *Irish Press*, March 23, 1918. Joseph McGarrity served as the editor and publisher.

[7] *Ibid.*, April 6, 1918.

"the application to Ireland now of President Wilson's noble declaration of the right of every people to self-rule and self-determination" and specifically asked Wilson to "exert every legitimate and friendly influence in favor of self-determination for the people of Ireland."[8]

One student of the Irish in America, Charles C. Tansill, has concluded that these activities had little effect upon Wilson. According to Tansill, when Senator Phelan asked Wilson if he would make a brief reference to "Ireland's right to autonomous government and the prompt granting of it," the President replied, "I do not think that it would be wise for me in my public utterance to attempt to outline a policy for the British government with regard to Ireland."[9] This and similar statements found among his private papers caused Professor Tansill to accuse Wilson of having little real interest in the Irish question. Tansill writes: "There is little doubt that he was anxious that some excuse should arise that would permit him from pushing the claims of Ireland at the peace conference. He was determined not to embarrass the British government by suggesting a settlement of the Irish question."[10]

This evaluation seems excessively harsh, because in the summer and early fall of 1918 Wilson's words and actions actually increased Irish-American hopes. On July 4, he declared that America wanted every question settled "upon the basis of the free acceptance of that settlement by the people immediately concerned, and not upon the basis of the material interest or advantage of any other nation or people which may desire a different settlement for the sake of its own exterior influence or mastery."[11] In responding to this speech, one Irish-American editor declared, "If the

[8] Tansill, *America and Irish Freedom*, 271.
[9] *Ibid.*, 268.
[10] *Ibid.*, 249.
[11] *Messages of Wilson*, I, 500.

Irish question is not included, we have yet to learn the meaning of the English language."[12] Then on September 3 Wilson's administration officially recognized the Czech-Slovak National Council as a de facto belligerent government. Within weeks the Yugoslavs appeared before Secretary of State Robert Lansing, asking for similar recognition. In his address to the American people on war aims, in late September, Wilson enumerated Five Particulars as the basis for the settlement; two of these drew praise from the Irish: "First, the impartial justice meted out must invoke no discrimination between those to whom we wish to be just and those to whom we do not wish to be just. It must be a justice that plays no favorite and knows no standard but the equal rights of the several peoples concerned; second, no special or separate interest of any single nation or any group of nations can be made the basis of any part of the settlement which is not consistent with the common interest of all."[13] Some declared that "President Wilson made it clear in his New York speech for the benefit of German and English statesmen that Ireland was included among the list of peoples and nations which must be made free as a result of this great war."[14] Even John Devoy, who had been known to be skeptical of Wilson in the past, declared "Wilson is for self-determination of all people."[15]

[12] Philadelphia *Irish Press*, July 13, 1918.

[13] *Messages of Wilson*, I, 524.

[14] Philadelphia *Irish Press*, October 12, 1918.

[15] New York *Gaelic-American*, October 22, 1918. These events received wide coverage in the Irish-American press. Even the telegram which Wilson sent to the Serbian National Defense League on June 17, 1918, was printed in the June 22, 1918, issue of the Philadelphia *Irish Press*. It is interesting to read the words of that telegram. "The struggle of the Serbian people for liberty and for right and the aspirations of all that great glorious people for the recognition of their national identity and their right to determine their own allegiance and their own political actions hold now more than ever the attention of the world and must engage the sympathy of everyone who sees what is now being every day made more clearly manifest to statesmen everywhere that the future peace of the world depends upon

How can one reconcile the difference between the hopes that such actions obviously raised and Professor Tansill's evaluations. The statements of July and September, 1918, were of a more general nature than those of the original Fourteen Points address; anyone who desired freedom for any oppressed nationality could find comfort in them. There can have been only three purposes in Wilson's generalizations: to win votes in the congressional elections, to achieve a propaganda effect on enemy populations, or to express a sincere idealism. There seems to be no conclusive evidence that, as far as the Irish were concerned, Wilson acted for political reasons. On the contrary, as Professor Tansill has indicated, he seems to have done just the opposite. For some unexplainable reason I cannot see Wilson as a hypocrite, one who used his idealism merely as a tool to weaken the unity of the enemy. To call him a realist one must, in effect, call him a liar—which no one will do. Was not Wilson merely living the role of the sincere, honest ex-college professor who believed in the social-Darwinian myth that man, by using his infinite power of reasoning, could solve all social and political problems? Along with Walter Lippmann he believed that man could "educate and control" life through science. Wilson, the product of the naive optimism of the nineteenth century, believed that man could create a world free of sin and suffering, and he wanted to make the world safe for peace-loving nations, for democracy, for everyone, including the Irish. Where then did he go wrong? His problem was that he devoted more time to the wording of his policy speeches than to the understanding of what these speeches actually meant or how he could accomplish what he was promising to accomplish. Wilson, in the summer of

---

the acquiescence of its several peoples in every settlement which affects their fortunes and their happiness." These words served as another example of Wilson's idealism.

1918, saw himself as the supreme policy-maker—as Thomas A. Bailey put it, the Messiah—and what messiah or supreme lawmaker ever found time for detail?[16] This was the work of subordinates. They dealt with the details of Ireland. They understood the problem. Wilson did not.

Although Wilson did not necessarily raise the point, the question of American support of Ireland's claim to self-determination entered the Congressional campaign. In Pennsylvania the local branches of the Friends of Irish Freedom mailed to all candidates for major office a questionnaire that included the question: "Will you, if elected to the public office for which you are a candidate, openly and unequivocally support Ireland's claims to complete independence, the form of government to be determined by the whole male and female population of Ireland? . . ."[17] It is interesting to note that eight congressional candidates, both Republicans and Democrats, and the two candidates for governor endorsed this statement on the front pages of the Philadelphia *Irish Press*.[18] What influence this had upon the campaign is difficult to assess; but the fact that candidates for high office would endorse publicly such a statement indicates, to some extent, the political power of the Irish at election time.

While the politicians debated the question, mass meetings continued. Petitions were passed and congressmen notified. Letters came from the citizens of Butte, Montana, the executive board of the Clan-Na-Gael, the Irish Progressive League, citizens of Cleveland, the New York Central Federated Union, and the Friendly Sons of St. Patrick. The clergy of Philadelphia, San Francisco, New York, Chicago,

[16] Walter Lippmann, *Drift and Mastery* (1911), 147-48; Thomas A. Bailey, *A Diplomatic History of the American People* (1955), 664.

[17] Philadelphia *Irish Press*, October 26, 1918.

[18] *Ibid.*, November 2, 1918. Devoy argued that support for the Democrats was the surest way to achieve Irish freedom.

St. Louis, Newark, Boston, and Catholic University, and the bishops of the Province of Pennsylvania sent similar letters. The tempo of the mass meetings increased, especially after the signing of the armistice, reaching a climax during the week of December 8-15, 1918, which was designated as Self-Determination Week. A huge gathering in Madison Square Garden on December 10 heard William Cardinal O'Connell of Boston declare: "This war, we are told again and again by all those responsible for the war, is for justice for all . . . for the inalienable right, inherent in every nation, of self-determination. The war can be justified only by the universal application of those principles. Let that application begin with Ireland."[19] The meeting ended with the passage of a resolution, which Wilson received as he sailed across the Atlantic, urging him "to demand at the peace conference self-determination for the people of Ireland."[20] Similar meetings producing similar resolutions were held in Chicago, Philadelphia, Denver, Baltimore, Louisville, Portland, New Haven, Omaha, Buffalo, Seattle, New Orleans, Manchester, San Francisco, Brockton, Mass., and Chester, Pa. By December these meetings had had some effect on Wilson; in answering a letter from Senator Thomas Walsh, who had asked Wilson if he would support Ireland's claims, the President replied, "He would do his utmost to bring about a just and satisfactory solution to a delicate problem."[21] At least he had shifted from the more negative position he had taken in June.

By the time the peace conference opened in late January, the problem had become much more delicate than Wilson imagined. In the British Parliamentary elections of December 14, 1918, the Sinn Fein—the Irish republican party that would settle for nothing less than complete independence—

[19] Tansill, *America and Irish Freedom*, 280.
[20] New York *Gaelic-American*, December 14, 1918.
[21] Tansill, *America and Irish Freedom*, 291.

won seventy-three seats. Irish-Americans immediately proclaimed that the Irish people, having exercised their right of selfdetermination, had voted for independence.[22] On January 7, 1919, twenty-six of the elected republicans—the remainder were either in prison or in hiding—met in Dublin and organized a constituent assembly. Two weeks later, this assembly adopted a constitution, issued a declaration of Irish independence, and authorized a delegation, composed of Eamon De Valera, Arthur Griffiths, and Count George Plunkett, to represent Ireland at the Paris Peace Conference. As a result of these events, the statesmen who assembled in Paris found a virtually independent nation pounding on their doors instead of an oppressed national minority.

These changes also greatly influenced events in America. Many Irish-Americans, after January 1919, no longed accepted selfdetermination as the solution to the Irish question; the people of Ireland, they argued, had in effect exercised that right in the December elections. Since the Irish people had indicated a preference for independence, the solution to the Irish question was simply official recognition of the Irish Republic. Others, of course, realized the gap between Irish declarations of independence and their acceptance by the English. They continued to argue that the statesmen at Paris would have to confer upon Ireland the right of self-determination since this was the only way in which England could be forced to recognize Ireland's right. In either case, the action of the President of the United States was significant, and both groups wanted Wilson to present the representatives of the Irish people to the Peace Conference. In order to do this, however, Irish leaders felt that public opinion had to be aroused.

With these thoughts in mind, Irish-American leaders decided to convene the Third Irish Race Convention. They

22 Philadelphia *Irish Press,* January 4, 1919.

selected Philadelphia as the convention city and February 20 as the opening day. Over 5,000 delegates arrived in time to hear James Cardinal Gibbons of Baltimore, the foremost Catholic churchman in America, declare, "All Americans should stand as one man for Ireland's inalienable right of self-determination."[23] The delegates cheered wildly for a resolution calling upon the Paris Peace Conference to "apply to Ireland the great doctrine of national self-determination." A committee headed by Justice Goff presented this resolution to Wilson, who was at that time in the United States. Wilson hedged when Goff asked him to raise the question of Ireland's right to selfdetermination at the peace conference and to request that the Irish delegates be given an opportunity to present their case. According to Professor Tansill, "The audience with the American Chief Executive came to a fruitless end."[24] Wilson was quoted as telling R. S. Baker after the meeting, "They were so insistent that I had hard work keeping my temper."[25]

In other quarters, however, particularly among politicians, the work of the Irish-Americans began to show some evidence of success. On February 7 the Governor of Missouri declared he "strongly favored self determination for Ireland."[26] Legislative bodies in Pennsylvania, Missouri, Colorado, and California passed resolutions that called for American support for Ireland. The Massachusetts legislature had declared in favor of an independent Ireland as early as March, 1918.[27]

Even the Committee on Foreign Affairs of the House of Representatives discussed a number of resolutions expressing

[23] John Tracy Ellis, *The Life of James Cardinal Gibbons* (1952), II, 226.
[24] Tansill, *America and Irish Freedom*, 301.
[25] Seth P. Tillman, *Anglo-American Relations at the Peace Conference, 1919* (1961), 198.
[26] Philadelphia *Irish Press*, February 22, 1918.
[27] *Ibid.*, March 23, 1918.

similar sentiments, and by late January had narrowed its discussion to the one introduced by Representative Thomas Gallagher of Illinois. Although the administration tried to delay committee action on the resolution, Frank L. Polk, the acting Secretary of State, came to feel that delaying tactics were useless; on February 3 he informed Lansing in Paris that "both sides are playing politics with the resolution in order to get the Irish vote."[28] By then even Wilson had intervened, asking Tumulty to explain to the congressional leaders that he opposed Gallagher's resolution because it would disrupt Anglo-American relations.[29] Although Tumulty later claimed that his intervention caused the committee to report an amended version on February 14, the change should not be wholly attributed to pressure from the administration. As was mentioned, Chairman Flood had in the previous year foreseen the possibility that congressional approval of resolutions favoring Ireland would disrupt Anglo-American unity. This belief must have been shared by other members of the committee. It may thus be that Wilson's intervention only confirmed what Flood and others believed. In this view the amended version was at least as much the result of their own convictions as Wilson's pressure. At any rate the interest generated by the favorable report caused Flood to ask for permission to publish 5,000 copies of the hearings.[30]

Some scholars have regarded the approval of the amended version by the committee and its subsequent passage as a sign that Congress favored Irish hopes. A comparison of the original with the amended text, however, fails to support this view. The original reads as follows: "that the commissioners of the United States of America,

[28] Tansill, *America and Irish Freedom*, 308.
[29] Tillman, *Anglo-American Relations*, 198.
[30] *Congressional Record, 65th Congress, 3rd Session*, Part 5, 4351.

representing the United States at the International Peace Conference soon to assemble at Versailles, be, and are hereby, requested to present to and to urge upon the said International Peace Conference the right to freedom, independence, and self-determination of Ireland, predicated upon the principle laid down by the President in his plea for an International League that all governments derive their just power from the consent of the governed."[31] The House committee, controlled by Democrats, offered a complete substitute, "that it is the earnest hope of the Congress of the United States of America that the peace conference now sitting in Paris, in passing upon the rights of various peoples, will favorably consider the claims of Ireland to the right of self-determination." Two important points should be noted here. First, since the original was merely a House resolution it needed only the approval of the House to possess a degree of legality. The substitute, however, was a concurrent resolution, which both the House and the Senate would have to pass before it had any degree of legality; at that time there was little hope for such joint action. Representative Mann, a Republican, raised this point when he declared that the Democrats had reported a concurrent resolution which would never reach the President because "it has as much chance of passing the Senate as a snowflake has in hell." Second, the original requested Wilson "to present and to urge" Ireland's case before the conference, while the substitute merely expressed congressional hope that the peace conference would "favorably consider" Ireland's claims. Since it did not mention the American delegation, even if it had passed both houses it would not have committed Wilson in any way. In addition the Democratic leaders of the House deferred debate until March 3, the last

[31] *Ibid.*, 5042. This quote and the others on the debates can be found on pages 5027-57.

day of the session, when it was obviously too late for Senate action.

The debate lasted for about three hours and carried into the late evening. One Democrat accused the Republicans of filibustering to prevent the vote on the resolution and declared that they were "fooling with dynamite." Mason, the Republican Irish-lover from Chicago, replied that the Democrats had held the resolution in committee for at least a year, "ever since the President announced his Fourteen Points and ever since he spoke in favor of self-determination." While speaker after speaker from both parties passionately pleaded for Irish freedom, Representative Connolly of Texas opposed the resolution on four points: it would force the United States to interfere in the domestic affairs of England; the House had no jurisdiction in such matters; the resolution would destroy allied cooperation, which was necessary to maintain the peace; and it would be useless because it would not change the results of the peace negotiations.

Connolly's arguments curiously enough paralleled those offered by Flood and Wilson. When Wilson learned about the agitation caused by Gallagher's resolution, he admitted to R. S. Baker that the United States could not possibly interfere in the Irish question since it was a domestic issue of the British Empire. Professor Tansill was right. Wilson did not want to raise the Irish question at the peace negotiations—at least in any official capacity—and he did not want Congress to force him to do so. This was less the result of any hatred of the Irish, however, than of his awareness of the realities of the situation. Yet even at this point he attempted to raise the question unofficially, at the same time hoping that the league would eventually solve it to everyone's satisfaction.[32] When the House finally approved the

[32] Tillman, *Anglo-American Relations*, 198.

watered version of the resolution, by a vote of 216 to 45 in the closing minutes of the session, it had no effect upon Wilson since the Senate never had the opportunity to take it up. Even if there had been time, there are indications that the Senate would not have approved the resolution. During the debate in the House a similar resolution, introduced by Senator Phelan, gathered dust in committee. The refusal to consider it cannot have been entirely the result of pressure from the administration, as some have claimed,[33] since arguments similar to those of Flood and Connolly must have had some sympathizers among senators. This can be seen in the Senate debate on the peace treaty, which began within three months. Arguments that Wilson was the real villain in the failure of the United States actively to aid the fight for Irish freedom are thus weakened. Even in a Democratic Congress, where one would expect Irish political power to produce results, the House passed a resolution which, although it tended to please the Irish, avoided any possible embarrassment for Wilson, while the Senate refused to consider a similar resolution.

This does not mean that Democrats in general took the Irish issue for granted. On the contrary, as the mass meetings continued, the Democrats became somewhat concerned. On March 28, five Democratic Senators sent a letter to Wilson in which they called his "attention to the necessity of seeing that some progress is made before the peace conference adjourns toward a solution of the vexing question of self-determination for Ireland. It is not alone that the future of our party imperatively demands that something be done before the work of the peace conference comes to an end to meet the reasonable expectations of the Irish people, but we will all concur in the view that the prospect of early ratification of the treaty by the Senate will be jeopardized

[33] Tansill, *America and Irish Freedom,* 310.

otherwise."[34] Irish pressures were slowly but surely getting results; at this critical point, Irish-Americans took a relatively bold step in pressure politics. During the Third Irish Race Convention, the delegates had selected an American Commission for Irish Independence, composed of Frank P. Walsh, a former member of the Federal Industrial Commission and a joint chairman with William Taft of the War Labor Board; Edward F. Dunne, ex-mayor of Chicago and ex-governor of Illinois; and Michael J. Ryan, ex-city solicitor of Philadelphia and a candidate in 1915 for the Democratic nomination for the governorship of Pennsylvania. The convention authorized this commission to travel to Paris to represent the Irish in America at the Peace Conference and to do all in its power to convince world statesmen that Ireland should be free. This, of course, had little significance as long as the commission failed to gain any official recognition from the statesmen assembled in Paris. On April 17, however, Wilson unofficially recognized its existence when Chairman Walsh asked him to intervene on behalf of the Irish representatives.[35] Wilson did not commit himself at the time; according to Colonel House, both Wilson and Lansing were in favor of refusing Walsh's request for safe conduct for the delegates of the Irish Republic. In fact, according to Thomas A. Bailey, Wilson at one time wanted "to tell him 'to go to hell.' "[36] Professor Tansill says Wilson suppressed this urge "because it was a political imperative to curry favor with Irish-American voters."[37] Although, as we have seen, Wilson wanted to avoid raising the Irish question, it is hard to prove that he acted from political motives. He could hardly have been interested in currying favor with Irish-American voters when

[34] Tansill, *America and Irish Freedom*, 310. Thomas J. Walsh, Peter W. Gerry, David D. Walsh, Key Pittman and John B. Kendrick signed the letter.
[35] *Ibid.*, 313.
[36] Bailey, *Woodrow Wilson and the Great Betrayal* (1945), 27.
[37] Tansill, *America and Irish Freedom*, 313.

he authorized the secretary of the American delegation, Joseph Grew, to inform Walsh and his friends that "it is not within the province of the American delegation to request the Peace Conference to receive a delegation composed of citizens of a country other than our own."[38] Some historians claim that Wilson did in an unofficial manner raise the question with the British and that at one point Lloyd George was willing to permit De Valera and the others to come to Paris. In May, however, Walsh and his committee toured Ireland and delivered a number of speeches which, according to Wilson, were so extreme that they destroyed any hope he had of getting the British to accept De Valera at the conference.[39] British refusal did not deter the Irish-Americans, however, and at another conference with Walsh on June 11 the President intimated that he might have made a mistake with the whole selfdetermination proposal.

> You have touched the great metaphysical tragedy of today. When I gave utterance to those words, I said them without knowledge that nationalities existed which are coming to us day after day. Of course, Ireland's case from the point of view of population, from the point of view of the struggle it has made, from the point of interest it has excited in the world and especially among our own people whom I am anxious to serve, is the outstanding case of a small nationality. You do not know and you cannot appreciate the anxieties I have experienced as the result of these millions of people having their hopes raised by what I have said.[40]

After this remarkable statement Wilson admitted that he could not permit the Irish issue to rise to the surface of the conference because it would have destroyed Anglo-American

[38] *Ibid.*, 316.
[39] Tillman, *Anglo-American Relations*, 200.
[40] Tansill, *America and Irish Freedom*, 319.

unity, without which he feared he could not have his league.[41]

By June, 1919, Wilson, who had at one time believed that man could remake the world, realized that, by himself, he could do no such thing. In reality, Wilson was finally reaping the painful results of his failure to think more realistically before January, 1919; of his failure to understand all the implications of his phrases; and of his failure to think out the means of accomplishing what he hoped to accomplish. Professor Tansill may well have been right, at least in the Irish case, in calling Wilson a "phrase-maker and not a peace-maker." Yet it must be remembered that when Wilson coined his phrases he spoke to the whole world, not to the Irish alone, and that even in June, 1919, he still believed that his league would solve the Irish Question.

While Wilson toyed with the American Commission for Irish Freedom, the Irish in America continued to work. On May 29, 1919, Senator William Borah, who had by then earned a reputation as a friend of Ireland, introduced a resolution in the Senate "that the Senate of the United States earnestly request the American Peace Commission at Versailles to secure, if possible, for the representatives chosen by the people of Ireland . . . a hearing before said Peace Conference in order that said representatives may present the case of Ireland and ask international recognition of the government, republican in form, established by the people of Ireland."[42] Two weeks later Borah himself asked that this resolution be returned to the Committee on Foreign Affairs for amendment. It must have been obvious to Borah that the resolution, as he had presented it, would not have received Senate approval. The new resolution, reported to the floor on June 5, read simply, "Resolved that the Senate

[41] Tillman, *Anglo-American Relations*, 200.
[42] *Congressional Record, 66th Congress, 1st Session*, Part 1, 393.

of the United States earnestly requests the American Commission at Versailles to endeavor to secure for Eamon De Valera, Arthur Griffiths, and Count George Noble Plunkett a hearing before said Peace Conference in order that they may present the case of Ireland."[43]

It is interesting that while the original referred specifically to the representatives "chosen by the people of Ireland" and asked recognition of the government "established by the people of Ireland," the substitute indicated merely that three individuals wanted to present the case of Ireland to the conference, avoiding the implication that Ireland was an independent republic. As had happened with the Gallagher resolution, Irish-Americans could force the introduction, but not the passage, of a strong statement. Borah, realizing this, deliberately watered the resolution to guarantee its passage. The technique worked; on June 6, sixty senators voted for the amended version while only one, Senator John Williams of Mississippi, voted against it, on the ground that the Senate did not have the right to intervene in the affairs of other nations.

An interesting aftermath of this vote came in late June, when Senator Thomas Walsh condemned the Senate for approving Borah's resolutions. "It was passed for political purposes only," he declared, and "in entertaining this resolution, we forced ourselves into the domestic affairs of one of our allies, inspired only by the promoting of partisan selfishness."[44] This speech brought down upon the senator a storm of protest letters, one of which he read to the Senate.

> The Irish people in the north are the backbone of the Democratic party in many states. Senator Phelan can tell you that the almost solid vote they gave the president in San Francisco saved the elec-

43 *Ibid.*, 671.
44 *Ibid.*, 1374.

tion of 1916. Members of the Democratic National
Committee . . . and others are fearful that the *failure*
of the Irish question may lose us much of our
remaining members of the party in the north. The
only place where we made any gains last fall was
in the districts heavily populated by the Irish. I
wonder if you have given any consideration to the
thought that such an attack as you have delivered
against the Irish people may not result in further
destruction of the party. . . . The sooner that the
Democratic Party encourages and supports the aspirations of the Irish race, the better for its safety and
promotion; for without the support of the Irish
people our party will remain in a hapless minority
for a long time to come.[45]

In reply Senator Borah, admitting that "there was politics
in the resolution," defended the action, declaring that Ireland
should have received the same treatment afforded other
oppressed peoples. Even as he spoke, however, Borah played
politics, for he knew that the Paris Peace Conference had
adjourned without even hearing the Irish case. The Irish in
America had marshaled all their forces, but these were not
enough for the task.

From January, 1918, to June, 1919, the Irish in America
earnestly hoped that Wilson would win for them their most
cherished dream, a free and independent Ireland. Yet when
on May 7, 1919, a draft of the proposed treaty was released
to the press, they realized that this was not to be. As the
realization that Ireland had been cheated sank slowly into
the Irish-American mind it produced a profound bitterness.
At the same time Wilson returned to the United States with
his treaty and his league. Bitterness, which seeks a scape-
goat, found three this time: Wilson, the treaty, and the
league. From June, 1919, to March, 1920, Irish-Americans

[45] *Ibid.,* 1727.

worked with the same ferocious vigor that had characterized their stand for selfdetermination, but now it was directed against Wilson's principles.

The reaction against Wilson's treaty began shortly after the text was released. On May 24 an Irish editorial declared, "If the League of Nations goes into effect as now presented, Americans will be found to assist England in crushing any insurrection that might occur in Ireland."[46] On June 1 Senator Borah, who already was interested in generating Irish opposition to the league, implied in a letter read at an Irish-American meeting in Oregon that article 10 would enforce the subjugation of Ireland, since it would force Americans to guarantee boundaries established by the peace conference.[47] In other words, it would freeze the status quo; Ireland would remain under the paw of the "British Lion."

Similar arguments appeared in the Senate in the midst of the debate on Borah's Irish resolution. At that time, Senator Albert B. Fall, Republican from New Mexico, compared the proposed league to the Troppau Protocol when he declared that "if a revolution arose in Ireland, or in any other nation, it would become the duty of the League of Nations to send assistance to put down that revolution, exactly as France acted as mandatory and as Austria acted as mandatory for the Holy Alliance in 1822 and 1823."[48] Senator Phelan immediately challenged this argument, showing that article 10 was expressly limited to external attack. Before he could sit down, however, another Republican, Senator J. Medill McCormick of Illinois, was on his feet shouting that, according to article 3, "the assembly may deal at its gatherings with any matter within the sphere of action of the League affecting the peace of the world." Phelan then denied that

[46] Philadelphia *Irish Press*, May 24, 1919.
[47] Tansill, *America and Irish Freedom*, 328.
[48] *Congressional Record, 66th Congress, 1st Session*, Part 1, 729.

a revolution in Ireland would come within the sphere of the action of the league or disturb the peace of the world, and that to try to extend the clause "external aggression" to cover internal revolt was utterly ridiculous. McCormick in rebuttal quoted the President's statement that "under the League, armed forces would intervene to protect the right of national minorities." If the league had this power, it obviously had the power to intervene in a local revolution. Phelan offered no comment.

While Congress debated the issue the Friends of Irish Freedom completed their victory fund drive, which netted over $1,000,000. With this sum, the Friends entered the fight against the league. They distributed over 1,300,000 pamphlets; they published full- and half-page advertisements in newspapers across the country; and when Woodrow Wilson toured the United States they financed the publication of full-page rebuttals in the newspapers of the towns in which he had spoken. Judge Daniel Cohalan, the moving spirit of the Friends, heard that Senator Frelinghuysen of New Jersey was debating whether to accept the treaty. Within a matter of days, Cohalan organized a campaign that filled the senator's office with 70,000 postcards.[49]

Although such activity alone would have made things difficult for the advocates of the league, on June 25 a distinguished visitor from Ireland, Eamon De Valera, arrived in the United States. He immediately began a whirlwind tour that was to last for months, taking him to every corner of the United States. Everywhere he went, officials received him with open arms. Every edition of an Irish-American newspaper carried article after article concerning his visits and his receptions. His continued appearances and inflam-

[49] Tansill, *America and Irish Freedom*, 332. Tansill is especially useful when it comes to the work of Cohalan and the Friends of Irish Freedom, mainly because he had access to Cohalan's papers.

matory speechmaking forced Irish tempers to a fever pitch.[50]

These activities increased the number of mass meetings held on the issue, the number of resolutions passed, and the number of petitions sent to Congress.[51] Even non-Irish organizations supported the Irish cause. The American Federation of Labor, meeting in its national convention, called for congressional recognition of the Irish Republic. The city council of Cincinnati and numerous state legislatures demanded Irish freedom.[52] It seemed that the entire force of Irish-American opinion, and whatever else it could bring with it, was converging upon the Senate.

Wilson's friends met this onslaught with two basic arguments. The first was an attempt to justify Wilson's failure to include Ireland in the scope of American war aims. Senator Phelan declared that the peace conference had necessarily confined itself to the territory "which had been as a result of the war wrested from the enemy. And therefore, Wilson was unable to raise the question." Agreeing that Ireland had all the qualifications for independence, he pointed out that the President, necessarily in a diplomatic way, had interested the English statesmen in her cause. At the same time, he contended, Wilson could not have demanded that the English give Ireland selfdetermination since that would have completely disrupted the peace conference.[53] Thus Wilson was forced by circumstances to exclude Ireland from his scheme.

The second line of defense against the Irish onslaught

[50] James P. Walsh, "De Valera in the United States, 1919," *Records* of the American Catholic Historical Society of Philadelphia, LXXIII (1962), 96. Mr. Walsh claims that "the mathematics professor" in the speech in Chicago "put a stop to this behavior"—the Irish-American effort to use his visit to stir up opposition to the league and Wilson's treaty. Yet on page 101 he shows how Hearst used De Valera's visit to do just this and later how De Valera himself denounced the league.

[51] *Congressional Record, 66th Congress, 1st Session,* Part 1, 496, 729; Part 5, 4822.

[52] Philadelphia *Irish Press,* June 21, 1919, July 5, 1919.

[53] *Congressional Record, 66th Congress, 1st Session,* Part 2, 1787.

argued that although Wilson was unable to win selfdetermination for Ireland he gave the world the League of Nations,
which would aid Ireland in her struggle "because it would
embarrass the British into giving self-determination to her."[54]
Borah, the chief opponent of the league, with an interest in
arousing Irish opposition, dismissed this as rubbish and
declared that the treaty would never help Ireland recover
her independence because she could not revolt successfully
without aid. As Borah indicated, the treaty precluded the
effectiveness of such outside aid, since if any third nation
supported the Irish revolution article 10 would require
even America to aid England. If this happened, Irish-
Americans would in effect suppress an Irish revolt. At this
point Senator Walsh of Montana placed Borah's arguments
in their true perspective: "It is not difficult to discern in the
discussion in relation to Article 10 a studied effort, usually
insidious, but not infrequently direct, to arouse the prejudice
of the citizens of our Irish birth or descent against the
League." Unfortunately for Wilson and his friends, Walsh's
interpretation was only too true and the effort only too
successful.

Borah's efforts continued through the summer of 1919; in
late August the Senate Committee on Foreign Affairs held
open hearings on the question of the league. In the midst
of these hearings, when Irish-Americans were invited to
testify, the Friends of Irish Freedom arrived in Washington
at full strength to hear Judge Cohalan explain to the committee why such Americans were against the league. The
Judge declared that the Irish were opposed to the league
because it would be a "superstate" that would deny freedom
of the seas to other nations and, thus, give England that
control of the seas which Americans had fought for years.
Cohalan declared that this was precisely why England

54 *Ibid.*, 2077.

wanted Ireland, "because with it she could control the seas."[55] Other speakers included members of the committee that had haunted Wilson for two months in Paris. In fact, that committee's correspondence with Wilson (at least the part the Irish gave to the Senate) was published as part of the hearings. If nothing else resulted, at least the hearings generated additional Irish opposition.

Some scholars have taken this gesture by the Senate to mean that the Irish received special treatment, but even a rapid study of the published hearings will show that the Irish were allowed two hours to present their cause—exactly the amount of time allotted to the Greeks, the Armenians, and many others.

As a result of such activities, petitions began to flow into the Senate. On July 26, the Democratic Committee of Massachusetts adopted the following resolution: "it was opposed to the attempt of England and her allies to force upon the American people so-called covenant of a League of Nations which attempts to commit this republic to recognize and hold forever the title of England to own and rule Ireland against the expressed will of an overwhelming majority of Irish people."[56] Two months later, the annual Democratic convention of New Jersey resolved: "that the Democratic Party of the state of New Jersey in convention assembled demands that any covenant of a League of Nations shall have these principles incorporated therein, to the end that the independence of the Irish Republic be acknowledged."[57] These and other resolutions, all demanding that Irish independence be recognized, finally forced the Democrats in the Senate to act.

[55] *Ibid.*, Part 5, 4651-718.
[56] Tansill, *America and Irish Freedom*, 331.
[57] *The News Letter*, October 10, 1919. This was published weekly in Washington by the Irish National Bureau, the lobbying arm of the Friends of Irish Freedom. It began in the summer of 1919 and lasted beyond the second defeat of the treaty.

In late October Senator Thomas Walsh, whose speeches indicated that he favored the league, offered a resolution proposing that the United States government approach the League of Nations on the question of Ireland "and the right of its people to self-government."[58] Irish-Americans immediately attacked the resolution, agreeing with Senator Lodge when he declared that it was "an attempt to save the League."[59] If it was such an attempt, however, it failed; on November 19, 1919, the Senate rejected Wilson's dream.

Although the role the Irish played in its defeat is hard to assess, some understanding of the results of their labors may be gained from two statements. The first was made by Senator Walsh of Montana when he declared before the vote, "It now seems apparent that the vote on this treaty may depend largely upon the possession of the Irish vote."[60] The second can be found in a telegram sent by Senator Borah to Judge Cohalan immediately after the treaty's defeat. It read simply, "Greatest victory for country and liberty since revolution, largely due to you."[61]

While the majority of Irish-Americans welcomed the defeat of the league, they were unhappy that Ireland's position remained unimproved. In the aftermath they immediately turned their attention to the main problem, Irish freedom, and in their search for useful tools rediscovered the Mason Bill, which had been introduced on May 28, 1919, by Representative William F. Mason, Republican from Illinois. By providing $14,000 for the establishment of a diplomatic mission to Ireland, the bill called in effect for official recognition of the Irish government. Although it had attracted little attention during the fight against the league, it came to prominence in late November

---

[58] *Congressional Record, 66th Congress, 1st Session,* Part 7, 7048.
[59] *Ibid.,* 7156.
[60] *Ibid.,* 7164.
[61] Tansill, *America and Irish Freedom,* 338.

when the Irish-American forces started to apply pressure for its passage.[62] On December 12 and 13, the House Foreign Affairs Committee held hearings on it. Within a week an Irish editor reported that the Democrats on the committee wanted to substitute a resolution for the bill, a move he interpreted as an attempt to "regain the large number of lost adherents to the party."[63] For months the question reappeared in congressional debates, while Irish papers continued their demands that the committee report the bill to the House. Finally, on May 27, Mason himself reported a substitute resolution that, first, related the statement of sympathy for the Irish cause to the general American sympathy for all oppressed nationalities and, second, claimed that conditions in Ireland threatened world peace and British-American friendship.[64] For "world peace and international good will," the resolution concluded, the House of Representatives felt compelled to issue a statement of sympathy "with the aspirations of the Irish people for a government of their own choice."[65] But even the Republican Congress refused to interfere with the executive role in foreign affairs, and the resolution did not get to the floor.

In the middle of the long debate on the Mason Bill, Wilson's followers wanted the Senate to reconsider the treaty and league. Senator Peter G. Gerry of Rhode Island, realizing that the earlier defeat was to some extent caused by Irish opposition, offered the fifteenth reservation to the treaty. "In consenting to the ratification of the treaty with Germany, the United States addresses to the principle of self-determination and to the resolutions of sympathy with the aspirations of the Irish people for a government of their

[62] Philadelphia *Irish Press*, December 6, 1919; New York *Gaelic-American*, December 19, 1919; *The News Letter*, December 19, 1919.

[63] Philadelphia *Irish Press*, December 20, 1919.

[64] *Congressional Record, 66th Congress, 2nd Session*, Part 8, 7767.

[65] *Ibid.*, Part 9, 9293.

own choice, adopted by the Senate on June 6, 1919, and declares that when self-government is attained by Ireland, a consummation it is hoped is at hand, it should promptly be admitted as a member of the League of Nations."[66] After a lengthy debate the Senate accepted the reservation on March 18, by a vote of 36 to 30, but the treaty was again rejected two days later. Although the Irish had gained some official recognition, the treaty was defeated. After twenty-four long, hard months both Wilson and the Irish lost.

[66] *Ibid.*, Part 5, 4522. The debate is on pages 4492-522. Gerry was also interested in the Irish vote.

THE BRITISH

Dennis J. McCarthy

The study of the British-Americans is quite different from
that of other immigrant groups. In the first place, they were
not an easily identifiable ethnic group like the Irish-Americans, Polish-Americans, or Italian-Americans. The very term
"British-Americans" is in fact merely a useful label, which
many of those who should be included in this study refuse
to accept. Americans of Scottish or Welsh descent, proud of
their Celtic origins, would hardly welcome a description as
"British-Americans;" "Anglo-Americans" or "English-Ameri-
cans" would be even less acceptable, and a label such as
"English-Scot-Welsh-Americans" would be inordinately cum-
bersome. Moreover, it would be proper to include in the
term some who do not trace themselves to the island of the
English, the Welsh, and the Scots. There were people in
Ireland—and they were not all in Ulster—who were happy
in the British connection. Certainly, their counterpart among
the Irish-Americans should be included in the British-
Americans. For them especially, was it not the United Kingdom of Great Britain *and* Ireland? The not inconsequential
numbers who traced their families to dominions of the British
Commonwealth of Nations, particularly Canada, may be
justifiably included on the basis of community of interest
and ancestry.

However broad or narrow the definition, the British-
Americans constitute other perplexing problems for the historian. For one they would most probably resent classifica-
tion as an immigrant group. Were not the colonies that
developed into the United States settled predominantly by
people from the British Isles? Were the colonists not English

subjects until the revolution made them Americans? Were not emigrants from the British Isles the core of the population of the United States? How then an immigrant group? Yet the essence of an immigrant group is to be found not in birth but in community or identification of interest with some foreign land or ethnic group; and the British-Americans constituted such an ethnic pressure group.

Conceived, then, in terms of an ethnic pressure group, the British-Americans doubly perplex their investigator because anglophilia was not limited to those with some ancestral connection to Great Britain. Although British-Americans were concerned with promoting Anglo-American friendship and cooperation before World War I, as well as during and after that conflict, so too were many Americans who had no ancestral bond with Britain. How can one differentiate between Americans and British-Americans who were propagandizing the same thing? Where does the river end and the bay begin?

Still another problem confronting the historian is that the British-Americans, unlike other ethnic pressure groups, were, in the terminology of the sociologists, an *in* group. They were part of the American scene, not readily recognizable as an ethnic pressure group.

If these points needed clarification, it may help to define further the limits of this study. Although the title of this book refers to Wilson's peacemaking, this chapter deals with peacemaking by the United States; for in our constitutional system the Senate has a role in treaty-making—a point which Wilson neglected, to his loss and the world's. We must therefore concern ourselves with the British-Americans, Wilson, the Senate, and, insofar as it bears upon either, public opinion.

Before America's entry into the war there was, of course, formidable British propaganda aimed at winning American sympathy for the Allied cause and inducing the United States to join the conflict against the Central Powers. Although it is not our purpose here to examine this propaganda, it should be noted that the wartime propaganda activities of Britain in the United States, under the guidance of Sir Gilbert Parker, director of the American subdivision of Wellington House, the British propaganda agency, made full use of British-Americans. The British propagandists emphasized personal contacts and the use of American citizens to present the British case. As one historian expressed it: "It was the social lobby, the personal conversation, and the casual brush which forged the strongest chain between America and Britain."[1]

British propaganda did not lead America into the war, but it helped secure American sympathy and eventually disposed Americans more favorably toward entry. In addition, it influenced Woodrow Wilson and his administration. Whatever their tendencies may have been before 1914 it seems that Wilson and his advisors came to believe the chief points asseverated by Wellington House after 1914, so much so that despite his call for "peace without victory," Wilson came to want an Allied victory so badly that to it he subordinated his desire for peace.[2]

Strong as were Wilson's leanings toward Britain and the Allies during the war, when it came to peacemaking he was the leader. In September, 1918, when the long-cherished Allied victory loomed on the horizon, Wilson told his secretary, Joseph Tumulty, that he feared Allied victory might

[1] Harold D. Lasswell, *Propaganda Technique in the World War* (1927); James D. Squires, *British Propaganda at Home and in the United States 1914-1917* (1935); Parker summarized his work, stressing the use of American citizens, in "The United States and the War," *Harper's Magazine* (1918), 521-31.

[2] H. C. Peterson, *Propaganda for War: the Campaign Against American Neutrality* (1939).

mean a return to the old days of alliances and competing armaments. "We must now serve notice on everybody that our aims and purposes are not selfish. In order to do this . . . we must be brutally frank with friends and foes alike."[3] Believing that "the common will of mankind has been substituted for the particular purposes of individual states,"[4] Wilson was not now to be influenced by the propaganda of Britain, the Allies, or the British-Americans. From his position as leader of a disinterested nation and author of the Fourteen Points, Wilson became *the* peacemaker.

This is not to say that the principles upon which Wilson wished to establish the peace were all of his creation; once he grasped them, however, he became their outstanding champion. Within a month of his Fourteen Points speech, the American President was championing the principle of selfdetermination: "National aspirations must be respected; peoples may now be dominated and governed only by their own consent. 'Self-determination' is not a mere phrase. It is an imperative principle of action, which statesmen will henceforth ignore at their peril."[5]

Throughout 1918, Allied propaganda stressed national selfdetermination. The collapse of the Central Powers in the autumn was accompanied by the birth of new nations and a scramble for ethnic territories. Nationalism had triumphed. In all this the British-Americans played no part. Their one great desire was to continue the connection between the United States and Great Britain that had been forged on the anvil of war. Friendship, cooperation, solidarity, unity —these were the words of American and British leaders and of the British-Americans. Their paramount objective during the peacemaking period was to promote closer ties, deeper

[3] Joseph P. Tumulty, *Woodrow Wilson as I Knew Him* (1921), 302.
[4] *Ibid.*, 303.
[5] *The Messages and Papers of Woodrow Wilson*, 2 vols. (1924), I, 475.

friendship between America and Britain. A corollary objective was to counter anti-British propaganda in the United States.

The promotion of Anglo-American cooperation and friendship was carried on through the press, the lecture platform, the pulpit, the banquet table, the movies, exchange professorships, and the revision of American history textbooks.

There was a large number of British-American organizations, particularly in New England and in such cities as New York, Philadelphia, Chicago and San Francisco. Among them were such national organizations as the Sons of St. George, the Order of Scottish Clans, the American Association of True Ivorites, the Loyal Orange Association, and the Daughters of the British Empire. Each of these had its local lodges or units. There were also local societies like the Victorian Club of Boston, the Albion Society of Philadelphia, the English Social and Mutual Improvement Club of Lawrence, Massachusetts, and the British-American Association of Paterson, New Jersey. These organizations were primarily social, though they served as useful channels for British wartime propaganda, and they constituted a formidable means for promoting Anglo-American friendship and cooperation.

The British-American press had many organs, if not a large circulation. Among their publications were the *British-American* and the *English-Speaking World* published in New York, the *Cambrian* in Cincinnati and Utica, the *Druid* in Scranton and Pittsburgh, the *British-Californian* in San Francisco, the *Fiery Cross* published by the Order of Scottish Clans, and the *Landmark,* the organ of the English-Speaking Union published in London but circulated in the United States.

Formidable though the organizations and publications of the British-Americans might have been, they did not possess a centralized organization, as one might expect of an efficient pressure group.

The Anglo-American cooperation which the British-Americans wished to promote was a natural outgrowth of already close ties. Official relations between the United States and Great Britain had been quite cordial for two decades or more, and when the United States entered the war the British-Americans could speak, write, sing, and toast Anglo-American friendship. What was more natural for allies who shed their blood and spent their treasure in the common cause? Understandably, the British-Americans, along with many other Americans, wished to see a continuation of the entente.

Particularly outstanding in cementing better relations between the two countries was the English-Speaking Union. This organization, dedicated to closer ties among all English-speaking peoples, had its headquarters in London but was very active in America. Although it sought the support of all English-speaking people, the membership of the Union in the United States appears to have been largely British-American.

The English-Speaking Union was founded July 4, 1918, chiefly through a gift from an American, Alexander Smith Cochrane, a grandson of the founder of the Alexander Smith Carpet Company. At the outset of World War I, Cochrane, obviously an anglophile, gave his yacht to the British Navy, and in 1916 he obtained a commission as a commander in the Royal Naval Reserve, serving in West Indian and North Atlantic waters.[6]

The aims of the English-Speaking Union were thus described: "The English-Speaking Union aims at increasing the knowledge of one another possessed by the English-

[6] *Dictionary of American Biography* (1946), II, 250.

speaking peoples. It aims at no formal alliances, it has nothing to do with governments, but it is merely an attempt to promote good fellowship among the English-speaking democracies of the world."[7]

The Union did not gain a large membership, but it compensated for numbers with the prestige of its members —men in government, college professors, and members of the press. It was somewhat topheavy with officers. In May, 1919, it could boast of only 1,786 members, 614 of whom were Americans. William Howard Taft and Lord Balfour were honorary presidents, and there were no fewer than eighty-two vice presidents! Among the vice presidents were Franklin D. Roosevelt, then Assistant Secretary of the Navy; Carter Glass, Secretary of the Treasury; Senator George Wharton Pepper; Gifford Pinchot, well known progressive; and the Vice President of the United States, Thomas R. Marshall.[8]

George Haven Putnam, probably the chief promoter of the English-Speaking Union in the United States and head of the Putnam publishing house, sought to induce Teddy Roosevelt to lend his name and prestige to the organization. Roosevelt politely declined membership, because he was seeking "to secure in this country a spirit of individual American nationalism, based on an Americanism which disregards all questions of national origin."[9] The former president expressed his agreement with the general purposes of the Union, however, and suggested that the United States and Great Britain should sign a universal arbitration treaty that would forever ban war between them through the submission of all disputes to arbitration.

The correspondence between Putnam and Roosevelt was

[7] *Landmark* (1919), 231. The aims appear on the masthead page.
[8] *Landmark* (1919), 165, 229; (1920), 30.
[9] *English-Speaking World* (1919), 9.

published in the *English-Speaking World* under the sub-title "An Alliance of English-Speaking Peoples of the World," even though the word "alliance" appears nowhere in Roosevelt's letter. Further, the same issue carried an advertisement for a nine-inch bronze bust of Roosevelt, billed as "A Friend of the English-Speaking Union."

Many college and university presidents and professors were members of the English-Speaking Union. Charles F. Thwing, president of Western Reserve; Frank J. Goodnow, president of Johns Hopkins; Lyman P. Powell, late president of Hobart; C. H. Van Tyne of Michigan; Alfred M. Brooks of Indiana; Richard Gottheil of Columbia; and Andrew C. McLaughlin of Chicago were among the many academic supporters of the union.[10]

A number of newspapers helped promote Anglo-American cooperation, giving editorial support to the aims of the union. The magazine *Living Age* reproduced several articles from the *Landmark*. Journalist members or supporters included S. J. Duncan-Clarke of the Chicago *Evening Post;* Edward Price Bell, the European manager of the foreign service of the Chicago *Daily News;* F. R. Kent, editor of the Baltimore *Sun;* Lafayette Young, editor of the Des Moines *Capital;* and Franklin Glass, editor of the Birmingham *News.*[11] The El Paso *Morning Times* devoted a leading article to the Union.[12] Wright H. Patterson, of the Western Newspaper Union, reported that he "talked up" friendship among the English-speaking peoples to newspaper men at conventions in several states.[13] Professor E. F. Gay resigned from Harvard to take editorial charge of the New York *Evening Post* in order to promote British-American understanding and to support the League of Nations. At a lunch-

---

[10] *Landmark* (1919), 22, 652, 685; (1920), 111.
[11] *Ibid.,* 150, 232, 652, 723.
[12] *Ibid.,* 372.
[13] *Ibid.,* 761.

eon tendered Gay by the London branch of the Union, a speaker expressed his expectation that the *Post* would be "a vehicle for the expression of the highest, noblest, and most abiding sentiments and truths between the two nations."[14]

Charles Hanson Towne, editor of *McClure's Magazine,* was a member of the English-Speaking Union and contributed to *Landmark,* as did Albert Shaw, editor of the *Review of Reviews.* Mark Sullivan was another journalist member of the Union, and publishers Putnam and Doubleday added to its impressive support among the American press.[15]

The leading branch of the English-Speaking Union was in New York; other branches were established in Philadelphia, Baltimore, Los Angeles, Chicago, Boston and St. Joseph, Missouri. One eager member suggested that Masonic members form an English-Speaking Union lodge.[16]

Though its membership was not large, the English-Speaking Union was active and influential. Its first public function in the United States was a luncheon in honor of Rear Admiral William S. Sims, U.S.N., himself a member of the Union. The Canadian-born admiral was a staunch supporter of Anglo-American solidarity; indeed, a speaker referred to him as the real founder of the Union, because in 1910, while visiting England, he had given a speech in the Guildhall in which he said that if Great Britain were ever menaced she could count on "every man, every dollar and every drop of blood" of the United States.[17]

The English-Speaking Union initiated the sending of an illuminated "Goodwill Address" to President Wilson, signed by the Lord Mayors, Lord Provosts, and mayors of the chief cities of the United Kingdom. It was presented to the

[14] *English-Speaking World* (1919), 33.
[15] *Landmark* (1919), 169, 262, 270, 748.
[16] *Ibid.,* 229.
[17] *English-Speaking World* (1919), 7.

American ambassador, for transmission to the President, at a dinner sponsored by the Union in London on November 15, 1919.[18]

A novel type of propaganda was the promotion of joint celebrations of "common" events, such as the birthdays of Lincoln, Washington, and Shakespeare, Magna Carta Day, July 4th, Thanksgiving, the centenary of James Russell Lowell's birth, and the tercentenaries of the landing of the Pilgrims and the establishment of the Virginia House of Burgesses. This kind of promotion of Anglo-American fraternalism was better in theory than in execution, at least on this side of the Atlantic. While the London members of the Union marked the birthdays of Lincoln and Washington with appropriate dinners, speeches, and messages, neither these holidays nor Shakespeare's birth were the subject of any conspicuous joint celebrations in the United States. The *New York Times,* for example, reported observances of Lincoln's birthday ranging from a "Big Sing" in Bryant Park for five thousand Boy Scouts to a Women's Republican Club luncheon, but carried no mention of any celebration by British-American organizations.[19]

The London *Times* published a special American supplement on July 4, 1919. While this was Anglo-American propaganda directed at a British audience, it is interesting to note some of the American contributors. There were greetings from William Howard Taft, Samuel Gompers, H. Pratt Judson, president of the University of Chicago, and Nicholas Murray Butler, president of Columbia University. The anglophile bias of Butler was rather extreme: "The world desperately needs for its leadership, its guidance, and its safety, precisely those qualities of mind and character which are known in modern history as Anglo-Saxon."[20]

---

[18] *Landmark* (1920), 155.
[19] *Ibid.* (1919), 168, 175, 227, 229; *New York Times,* February 12, 1919.
[20] *The Times* (London), July 4, 1919.

Articles were written for this supplement by Franklin P. Lane, Secretary of the Interior, David F. Houston, Secretary of Agriculture, and Franklin D. Roosevelt.

The celebration of the Lowell centenary came off somewhat better as a joint enterprise. Sponsored by the American Academy of Arts and Letters, this observance of the birth of a distinguished American writer, who had served as ambassador to the Court of St. James from 1880 to 1885, was graced by the presence of a number of British men of letters, headed by the Nobel-prize-winning playwright and novelist, John Galsworthy. The four-day celebration in New York was profuse in speeches promoting and promising lasting amity among English-speaking peoples.[21]

British-Americans were naturally prominent in commemorating "Britain's Day," December 7, 1918. The contributions of Great Britain to the war were duly recognized in editorial columns, in parades, and at banquet tables throughout the nation. "Empire Day," which was also the centenary of Victoria's birth, was celebrated by the United British Societies of Philadelphia on May 24, 1919. With twenty-eight British-American organizations participating, there was a parade, a dinner at the Manufacturers Club, and a mass meeting at the Metropolitan Opera House.[22]

One of the more unorthodox promotions of Anglo-American friendship was a contest, proposed by the World Trade Club of San Francisco and supported by the English-Speaking Union, which offered $1,000 for the best name for denoting the United States and Great Britain. Among the suggestions were: "Usanglia," "Brittusa," "Britusam," "Usabritain," and "Britusannia."[23]

The activities of the English-Speaking Union were sum-

21 *New York Times,* Feb. 9, 1919.
22 Philadelphia *Public Ledger,* May 25, 1919; *English-Speaking World* (1919), 21.
23 *Landmark* (1920), 158.

marized, though not detailed, by the *English-Speaking World* as: distribution of the *Landmark* and other literature, establishment of scholarships and professional chairs in American universities, cooperation in the revision of American school history texts, arranging lectures, entertaining distinguished foreign guests, and participating in the tercentenary of the landing of the Pilgrims.[24]

Other British-American organizations were active. The Sons of St. George and the Daughters of the British Empire, with "thousands of members," were doing "their utmost among their U. S. friends to bring about the desired friendly bonds. . . ." Also prominent were the two branches of the Pilgrim Society, one in Britain and one in America. The former was founded in London in 1902 to promote Anglo-American friendship. An American general, Joseph Wheeler, and George T. Wilson of New York were among the founders. The American Pilgrims were organized in the following year with Episcopal Bishop Henry C. Potter of New York as president and Cornelius Vanderbilt as a member of the executive committee. Perhaps in keeping with the pilgrim tradition of Thanksgiving, the society banqueted virtually every prominent Englishman who came to America. On these occasions, a toast was always offered to "The President and the King."[25]

The sentiment of wartime comradeship also gave birth to new organizations dedicated to Anglo-American cooperation. The Society for American and British Friendship was founded in New York by a group of men described as prominent in the business, professional, and literary worlds. Fifteen hundred people attended the society's first public meeting in November, 1919.[26] The society was zealous in propagandizing Anglo-American partnership and in attempt-

---

[24] *English-Speaking World* (1920), 30.
[25] *Ibid.* (1919), 24, 28-29; (1920), 16, 27.
[26] *Ibid.*, 28.

ing to combat anti-British propaganda in America. The society supplied "dozens of newspaper articles and data for magazine stories;" provided speakers for various meetings; interviewed writers and "placed resources at their disposal;" sought the support of "dozens of prominent people;" and distributed "thousands" of pamphlets, leaflets, and booklets. It also arranged the itinerary for the "Loyal Coalition," a group of Irish Unionists brought to America in 1919 in an effort to counter Sinn Fein propaganda. The society also protested against such propaganda in the public schools at a hearing of the New York Board of Education.[27]

The Allied War Veterans Brigade and the Anglo-American Society for Americans of British Ancestry, also new organizations, were apparently less active than the Society for American and British Friendship.[28]

Some purely American organizations that were heavy with British ancestry willingly extended "hands across the sea." The Daughters of the American Revolution honored the founder of the Imperial Order of the Daughters of the British Empire at their convention in Washington in 1919. The Sons of the American Revolution presented "Old Glory" to the Sons of St. George at a victory dinner in July, 1919. The Montclair (New Jersey) chapter of the Sons of the American Revolution also honored Lt. Col. G. G. Woodwork, a special representative of the British Ministry of Information.[29]

It is impossible to gauge what influence this wining and dining in behalf of Anglo-American friendship exerted upon the people of the United States. One interested commentator believed the British-American rapprochement was merely at the "dinner stage." He noted that there were numerous

[27] *Ibid.* (1920), 15.
[28] *Ibid.* (1919), 15, 29, 33.
[29] *Ibid.*, 22, 27.

societies that met once or twice a year, "eat more or less excellent meals," and listened to speeches that were "always full of general expressions of mutual sympathy, respect and regard and sometimes replete with wit, but rarely contain a specific suggestion of any particular political end." This erstwhile analyst, a certain William M. Coleman, proposed a political union of Great Britain and the United States![30]

So skillful and subtle were the British propaganda techniques before American entry into the war that there is great difficulty in distinguishing between British propaganda, official and unofficial, and that of the British-Americans. Although the British-Americans helped to circulate British propaganda, Sir Gilbert Parker, who headed Wellington House's subdivision for propaganda in America, did not direct his efforts primarily at British-Americans. Americans who had no obvious connection with Britain were much better instruments for disseminating propaganda. As part of a study of British wartime propaganda, George Viereck, a noted author and leader of the German-Americans, interviewed many Wellington House officials after the war. He reports a pseudonymous "Master of Propaganda" as explaining: "Our men merged with the crowd. They 'passed' as Americans. In every newspaper office, in every great industrial concern, there were Englishmen whose national origin no one suspected or questioned." On the use of Americans, Viereck quotes the propagandist: "The war showed us that it was not necessary for us to employ or bribe Americans. They did our work for nothing."[31]

Official and unofficial British propaganda did not end with America's entry into the war but continued emphasizing Britain's contributions to the war, the "partners-in-war" theme, and the continued need for Anglo-American partner-

[30] *Ibid.*, 7, 8.
[31] George S. Viereck, *Spreading Germs of Hate* (1930), 122.

ship. Did it end with the Armistice? Lord Northcliffe, head
of the British War Mission to the United States in 1917, was
reported to have left behind "one hundred and fifty million
dollars and ten thousand trained agents," when he returned
to England in November 1917.[32] Justice John W. Goff, an
Irish champion and hardly an unbiased witness, maintained
in November, 1919, that the British were spending hundreds
of millions of dollars on propaganda in the United States.[33]
While these figures might be viewed with some skepticism,
Lord Northcliffe did establish the British Bureau of Information, a continuing propaganda agency, in New York City.[34]
The important point is that, whether from British or British-
American sources, there still flowed a propaganda that did
not differ in general character from that of wartime. Anglo-
American friendship and solidarity were still the paramount
goals.

As in wartime propaganda, the social lobby, the pulpit,
the rostrum, and the press were employed to promote Anglo-
American fellowship. American hosts and hostesses, the
latter especially, vied with one another to entertain visiting
dignitaries and to present them to their American friends,
including members of Congress and high-ranking officials.
One hostess of "strong English affiliation" leased a residence
in Washington for ten days at $100 per day in order to
entertain the Prince of Wales at tea.[35] In delivering a bac-
calaureate sermon at Columbia University in June, 1919, the
Reverend Edward E. Braithwaite, president of Western
University, London, preached closer union between the
United States and Britain. The president of Brown Univer-

[32] *Ibid.*, 275. Viereck cites a conversation with C. G. Miller, author of
The Poisoned Loving Cup, as his authority for this statement. James D.
Squires, *British Propaganda at Home and in the United States, 1914-1917*
(1935), 41, believes that it did stop.
[33] *New York Times*, November 19, 1919.
[34] Viereck, *Germs of Hate*, 275.
[35] *New York Times*, November 16, 1919.

sity, William H. P. Faunce, urged that Anglo-American relations be encouraged.[36]

W. Lanier Washington, a direct descendant of two of Washington's brothers, wrote an article for *Landmark* speculating upon "George Washington and a League of Nations" and proclaiming that had George Washington lived in the days of "the great German aggression . . . he would have taken his stand by the side of the Mother Country. . . . The sword of Washington would have flashed forth, to lead in the fight to preserve the liberties of mankind." Lanier Washington also made the common charge of British-American revisionist historians that George III was a "British monarch of German blood and instincts."[37]

Few men equalled George Haven Putnam in zeal for, and activity in behalf of, Anglo-American friendship. One of the organizers of the English-Speaking Union in the United States, Putnam was indefatigable in promoting its cause. Born in 1844 in London of American parents, he was eligible for both American and British citizenship at the age of twenty-one. Since he was a Union officer at that time, he "took his [United States] citizenship for granted," but, as a property-holder in London, he voted in parish elections for fifty years and once stumped for Gladstone.[38]

Major Putnam, as he was often called, was active in organizing branches of the English-Speaking Union and writing in behalf of the League of Nations and Anglo-American unity. He maintained that it was the "duty" of the people of the United States to cooperate with Britain and to support the league. He felt that the English-speaking peoples would come together within the league in a special

---

[36] *English-Speaking World* (1919), 28; *Landmark* (1920), 128-32.

[37] *Landmark* (1920), 89, 90. Washington's nephew, William Augustine Washington, married his cousin, Jane Washington. *Who Was Who in America* (1943), I, 1305.

[38] *Dictionary of American Biography* (1946), XV, 278.

informal association of their own, which would strengthen
the league. Indeed, he believed their power would be "alone
sufficient to assure the peace of the world."[39]

Another leading British-American was George T. Wilson,
one of the founders of the Pilgrim Society. With Joseph H.
Choate, former ambassador to Great Britain, he headed a
committee to welcome Lord Balfour and the British War
Mission in 1917. He served on many other welcoming
committees and was reputedly known by more prominent
Britishers than any other man in New York. The story was
told that when a British officer returned from America, he
was asked who had most impressed him. He replied: "Wilson." "The President?" asked the friend. "No, no!" he
answered, "George Wilson of New York, one of the best
friends England has over there."[40]

British and British-American propaganda did not neglect
the American weaker sex. Mrs. Burnett Smith came twice
to the United States as an official representative of the
British government. On the first occasion, she sought wheat
flour; on the second, understanding. She spoke throughout
the country in the spring of 1919, and wrote a rather bland
article, entitled "Let Us Be Friends," for the *Woman's Home
Companion*. Readers of the *English-Speaking World* were
treated to a reprinting in installments of a novel, *His Royal
Happiness*, by Mrs. Everard Cotes. The novel, serialized by
the *Ladies Home Journal* in 1914, dealt with a prince of
the royal blood who wooed and won the daughter of a man
fated to become President of the United States.[41] Even
romantic love might serve the cause of Anglo-American
friendship!

[39] George H. Putnam, "The Duty of the English-Speaking Peoples in the
United States," *English-Speaking World* (1919), 11.
[40] *English-Speaking World* (1920), 27.
[41] *Woman's Home Companion* (1919), 4; *English-Speaking World*
(1919), 23-27; and subsequent issues.

The cinema was not neglected as a means of influencing the American people. Lord Northcliffe sent W. G. Faulkner, a film expert, "to enlist the cooperation of the film industry in a plan to use the screen for the purpose of furthering Anglo-American relations." Faulkner was entertained at a luncheon for two hundred film producers. In reporting this, the *Landmark* expressed the hope that producers on both sides of the Atlantic would never produce a picture distasteful to any part of the English-speaking world, but would emphasize the great achievements of the English-speaking peoples.[42]

International goodwill and cooperation were advanced through exchange professorships. The Sulgrave Institution, named from Sulgrave Manor, the ancestral home of Washington, sought to establish chairs of British history in the United States, and the Rose Sidgwick Memorial Fellowship was established to provide facilities for British women "to finish" in America. In the same vein, a committee for the interchange of ministers of the gospel was affiliated with the English-Speaking Union.[43]

Visiting British dignitaries were wined and dined by British-American organizations and civic groups, and their activities were reported in the press to an extent consistent with their stature. The visit of Edward Albert, Prince of Wales, in November, 1919, quite naturally received the most extensive verbal and pictorial coverage in the newspapers. After being hosted in Washington by the Vice President, the prince was feted for five days at dinners and balls by British-American organizations and by prominent citizens in New York.[44]

One of the more interesting aspects of the British-

[42] *Landmark* (1920), 223-24.
[43] *Ibid.*, 55, 133; (1919), 680.
[44] *New York Times*, November 18-22, 1919; *English-Speaking World* (1919), 7-13, 18.

American propaganda was the attempt to revise the history of Anglo-American relations, especially of the American Revolution. Granted that the revision of American school histories was long overdue, the propagandists went to extremes in their efforts to remove the black garb of the villain from the Britain of 1776. "It was not England, it was a superimposed German method . . ." that drove the colonies to revolt, argued Mrs. Henry F. Osborn in a letter to the *New York Times*. George III was a German king, she claimed.[45]

A more formidable attack was made by the "History Circle" in a little volume called *British-American Discords and Concords*, published, significantly, by Putnam. The "History Circle," most of whose members remained anonymous, first met at the City Club of New York in May 1917. It was apparently composed of a number of prominent men, including some professors, whose attitudes were strongly anglophilic.[46] According to the introduction, *Discords and Concords* was undertaken to help develop an "unprejudiced knowledge" of past British-American relations in order that "sound judgements" might be made on America's present and future plans. Interpreting the American Revolution, the authors maintained that the Hanoverian George III, who came to the throne with the avowed purpose of establishing an autocracy, could not comprehend the temper of the colonies or their representative governments. "The American Revolution," they said, "was in fact a civil war fought by men of the same race, with democracy on one side and autocracy on the other." Further, they declared, the war was won in Parliament because the liberal-minded members hampered the King and the ministry, eventually forcing their will upon them. Indeed, the "History Circle" found

[45] *New York Times*, February 9, 1919. Mrs. Osborn enlarged this letter to an article, "American School Histories and Past Misunderstandings," for the *Landmark* (1919), 735-42.

[46] *New York Times Book Review*, February 2, 1919.

that the revolution established the "final supremacy of the British Parliament over the Crown, thus ending in the reign of George III the six-hundred years' struggle since Magna Carta." Washington was seen as the "founder of the British Empire," because he showed Britain how to evolve the British Commonwealth of Nations![47]

So well known a historian as Andrew C. McLaughlin, of the University of Chicago, was also carried to extremes in his revisionism. Under the title *America and Britain,* he published a paper he had read to the Royal Historical Society and a series of lectures he had presented at the University of London in May, 1918. Typically revisionist, he referred to George III as a German monarch who, under the sway of a "junker aristocracy," was the cause of the American Revolution. McLaughlin also accepted uncritically the *British Blue Book* on the causes of the war with the Central Powers and the Bryce Report on atrocities in Belgium. Of course this was not a historian talking, but a partisan in wartime. Professor McLaughlin published the lectures "in the hope that they may be of some slight service in helping to strengthen the good feeling and sense of comradeship between the British and American peoples."[48]

Another revisionist, Professor H. H. Powers, maintained that the "old history" had fulfilled its purpose in developing a national consciousness; now the time to change had come. He wrote: "I am tired chasing red-coats down Bunker Hill. It was a pastime suited to an earlier day."[49]

The British-Americans were, as would be expected, strong in their support of the League of Nations. They seem to have taken for granted American participation in the league, and to have believed that Anglo-American

[47] The History Circle, *British-American Discords and Concords* (1918), 8, 15, 16, 17, 65.

[48] Andrew C. McLaughlin, *America and Britain* (1919), v-vi, 15-16, 56.

[49] *Landmark* (1920), 22.

cooperation (always their paramount objective) was essential to its success.[50] So far as I can determine, they directed no special propaganda effort at the Senate, no doubt relying on public opinion, which, judged by the editorial support of newspapers and by certain polls, overwhelmingly favored the league in early 1919. In any case most Senators approved the idea of a world organization, at least in some form. When reservations became likely, however, the British-Americans were willing to accept them[51]—perhaps, though I cannot demonstrate it here, because the British-Americans were to a large degree Republican in politics.

The only important effort to influence the Senate occurred when its Foreign Relations Committee, headed by Henry Cabot Lodge, heard Judge Cohalan and the Irish delegation in behalf of national selfdetermination for Ireland. On the same day, August 30, 1919, a group of British-Americans, some bearing conspicuously Irish names, presented a formal written protest. They argued neither for nor against the treaty or the league, but objected to the action of the Sinn Feiners and other Irish organizations in "thrusting" the Irish Question into the deliberations of the Senate. Their arguments can be summarized thus: the Irish faction was not a member of the Allies and had not supported the war in sentiment or in deed; Ireland had selfgovernment; Ireland had never been an undivided country; and consideration of the Irish Question by the Senate tended to raise racial and religious animosities.[52]

Although the Irish-Americans wanted an independent Ireland, the same was not true of the Scottish-Americans, except for a certain George J. Bruce, who addressed a telegram to the Foreign Relations Committee advocating self-

[50] *English-Speaking World* (1919), 14, 17.
[51] *Ibid.*, 7, 16.
[52] *Treaty with Germany: Hearings before the Committee on Foreign Relations, United States Senate, 66th Congress, 1st Session* (1919), 903-904.

determination for Scotland. Scottish-Americans quickly opposed him. The Executive Council of the Royal Clan, Order of Scottish Clans, sent a telegram to combat his "perniciousness." The council pointed out that Bruce did not represent the sentiments of Scots in America or in Scotland, and further asserted that Scotland had had selfdetermination for over 600 years—ever since Bannockburn.[53]

Failure of the Senate to ratify the Versailles Treaty in November, 1919, brought forth criticism in the *English-Speaking World;* the second failure, in March, 1920, evoked criticism of both the Senate and Wilson,[54] and even raised the "bogies" of bolshevism and the "yellow peril." According to one writer, while the United States debated the difference between "tweedle-dum and tweedle-dee," bolshevism threatened Germany, the Balkans, China and Japan. To save the world from a "Red and Yellow Plague," he maintained, it was necessary for the United States and Britain to assume the "White Man's Burden."[55]

It should be noted, however, that the official organ of the English-Speaking Union, in deference to American domestic politics, was more circumspect, thinking it "diplomatic to avoid any reference" to the failure of the United States to ratify the treaty and join the league.[56]

Finally, British-American propaganda was concerned with counteracting anti-British propaganda. British-Americans were very sensitive to the anti-British charges which were circulated, especially the attacks of the Irish-Americans.

Major Putnam, that zealous proponent of British-American solidarity, felt that it was the duty of the English-speaking people of the United States to counteract such propaganda. He urged them to make clear the nature and

[53] *The Fiery Cross* (1919), 4.
[54] *English-Speaking World* (1919), 29; (1920), 15, 21.
[55] *Ibid.,* 16.
[56] *Landmark* (1920), 284.

purpose of British policy, to correct the traditional histories, to emphasize the three years Britain had fought to defend the policies and liberties of the United States, to refute anti-British charges, and to stress that the peace of the world depended upon close association of the English-speaking peoples of the world.[57]

Another leading British-American, the volatile Admiral Sims, told a Victory Loan audience: "Don't criticize Pershing; don't criticize the army; don't criticize the Allies. Above all, stop criticizing England."[58]

Readers of the *English-Speaking World* were advised: "Turn a deaf ear to the one who would suggest an English-made League of Nations. Scout the man who says that the United States can care for itself and needs no European entanglements."[59] And the *Landmark* urged its readers to report unfair criticism and to "remonstrate" with local editors, that the press might realize that the English-Speaking Union was a force to be reckoned with.[60] Answering the charge that Britain wanted money from America, the same journal asserted that while the United States had lent £850,000,000 to Britain, Britain had lent £700,000,000 to her allies, and concluded that "British indebtedness to the United States was incurred solely on account of her loans to her Allies and not for some nefarious imperialistic project, as Mr. Hearst and the Anglophobes would have us believe."[61]

The greater part of British-American counterpropaganda was directed against the vociferous attacks of the Irish-Americans. Many columns and articles in the *English-Speaking World* and in the *Landmark* were devoted to combating the Irish in one way or another. Objection was made to the

---

57 Putnam, "The Duty of the English Speaking Peoples," 11.
58 Philadelphia *Public Ledger*, May 3, 1919.
59 *English-Speaking World* (1919), 10.
60 *Landmark* (1919), 230.
61 *Ibid.* (1920), 222.

reception of De Valera, the President of an Irish Republic which, they maintained, had no tangible existence; to the solicitation of money in the United States to promote secession in the United Kingdom; to the congressional bill to pay the expenses of an American ambassador to the fictitious Irish Republic; and to the willingness of the Senate's Foreign Relations Committee to hear every expression of discontent in the British Empire.[62]

Although the reception accorded Mr. De Valera by the mayor and city of New York must have caused considerable pique among British-Americans, the *Landmark* sought to depreciate it by comparing it to the "extraordinary demonstration of goodwill" for the Prince of Wales and by describing the reception of De Valera as largely "a question of internal politics and placating the Irish vote."[63] Others were more outspoken, however, urging the deportation of De Valera and objecting to the clergy (presumably the Irish-American Catholic clergy) who taught anti-British sentiments with the purpose of dismembering the British Empire.[64]

The British-Americans maintained that there were four Irelands—Sinn Fein, Nationalist, Ulster, and Southern Unionist—and that Britain was willing to give them any form of government within the commonwealth upon which they could all agree. Asking patience of Americans, *Landmark* noted that "if the doctrine of self-determination had been applied in the American Civil War, the Confederacy would have received the sanction of the World."[65] A letter writer to the *New York Times* challenged the Sinn Feiners to show the sincerity of their belief in selfdetermination by allowing

[62] *Ibid.,* 146, 150.
[63] *Ibid.,* 150.
[64] *English-Speaking World* (1920), 16.
[65] *Landmark* (1919), 198-200.

all parts of Ireland, each for itself, to decide upon its future connections.[66]

The Society for British and American Friendship sponsored a tour of the "Loyal Coalition," composed of Ulsterites and Southern Unionists, to combat the influence of the Sinn Feiners in the United States. The group, which arrived in December, 1919, included two bishops, a number of ministers, three editors and ten authors.[67] Their effort, however, had little or no influence upon opinion in the United States, where the case of Ulster was admittedly "hopelessly unpopular." "It was impossible to obtain the signature of any man of public prominence to the thesis that Ulster is politically right."[68]

This investigation of the British-Americans and President Wilson's peacemaking must be largely negative in its conclusions. There was no direct appeal to Wilson or to the Senate; there was no need for such. Although no evidence can be produced to show that either the President or the Senate was influenced by the activities of British-Americans, both lived in an atmosphere in which the parallel interests and views of the United States and Great Britain were obvious. The Wilson administration was infected with anglophilism. The counterpropaganda of the British-Americans may have served to improve the general attitude of the American people toward Britain, but the final failure of the Irish-Americans, despite their numbers and political importance, was not due to the counterefforts of the British-Americans.

The British-Americans were strong supporters of the league. When the league became a controversial issue, they doubtless divided for Wilson's League or Lodge's League,

[66] *New York Times,* February 9, 1920.
[67] *English-Speaking World* (1920), 16.
[68] *The Times* (London), July 4, 1919.

as did the Senate and the rest of the country; the Covenant of the League, however, was not argued in the British-American press. Since the paramount objective of the British-Americans was closer friendship and cooperation, when it became clear that the choice was between reservations or rejection of the league, the British-American organs, reflecting British and Allied views, accepted the reservations. The failure of President Wilson and the Senate to reach agreement, with the resultant defeat of the treaty and the league, must be regarded as a serious setback for the British-Americans. While relations between the United States and Great Britain did not seriously deteriorate, the closer union, the deeper friendship, and the fraternal solidarity that they hoped to advance were not realized. If the speechmaking, the writing, the dining and the toasting of Anglo-American partnership were not entirely in vain, the efforts expended nevertheless failed to achieve the glorious new day envisaged by the British-Americans in which Uncle Sam and John Bull would walk together and all would be right with the world.

THE ITALIANS

JOHN B. DUFF

The interest shown by the Italian-Americans in the proceedings of the Paris Peace Conference marks the political coming of age of the Italian element in the United States. Certainly the stirring of political consciousness among the Italians, as well as such other newer immigrant groups as the Jews, Poles, and Yugoslavs, had manifested itself at the turn of the century, when these groups cooperated with the Germans and Irish in opposing prohibition and the restriction of immigration. Some ten years earlier, when the Italian population became agitated over the lynching of eleven Italians by a New Orleans mob, the Italian-language press threatened political repercussions.[1] But not until World War I, when the great Italian migration that began in the 1880s ended, were the Italian-Americans sufficiently assimilated to be able to express themselves vocally on a policy question involving both their adopted country and their ancestral home. Although in the years 1918–1920 their political influence did not nearly equal that of other immigrant groups, they could not be ignored. Politicians of the great eastern cities, whose foreign policy platform had formerly consisted of but one plank, "All Ireland must be free," would soon add, "Fiume belongs to Italy."

Before the fourth quarter of the nineteenth century, comparatively few Italians had come to the United States. In 1880 the Italian population consisted of a handful of political refugees, intellectuals, priests, and merchants. But as the century ended, the period of mass migration began. By 1900 some 655,000 had arrived, and in the next decade no fewer than two million more reached America. This steady influx continued until 1914. With natural increases the population of Italian stock in 1920 numbered 3,336,941, and it would have been higher still if the Italians had not been prone to use the Atlantic Ocean as a two-way street. From 1908 to 1916, 1,215,998 Italians left the United States.[2]

The Italian immigration resembled the early Irish migration in that, although the great bulk of the newcomers were of the peasant class, they clustered primarily in the industrial centers of the North. Since by this time the Irish had moved from the menial day-laboring jobs into the skilled occupations and professions, their places were taken by Italians eager for quick employment even at very low wages. All the cities with large Irish populations—New York, Boston, Philadelphia, Chicago, Baltimore, Detroit—had considerable Italian colonies by 1920. Almost 85 percent of the Italians lived in the eight states that held three quarters of the Irish.[3]

Often, as in the north end of Boston, the Italians moved into the substandard housing abandoned by the Irish. Close contact between the two peoples produced friction, for although they were coreligionists language and class differences tended to separate them.

Conflict with the Democratic Irish tended to orient the Italians politically toward the Republican party. Less emotionally loaded factors, such as the innate conservatism of many of the newer immigrants and their literal faith in the full-dinner-pail philosophy of the McKinley era, strengthened such inclinations. The Republicans exploited their opportunity through the American Association of Foreign

[1] J. A. Kaplin, "The Italo-American Incident of 1891 and the Road to Reunion," *Journal of Southern History*, VIII (1942), 242-46.

[2] Lawrence F. Pisani, *The Italian in America* (1957); Oscar Handlin, *The American People in the Twentieth Century* (1957), 57; U. S. Bureau of the Census, *Fourteenth Census of the United States: 1920, Population*, II, 904; Carl Wittke, *We Who Built America* (1946), 437.

[3] *Fourteenth Census*, II, 902-904.

Language Newspapers, a party "front" directed by a Polish editor named Louis Hammerling, which contributed advertising contracts to the immigrant press in return for political support.[4]

The hold of the G.O.P. on the Italians and other new immigrant peoples was nonetheless quite tenuous. Democratic machines in the North, territorially organized, realized that they must conciliate the new populations in their districts or pass into political oblivion. Many adept Irish leaders overcame their initial distaste for the newcomers and responded to their demands, with the result that the Republican drive to recapture local control of the cities achieved only a modicum of success.[5]

On the national level, the Italian vote proved quite unpredictable. In 1912, despite a plethora of Hammerling-supplied pro-Taft editorials, the bulk of Italian and other newer immigrant votes appear to have gone to the Bull Moose ticket of Theodore Roosevelt. In 1916, when they deserted the Republican party en masse, Woodrow Wilson carried the Italian districts of New York, Boston, and Chicago.[6] Since Wilson had not run well in these areas in 1912, the explanation for his success four years later probably lies in the appeal of the Democratic platform of "peace with honor," plus the administration's neutrality policy, which frankly favored the Allies whom Italy had joined in May, 1915.

After the United States entered the war in April, 1917,

[4] Oscar Handlin, *The Uprooted* (1951); Wittke, *We Who Built America*, 442; Maldwyn Jones, *American Immigration* (1960), 238.

[5] Handlin, *The American People in the Twentieth Century*, 93-94; Wittke, *We Who Built America*, 442-44.

[6] Jones, *American Immigration*, p. 239. See the comparison in Italian-American voting between 1916 and 1920 in J. Joseph Huthmacher, *Massachusetts People and Politics, 1919-1933* (1959), 42-44; and David Burner, "The Breakup of the Wilson Coalition of 1916," *Mid-America*, XLV (1963), 32.

Italian life in America began a new phase. The Italian population in America had no problem of divided loyalties as did the Germans and, to a lesser extent, the Irish. Since their adopted country had joined their homeland in the great effort to create a better world, they could be enthusiastically "Italian" and still escape the stigma of hyphenism. The Italian-American press took a great pride in the achievements of Italy during the war, and in the estimated 300,000 Americans of Italian extraction who fought in the American armies. It was pleasant for a people whose country only a few years before had been viewed by many Americans as a breeding ground for the Black Hand Society and other nefarious organizations to hear such eminent Americans as Nicholas Murray Butler, President of Columbia University, declaring that Italy's neutrality in 1914 had been the decisive factor in preventing a quick German victory. They took a justifiable pride in the observation by George Creel, director of the Committee on Public Information, that while the Italians in the United States constituted only 4 percent of the population, the list of casualities showed that 10 percent were Italian. Editors delighted in pointing to the enthusiastic response of the Italian population to the Liberty Bond drives.[7]

No immigrant group surpassed the Italians in their admiration for the war President. When Wilson declared May 24, 1918, "Italian Day," Italian communities throughout the United States deluged the White House with telegrams saluting the "great champion of Liberty" in his gallant stand for world democracy. Italian-American societies in New York and Boston struck off commemorative medals to

[7] Pisani, *The Italian in America*, 129; Alfredo Bosi, *Cinquant' Anni Di Vita Italiana in America* (1921), 337-38; Giovanni Schiavo, *Four Centuries of Italian-American History* (1952), 327; Michael A. Musmanno, *The Story of the Italians in America* (1965), 140-41.

express gratitude and pledge their fidelity to the President.[8]

The Italian-Americans endorsed Wilson's peace program wholeheartedly, interpreting it in line with the aspirations of the mother country. Selfdetermination, and the promise of reorganization of Italy's boundary, meant to them an immense increase in territory and prestige for the homeland at the expense of the Austrian Empire.[9] They fully expected Wilson to accept the Italian claims at the peace conference as one method of acknowledging the importance of Italy's contribution to the victory.

Intimations of a possible reaction against President Wilson, if he failed to do his duty by Italy, appeared in the Italian press only days after the armistice. The most important Italian-language newspaper in New England, the *Gazzetta del Massachusetts,* warned its readers not to let the "enthusiasm of victory" allow them to forget Italy's rights, and spoke darkly of certain people who were beginning to question Italy's rights to the Adriatic, specifically mentioning the port of Fiume.[10] Yet few Italians believed that Woodrow Wilson, the same man who had gone to the Italian embassy on the night of the armistice to toast King Victor Emmanuel, would turn out to be one of the "certain people" about to question Italy's territorial ambitions. When the President sailed for Europe in December, 1919, to attend the peace conference, he carried with him the unquestioned support of America's Italian community.

The Italian problem at the Versailles Conference was a complex one, involving the disposition of the South Tyrol, Trieste, Dalmatia, and the Dodecanese Islands. The main point of contention, however, concerned the disposition of

[8] The nationwide expressions of Italian-American good will toward Wilson are collected in Woodrow Wilson MSS, Library of Congress, File VI, Box 315.

[9] Huthmacher, *Massachusetts People and Politics,* 12.

[10] *Gazzetta del Massachusetts,* November 16, 1918.

the Adriatic port of Fiume. Should it be awarded to Italy or to the newly formed Yugoslav state? The dispute that arose over this question came close to disrupting the peace negotiations.

The seeds of the Fiume controversy between Italy and her Allies had been planted in the diplomatic maneuverings of the early months of the war. In August, 1914, the Italian government had declared that it was not obliged by its Triple Alliance with Germany and Austria to enter the war on the side of the Central Powers. There then ensued several months of heated debate on whether Italy could get more by remaining a neutral than by becoming a belligerent. After protracted negotiations, Italy joined the Allies in May, 1915, in response to inducements offered by the Treaty of London. This pact among Italy, France, and Great Britain promised Italy a fulfillment of its policy of *sacro egoismo* ("sacred selfishness" or "consecrated selfishness"). It provided that the Brenner Pass would become Italy's border with Austria, thus incorporating into Italy the Tyrol, whose inhabitants were mainly Austro-German. In addition, Italy was promised territory along the eastern Adriatic, where the population was predominantly Slavic. In effect, about 500,000 unwilling Slavs would have passed under Italian rule. Most significantly, however, the vital port of Fiume was not awarded to Italy; it was specifically reserved to the yet unborn kingdom of the Serbs, Croats, and Slovenes (Yugoslavia).

To this arrangement the Italians made no objections, since until 1914 Fiume had not been an object of Italian expansionism. During the war the slogan *Italia Irredenta* (Italy unredeemed, or places where Italian populations still lived under foreign control) referred to Trente and Trieste. It would hardly be an exaggeration to say that Italian opinion, before and during the war, had been unaware of the existence of such a city as Fiume. Not until the fall of 1918 did the Italian government begin to press claims, based on the Wilsonian principle of selfdetermination, for Fiume's two-thirds Italian population, allegedly desirous of reunion with Italy. At the same time, Premier Vittorio Orlando and Foreign Minister Sidney Sonnino determined to press for everything promised Italy under the Treaty of London, even where the territorial agreements violated the principle of selfdetermination. Italy apparently wished to eat its cake and have it too. The contradiction in its position suggests, in fact, that Italy was merely putting forth its most extreme claims for bargaining purposes.[11]

It was widely believed that President Wilson would not consider the United States bound by any treaty to which she was not a signatory. But soon after his arrival in Paris, Wilson, despite the objections of American territorial experts, indicated his willingness to accept the Italian claims under the Treaty of London. Specifically, he assured Italy that the Brenner Pass would be its northern frontier, with the result that the South Tyrol with its 200,000 Germans was ceded to Italy. This decision was a flagrant violation of point nine of the Fourteen Points, which proclaimed that the frontier of Italy should be readjusted along "clearly recognizable lines of nationality." Moreover, it was poor diplomacy on the President's part, since he asked nothing from Italy in return for this remarkable concession. When Orlando demanded Fiume, Wilson had, by his hasty decision, forfeited a bargaining position.

Wilson soon realized his mistake in yielding the South Tyrol so easily. Attributing the error to his lack of knowl-

---

[11] For an extended account of the Italian problem at the peace conference, see René Albrecht-Carrié, *Italy at the Paris Peace Conference* (1938). See also Thomas A. Bailey, *Woodrow Wilson and the Lost Peace* (1944); and Douglas W. Johnson, "Fiume and the Adriatic Problem" in Edward M. House and Charles, eds., *What Really Happened at Paris* (1921).

edge of the ethnography of the region, he determined to be well informed on Fiume and worked on this problem as on no other. Thomas A. Bailey has observed that, if the Tyrol blunder resulted from too little study, Wilson's blunder on Fiume was perhaps the result of too much.[12]

At one point Wilson seriously considered making Fiume a free city, the solution earlier agreed upon for the German port of Danzig. But after studying lengthy reports from his Yugoslav experts, and poring over a large specially prepared map of the Dalmatian coast, he concluded that Italy had no legal or moral right to Fiume. The arguments advanced by the group of experts strongly impressed him. Although some of the President's advisors, among them Colonel House and David Hunter Miller, favored a compromise that would give the Italians actual, though not nominal, control of Fiume, the Adriatic experts contended successfully that, while the city of Fiume was Italian, the suburbs and the surrounding area were Slav. They argued that Fiume was vital to the economic life of Yugoslavia, but had no economic significance to Italy. They reminded the President that the Italian agitation over Fiume was only a few months old, and that until the armistice it had been generally admitted in high Italian circles that Fiume should go to Yugoslavia. Unanimously rejecting the proposal to make Fiume a free city, the Adriatic specialists recommended that Fiume be given to the Yugoslavs without restriction, and that the interests of the Italian minority should be assured by the establishment of adequate guarantees of protection.[13]

[12] Ray Stannard Baker, *American Chronicle* (1945), 433; Bailey, *Wilson and the Lost Peace,* 260.

[13] Memorandum to American Peace Commissioners from the Chiefs of the Italian Division, the Balkan Division, the Austro-Hungarian Division, the Division of Boundary Geography and the Division of Economics. Wilson MSS, File VIII-A, Box 32. This memorandum is dated April 4, 1919, but its essential points had been presented to Wilson on January 24, 1919. See also Ray Stannard Baker, *Woodrow Wilson and World Settlement* (1923), II, 144-46.

Accepting these conclusions, Wilson replied to the Italians that Italy must choose between the Treaty of London, with its violations of selfdetermination, and the principle itself, to be applied not only to Fiume but to the Tyrol, the Dalmatian coast, and other areas as well. She might not have both.[14] But it was well into 1919 before Wilson arrived at this final position. During his deliberations Italian opinion, both in Italy and the United States, had increasingly advocated the acquisition of Fiume to ensure Italian domination of the Adriatic.

"No nation at the Paris Peace Conference was more indefatigable with its propaganda than Italy." This was the considered opinion of Ray Stannard Baker, press officer of the American delegation, who was frankly impressed by the Italian public relations effort.[15] Since the Italians correctly surmised that Wilson's opinion would be decisive in any judgment on the Italian claims, they directed a great deal of their effort toward the United States.

In fairness, it should be noted that Italian propaganda for American consumption was, in great part, a reaction to the activities of the Yugoslavs. In January, 1919, the new Kingdom of the Serbs, Croats, and Slovenes established the Yugoslav Information Bureau in New York and began distributing thousands of pamphlets describing in great detail the Slavic culture and population of the disputed area, while ridiculing Italy's claims to historical rights in the Adriatic. From Washington the Yugoslav National Council emphasized in its press releases that Yugoslav claims were nationalistic, Italy's imperialistic.[16]

The Italian Ambassador to the United States, Count Macchi di Cellere, strongly urged the Italian government

14 Bailey, *Wilson and the Lost Peace*, 259.

15 Baker, *Wilson and World Settlement*, II, 139.

16 *Literary Digest*, February 1, 1919; Gerald G. Govorchin, *Americans from Yugoslavia* (1961), 124-25, 163.

to act to counter this campaign of "gigantic proportions," which, he charged, was being financed by Austria and Germany to sow discord among the Allies. The Orlando government responded by setting up the information bureau in New York and Washington and dispatching a "special mission," headed by Captain Pietro Tozzi, to the United States. Tozzi made a special effort to discredit the concept of "plucky little Serbia" then current in the United States. He stressed to his American audiences that they would be unable to appreciate his country's position unless they realized that the "Italians regard the Yugoslavs as the English regard the Prussians. . . . They are defeated enemies." A *Literary Digest* survey in February, 1919, indicated that the Italians were defeating the Yugoslavs in the battle for American public opinion. A majority of the American press supported the Italian position on Fiume.[17]

There was no question, of course, where the Italian element in the United States stood. In the early months of 1919, the question of "Italy's rights," for example to Fiume, dominated the news stories and editorials of the Italian-language press in the United States to the exclusion of almost everything else. Much of the news and comment was taken directly from papers in Italy. Like most of the foreign-language newsmen in America, Italian editors made good use of scissors and paste. This practice contributed to the unanimity of Italian-American opinion regarding Fiume.[18]

Such groups as the Sons of Italy and the Italia Irredenta Society asked their members to send petitions in behalf of Italy to the American delegates at Paris. In Chicago the Organization Italiana, established to counter "false Yugoslav

[17] Justus (pseud.), *V. Macchi di Cellere all' Ambasciato di Washington* (1920), 178; *Literary Digest*, February 1, 1919.

[18] This observation is based on my reading of the *Gazzetta del Massachusetts*, *Il Progresso Italo-Americano* (New York), *Il Telegrafo* (New York), and *Il Bolletino della Sera* (New York) for all of 1919.

propaganda concerning Fiume," urged all Italian-American societies in the country to protest any infringement of Italy's rights under the Treaty of London. It exhorted the Italians of the United States to remind their fellow Americans that the population of Fiume had "overwhelmingly approved a plebiscite of union with the mother country."[19]

Italian-Americans confidently expected that Woodrow Wilson would see the justice of the claims of America's ally. Upon Wilson's triumphant reception in Italy they pointed out with great pride that the Italians had outdone the French and the English. Enthusiastic endorsement from the Italian-language press greeted Wilson's plan for an association of nations, which it called the "solution of the world's problems." Under the "great leadership of Woodrow Wilson" it was certain to become an accomplished fact. History would place the American President "among the greatest of the world's leaders." And so it went.[20]

Some uneasiness existed, however, over indications that Wilson might be leaning too far toward the Yugoslav position on the Adriatic. The Italia Irredenta Society sent the President a telegram "agreeing to the wisdom of the concession of a non-fortified port on the Adriatic to Yugoslavia"—an area liberated by Italian sacrifices and bravery—but reminded Wilson of the military necessity that Italy control the Adriatic. The blatantly nationalistic monthly *Il Carroccio* (the War-Chariot) expressed alarm over the rumors emanating from Paris that Wilson had proposed making Fiume a free city.[21]

Both admiration for the President and the League of

[19] *Gazzetta del Massachusetts,* January 4, 1919.

[20] *Ibid.,* January 11, 18, 1919; *Il Progresso Italo-Americano,* January 26, 1919; *Il Telegrafo,* January 4, 1919. The President's visit to Italy occupied the news sections of the Italian-American press for the greater part of January.

[21] *Il Carroccio,* January, 1919.

Nations, on the one hand, and on the other disappointment
that the chief executive had not yet come out strongly for
the Italian position were reflected at a large rally held by the
Italy-America Society at the Metropolitan Opera House late
in January. The mention of Wilson's name brought repeated
cheers; resolutions endorsing the President and his peace
program were passed and dispatched to Paris; but the
speakers emphasized that no lasting peace could be achieved
unless the Allies recognized their sacred obligations to Italy.
Fiorello La Guardia, the popular Italian-American war hero
and congressman, found the mood of the rally when he
asked the American people not to be carried away in their
admiration for the Yugoslavs. Declaring that a good many
of his friends and colleagues "find it difficult to distinguish
between the Czecho-Slovaks and Yugoslavs," the "Little
Flower" suggested that the great difference was that the
"Czech-Slavs fought with us and the Yugoslavs against us."
Although Italy was "desirous" of helping and befriending
Yugoslavia, he declared, "Yugoslavia must realize the justice
of Italian claims."[22]

La Guardia's remarks were typical of the Italian-American reaction to what they considered unwarranted American
admiration for the Yugoslavs. The *Gazzetta del Massachusetts* complained that the "Yugoslavs fought with Austrians
against the Italians . . . yet a good part of the French and
English press . . . and some American papers too . . . are
freely giving their sympathy to the uncivilized Yugoslavs
who are arming against Italy."[23]

The characterization of the Yugoslavs as uncivilized
barbarians was a favorite device, along with the argument
that "the superior culture of Rome" must dominate the
Adriatic region. Nor was this racist feeling limited to a few

[22] *Il Progresso Italo-Americano,* January 27, 1919.
[23] *Gazzetta del Massachusetts,* January 25, 1919.

demagogic journalists. Gino Speranza, a cultured Italian-American diplomat and ardent Wilsonian who was American consul at Rome, writing to James Shotwell of the American Peace Commission at Paris of his impression of the Adriatic situation, contended that the Fiume question was essentially a matter of "honestly gauging the Yugoslav capacity for self-government." Doubting that the Yugoslavs possessed "political maturity," Speranza urged that any Adriatic settlement should recognize that a "race" like the Italians, dominant in "history, culture, and liberalism," would never entrust any of its members to "Croat rule."[24]

The rally at the Opera House opened an intensified campaign of Italian-American pressure on President Wilson and the American peace delegation at Paris. To make it easier for citizens to communicate their views directly to the President, the most important Italian-American daily in the country, *Il Progresso Italo-Americano,* printed a convenient petition, which it urged its readers to clip, sign, and mail to Wilson. This remarkable document, which the paper ran for six weeks, gave the impression that Premier Orlando and Baron Sonnino were representing the New York Italians at Paris! Thus: "We the undersigned, members of the Italian colony, living in this country, earnestly request your excellency, to bring to the attention of the Peace Conference, the determinate will of the Italian population of America on the subject of Italy's claims on the Adriatic. . . . We ask that the Peace Conference integrally accept the program of *our* national aims, as presented and is being defended by *our* representatives in Paris—We further ask as a matter of Justice, that America's sentiment and America's intervention will aid Italy's cause."[25]

[24] Speranza to Shotwell, January 13, 1919, Gino Speranza MSS, New York Public Library.
[25] *Il Progresso Italo-Americano,* February-March, 1919. My italics.

Rallies held in important Italian-American centers demonstrated a solidarity of support for the rights of the motherland. The appearance at the Boston rally of Senator-elect David I. Walsh testified to a growing awareness by politicians of the interest in Fiume. Walsh cabled Wilson that it was the sense of the Boston meeting that no possible advantage could come out of building a state (Yugoslavia), or a series of small states, at the expense of a proven ally like Italy.[26]

Although Wilson replied to Walsh that he was properly impressed, these pressures did not dissuade him from his determination to reject Italian "pretensions" in the Adriatic. During his brief return to the United States in late February, Wilson gave an indication of his position on the Fiume question. In a speech at Boston he referred in glowing terms to the aspirations of Yugoslavia, without mentioning the claims of Italy. Sentiments of shock, anger, and hurt ran through the Italian-American press. The *Gazzetta del Massachusetts* thundered: "The Italians of Boston, of the United States, of the whole world, have now just one thing to do . . . to arouse themselves, to agitate, and to cry out in a loud voice: We are disappointed, Mr. President!"[27]

Most Italian-Americans, not yet able to believe that Wilson would not ultimately support Italian aspirations, waited hopefully for a more encouraging statement. But the personal adulation of Wilson that had filled the Italian-language press in January became more subdued in March. Moreover, a perceptible change appeared in the general Italian-American attitude toward the Wilsonian peace program. While continuing to endorse the principle of a League

[26] Walsh to Wilson, January 30, 1919; Wilson to Walsh, February 10, 1919; David I. Walsh MSS, Holy Cross College.

[27] *Gazzetta del Massachusetts*, March 1, 1919. See also the special supplement on the Adriatic question in *Il Progresso Italo-Americano*, March 2, 1919.

of Nations, editors warned Wilson not to scoff at criticism
of the covenant merely because it originated from Republican spokesmen. The responsibility for keeping the league
issue out of politics, they claimed, rested with the President.
Italian-American papers gave front-page prominence to
speeches by Senators William E. Borah and James A. Reed,
both irreconcilably opposed to any kind of league. In part,
the Italian-American press merely reflected the outburst
against Wilson in the papers of Italy. Gino Speranza believed the attacks on the President were ordered from
"higher up," to prepare the ground for putting the blame
on the American delegates if the Italians at Paris were not
satisfied.[28]

Italian-American politicians, respecting the tremendous
sentiment created among their constituents, inevitably became champions of *Fiume Italiana*. State Senator Salvatore
Cotillo of New York led a delegation of Italian-Americans
to the White House, where they presented Wilson with a
detailed summary of Italian claims in the Adriatic and
assured him that the Italian colony in America wholeheartedly supported the position of the mother country. Cotillo
then introduced into the New York legislature a resolution
asking "President Wilson and the American Peace Commission to support Italy's claims to Fiume and Dalmatia."
Justice John Freschi, of the Municipal Court of New York,
charged that the pretensions of the Yugoslavs in the Adriatic
were no more than a German intrigue designed to split the
Allies at Paris. Most active of all was Fiorello La Guardia.
Although he had indicated in January his support of the
Italian position in the Adriatic, as a fervent supporter of
the League of Nations he hoped for a compromise acceptable
to both the Italians and the Yugoslavs. Having served as

[28] *Il Telegrafo*, March 7, 1919; *Gazzetta del Massachusetts*, March 8,
1919; Florence C. Speranza, ed., *The Diary of Gino Speranza* (1941), II,
277.

American consul at Fiume, he regarded himself as an expert on the Adriatic situation. Sent to Europe early in April with the House Military Affairs Committee to investigate army camps, La Guardia arranged to meet Colonel House in Paris. To House he proposed a plan under which Fiume would be an independent city, with the King of Italy as its sovereign and the Italian government handling its defense and foreign affairs.[29] Nothing came of La Guardia's scheme; in fact, we do not know whether Wilson was even apprised of it. It is of little consequence, however, for by then Wilson had already reached his decision on Fiume.

The Fiume crisis reached its climax at the end of April, 1919, when Wilson determined on a course that proved to be the most sensational and controversial incident of the Paris Conference. On April 20, Premier Orlando had warned the Council of Four that if Fiume was denied to Italy the Italian people would be aroused to the most violent explosion. Wilson thought Orlando's position "incredible."[30] Convinced that the Italian people did not want Fiume, that they had been aroused to an unwholesome attitude by their government and the poisoned Italian press, he made a dramatic appeal to the people of Italy to reject their government's greed and support his awarding of Fiume to Yugoslavia.

As he released his statement to the press, Wilson ventured a classic understatement. He thought there might be a "temporary uproar" over his message. An uproar there was, but hardly a temporary one. Orlando withdrew the Italian delegation from Paris and returned home to receive the overwhelming support of the Italian parliament and public

[29] Cotillo to Joseph P. Tumulty, March 1, 1919, Wilson MSS; *Il Progresso Italo-Americano*, March 5, 1919; *Il Telegrafo*, March 19, 1919; *Gazzetta del Massachusetts*, March 22, 1919; Arthur Mann, *La Guardia: A Fighter Against His Times, 1882-1933* (1959), 106.

[30] Seth P. Tillman, *Anglo-American Relations at the Paris Peace Conference of 1919* (1961), 321.

against Wilson. An earthquake of protest shook Italy and reverberated in the Italian colony across the Atlantic.

In New York the *Bolletino della Sera* took up the cry of the Italian newspapers: "Viva America! Down with Wilson!" The editorial reaction of the *Gazzetta del Massachusetts* is illustrative of the depth of Italian-American bitterness towards the President: "In this instance our sympathy is far from being with the American President. . . . (He) has put it into his head that Italy cannot recover the Italian city of Fiume and according to him Italy must not have it. But it's absurd for him to take such stands. Italy cannot depend for her future on the good will or bad will of others. Whether President Wilson favors it or not Italy will not sign a peace that does not give her Fiume and the greater part of Dalmatia." The Italian-Americans believed that, while the "drunken" Yugoslavs and their admirers would rejoice over Wilson's rejection of Italian claims, the great majority of Americans would condemn his action. *Il Carroccio* was comforted by its conviction that, despite the treachery of the American President, "America is Italy's friend."[31]

The reaction among other Americans to Wilson's statement and Orlando's subsequent departure from Paris was mixed. The antileague papers in general either opposed Wilson and defended Italy's claims or contended that the Fiume dispute was not a concern of the United States. Others condemned Italy's rapacity and applauded Wilson's courage. Many Americans believed that the Italians at Paris were merely grandstanding, or worse, playing into the hands of the Germans by withdrawing from the conference. Certainly, support for the Italian position had declined since late in March.[32]

An important boost for Italy's claims came, however,

[31] *Bolletino della Sera*, April 24, 1919, April 29, 1919; *Il Carroccio*, April, 1919; *Gazzetta del Massachusetts*, April 27, 1919.
[32] *Literary Digest*, May 3, 1919. See also the *Nation*, May 3, 1919.

from the senior senator from Massachusetts, Henry Cabot Lodge, who numbered among his constituents a large number of Italian-Americans. In March Lodge had assured Italian-Americans that "Italy has no stronger friend than I —no one who will urge the satisfaction of her just claims more strongly than I shall." He now assailed the President's lack of a proper appreciation of the situation. He stated his firm conviction that, while Italy's demands rested on the grounds of her national safety and protection, the reasons advanced for turning the port over to the Yugoslavs were purely commercial and economic. In an open letter to Boston's Italians, he affirmed Italy's right to military and naval control of the Adriatic: "Italy regards Fiume as the Founders of our Republic regarded the mouth of the Mississippi River when it was said that any other nation holding the mouth of the Mississippi was of necessity an enemy of the United States."[33]

Informed by the State Department of Lodge's attitude, Henry White, the lone Republican member of the American peace delegation who had been corresponding with Lodge on the progress of the Peace Conference, sadly wrote to his old friend: "I cannot help feeling that my efforts to keep you accurately informed have failed signally. Your comparison of Fiume to the mouth of the Mississippi applies to the Yugoslavs rather than to the Italians." The *New York Times* commented wryly, "By use of that illustration, Mr. Lodge dealt his Italian friends a blow under which they must have winced."[34]

Nonetheless, Lodge was now a hero to the Italian-Americans—an ironic honor for this long-time advocate of immigration restriction and proponent of the Anglo-Saxon

[33] *Il Carroccio,* March, 1919; Lodge to the Italian Societies of Boston, *New York Times,* April 29, 1919.

[34] White to Lodge, April 29, 1919, Henry Cabot Lodge MSS, Massachusetts Historical Society; *New York Times,* April 29, 1919.

theory of history. For a long generation Lodge had advocated legislation aimed directly at the "new" immigration of the Italians, Greeks, Poles and other peoples from southern and eastern Europe, believing that such peoples threatened to change the character of American civilization by destroying its national (i.e. Anglo-Saxon) character with their alien ways.[35] But the senator's previous racism was overlooked by his new supporters, who were more interested in Woodrow Wilson's views on the subject.

Although the President shared with Lodge a conviction of the superiority of the Anglo-Saxon culture, he had always questioned the existence of inherent differences in political capacity among the Slavic, Celtic, and Teutonic races. By 1919, as his veto of literary tests for immigrants demonstrated, Wilson had considerably modified his earlier ideas on the immigrant peoples.[36] Angry Italian-American editors nevertheless reminded their readers that Wilson had once described the "new" immigration in these words:

> But now there came multitudes of men of the lowest class from the south of Italy and men of the meaner sort out of Hungary and Poland, men out of the ranks where there was neither skill nor energy nor any initiative of quick intelligence, and they came in numbers which increased from year to year, as if the countries of the south of Europe were disburdening themselves of the more sordid and hapless elements of their population, the men whose standards of life and work were such as American workmen had never dreamed of hitherto. . . . The Chinese were more to be desired, as workmen if not as citizens, than most of the coarse crew that came crowding in every year at the Eastern ports.

[35] John A. Garraty, *Henry Cabot Lodge* (1953), 140-45.
[36] For a comparison of the racist attitudes of Wilson and Lodge, see Edward N. Saveth, *American Historians and European Immigrants 1875–1925* (1948), 51-65; 136-49.

This paragraph was printed under captions such as "Never Liked Italians," and readers were advised to clip the article and keep it as a remembrance of Professor Woodrow Wilson of Princeton University.[37]

Wilson's secretary, Joseph P. Tumulty—a man ever sensitive to the political aspects of any problem—became apprehensive that the enemies of the league might capitalize on the Italian disaffection. He cabled Wilson urging that the Foreign-Born Division of the Committee on Public Information not be disbanded as scheduled on May 1, 1919. Although confident that the President's position would be ultimately vindicated, Tumulty feared that the temporary consequences could be dangerous, and deemed it imperative to keep active "the one effective organ of communication between the government and the foreign speaking elements in the population." Such propaganda, he assured Wilson, "is more important now than ever." Wilson replied that "unhappily" there existed no more funds for carrying on the work of the Foreign-Born Division.[38]

Tumulty's fears were well founded. Enemies of the league hastened to take advantage of the Italian-American ire. To an even greater degree than Lodge, Senator Lawrence Y. Sherman of Illinois, who was unalterably opposed to the league, became a champion of "Fiume Italiana." To resounding applause from the Italian-Americans, Sherman introduced a resolution in the Senate expressing sympathy to the population of Fiume, and assurance that the representatives of the American people would do their duty in defense of the principle of selfdetermination.[39]

The Italian situation proved incapable of solution during

[37] *Gazzetta del Massachusetts*, May 12, 1919; *Il Telegrafo*, April 30, 1919. The quotation was taken from Woodrow Wilson, *A History of the American People* (1902), V, 212-14.

[38] Tumulty to Wilson, April 24, 25, 1919; Wilson to Tumulty, May 1, 1919; Joseph P. Tumulty MSS, Library of Congress.

[39] *Congressional Record, 66th Congress, 1st Session*, Part 2, 2050.

May and June. After the President's appeal, any Italian government that gave up Fiume would have signed its own death warrant. Hopes that Wilson could be persuaded to appease the Italians died quickly. Italian-American pressure succeeded in securing resolutions from the legislatures of New York, Illinois, and Massachusetts asking the President to accept Italian claims on the Adriatic, but Wilson was more convinced than ever of the justice of his position. Angry over the continued Italian agitation, he told Ray Stannard Baker, "They will never get Fiume while I have anything to do with it."[40]

As it became clear that the President could not be moved, a sense of frustration and bitterness pervaded the Italian-American community. Although Wilson had promised nothing to the Italian-Americans, the Italian language press preferred to create the impression that he had gone back on his word. When he returned to the United States in July to present the treaty to the Senate, the *Bolletino della Sera* was aghast that persons with "Italian names" would accompany Mayor Hylan of New York "to greet with sweet words the man who betrayed Italy at Paris."[41]

The position of the Italian-Americans during the great debate of 1919–1920 was determined entirely by personalities. The Treaty of Versailles settled nothing about Fiume, the Allies having failed to solve the impasse of April. Since Italy soon ratified the treaty and joined the League of Nations, the Italian-Americans had little reason to oppose the pact on the grounds that it discriminated against the mother country. Instead, despising Wilson and admiring Lodge, they endorsed the position of the Massachusetts senator that the treaty needed "de-Wilsonizing." The Italian-language press parroted his criticisms of the "Wilson League,"

[40] *Ray Stannard Baker Notebook,* May 19, 1919, Ray Stannard Baker MSS, Library of Congress.
[41] *Bolletino della Sera,* July 7, 1919.

urging its readers to demonstrate their reaction to Wilson's treachery and their gratitude to Lodge by supporting the senator's reservations to the treaty.

This rather paradoxical attitude, opposed not so much to the structure of the peace as to its creator, is illustrated by the activities of La Guardia during the treaty fight. On June 29, the day after the Germans signed the treaty including the Covenant of the League, La Guardia declared that the league was the only hope for peace. Two months later he appeared before Lodge's Committee on Foreign Relations to condemn Wilson's action in denying Fiume to Italy, a city that was "Italian in spirit, blood, language and in every way." In September, running for the office of President of the Board of Aldermen in New York, La Guardia indicated the tenor of his campaign by declaring, "We must have a Republican election this year to show the whole world that Woodrow Wilson is discredited at home."[42]

Similarly, Gino Speranza, erstwhile ardent Wilsonian and champion of the league, returned from his consul post at Rome deeply embittered over Wilson's "blunders" on the Adriatic. When the President, during his September trip in behalf of the league, argued that if the Italians were going "to claim every place where there was a large Italian population, we would have to cede New York to them, because there are more Italians in New York than any Italian city," Speranza retaliated that the President's remarks "perplexed" and "stunned the Italian people." Wilson had demonstrated, he charged, his ignorance of the Adriatic situation by using an argument that might better have been directed at the Slavs, who were the alien immigrants in Fiume.[43]

As the summer waned, events in Italy and partisan politics combined to keep the Fiume issue alive. Toward the

[42] Mann, *La Guardia*, 108; *New York Times*, September 30, 1919.
[43] *Il Carroccio*, October, 1919.

end of September the Italian-American community thrilled
to the news that the poet-adventurer, Gabriele D'Annunzio,
had launched a sudden and successful military foray against
Fiume. Italian communities throughout the United States
heaped extravagant praise upon the flamboyant proto-fascist.
The incident served to refresh their enmity toward Wilson,
for the administration heatedly condemned D'Annunzio's
coup d'état. Carlo Barsotti, publisher of *Il Progresso Italo-
Americano,* organized a fund to aid D'Annunzio and contended that, but for "President Wilson's domineering attitude," the Fiume question would have been satisfactorily
settled long before. D'Annunzio now joined Lodge as a hero
among the Italian-Americans. The Columbus Day celebration produced great ovations for these two patriots, along
with condemnations of Wilson and his treaty. In the Boston
observation, the crowd hissed Mrs. Wilson for having accompanied her husband on his trip to Europe.[44]

Not surprisingly, the Republicans exploited the Italian
antagonism toward Wilson. Senators Sherman and George
Moses of New Hampshire, both prominent opponents of the
Wilsonian peace, made conspicuous contributions to the
D'Annunzio fund. In New York City, the Fiume question
became a dominant issue in the local elections. Alfred E.
Smith complained that the Italo-Americans expected Tam-
many Hall to do something about Fiume. La Guardia
talked of hardly anything else in Italian districts. At one
point, carried away by his own demagoguery, he cried (in
Italian) "any Italo-American who votes the Democratic
ticket this year is an Austrian bastard." *Il Carroccio* interpreted La Guardia's November victory as a result of the
Italian-Americans' asserting themselves against Wilson.[45]

[44] *Il Progresso Italo-Americano,* October 17, 1919; *Gazzetta del Massachusetts,* September 13, 1919.
[45] *Il Progresso Italo-Americano,* October 17, 1919; Alfred E. Smith, *Up
To Now* (1924), 197; Mann, *La Guardia,* 114; *Il Carroccio,* November, 1919.

In Massachusetts, Italian-American organizations bought advertisements in Italian-language newspapers declaring that a vote for the Republican gubernatorial candidate, Calvin Coolidge, constituted a repudiation of Wilson and an endorsement of Senator Lodge. The *Gazzetta del Massachusetts* attributed Coolidge's large vote to the determination of the Italians and Irish to revenge themselves on Wilson, explaining "You will find no one in Republican ranks who after making fourteen promises kept only one of them."[46] Included among the "Republican" promise-keepers was George Washington!

The Democratic defeats preceded by a few weeks the defeat of the Versailles Treaty in the Senate. The Italian press expressed little regret over its demise. Attributing its failure to the obstinate refusal of the President to advise and cooperate with the Senate on the peace negotiations, most papers rejoiced at the discrediting of the chief executive. As one editor put it, "Let (the treaty) rest in peace, Fiume and Dalmatia will go to Italy without Wilson."[47]

Between the election and March, 1920, when the Senate reconsidered the Versailles Treaty, nothing occurred to mitigate the Italians' feeling against Wilson. Indeed, the Italian-Americans were further exasperated in February, 1920, when the State Department released a summary of a note sent by Wilson to the governments of France, Great Britain, and Italy. The President objected in the strongest terms to a proposed settlement of the Fiume controversy, which was favorable to Italy and contrary to the strong moral position he had taken against Italian aggrandizement.[48] The Italian-Americans were again in full cry. What business did Wilson have interfering in what they regarded

---

[46] *Gazzetta del Massachusetts*, November 8, 1919.

[47] *Ibid.*, November 22, 1919.

[48] Thomas A. Bailey, *Woodrow Wilson and the Great Betrayal* (1945), 252.

as a statesmanlike attempt by the European powers to settle a difficult situation?

As they had in November, Italian-American editors in March favored ratification of the treaty, but only with the Lodge reservations. Although it was acknowledged by leaders of both parties in the Senate that unconditional ratification was now impossible, Wilson remained adamant in rejecting the Lodge modifications. Hating even the sound of his antagonist's name, the ailing President demanded that his supporters reject any compromise. In the last analysis, as Thomas A. Bailey has observed, the treaty was killed in the house of its friends.[49] In March, if not in November, the Italian-American press was justified in placing on the President the burden of responsibility for this failure in American statesmanship.

The presidential election of 1920 provides an epilogue to the story of the Italian-Americans and Woodrow Wilson. The President, believing that the overwhelming majority of the people in the country desired ratification of the treaty, had asked that the election be considered "a great and solemn referendum" on the League of Nations. The Italian-Americans, taking up the challenge, declared that they viewed the presidential contest as an opportunity to administer a final humiliation to Wilson, and plunged energetically into the campaign to elect Warren G. Harding. To be sure, this enthusiasm reflected no great admiration for the insipid Ohioan. They would have greatly preferred Henry Cabot Lodge or Senator Hiram Johnson of California as the Republican standardbearer. Nor was there, at first, any considerable personal antagonism toward James M. Cox, the Democratic nominee. Italian-American editors found little in Harding's record to inspire confidence, and admitted they had nothing in particular against Cox. Italian-Americans

[49] *Ibid.*, chapter 17.

would vote for Harding, explained the *Bolletino della Sera,* simply to "rebuff the insults to Italy of Woodrow Wilson." Oscar Durante, the editor of the Chicago daily *L'Italia,* announced that Cox would be a victim of Italian retribution, since he "pledged to carry forward the policies of Wilson, which means he cannot be fair to Italy."[50]

The theme of anti-Wilsonism overrode partisan considerations. The Federation of Italian Societies in America sent firm instructions to its members to disregard party affiliations and vote unanimously for Harding, "as a protest against President Wilson and his party, for the shameful mistreatment the Italians received in the settlement of the Italian Adriatic dispute."[51]

Attacks on Wilson by the Irish, the Germans, and other disaffected immigrant blocs were every bit as violent, and as the 1920 campaign moved into its final month it became quite apparent to Cox that large blocs of America's immigrant voters were opposed to his election. In desperation, Cox decided to appeal to the "pro-American" vote by stigmatizing these groups (he carefully excluded the Irish, who were to be moved with promises of action on Ireland) as hyphenated Americans willing to place the interest of a foreign country over the wellbeing of America. Apparently Cox hoped to duplicate the success of Wilson's dramatic telegram to Jeremiah O'Leary in the 1916 election. Wilson had been able to convince many voters that the "hyphenate" opposition to his reelection was unamerican.[52] In a bitter speech on October 14 at Columbus, Ohio, Cox attacked what he described as a great "racial alignment" behind

[50] *Bolletino della Sera,* October 17, 1920; *New York Times,* September 6, 1920.

[51] *Foreign Born,* October, 1920.

[52] E. Morris (a Cox manager) to Tumulty, September 29, 1920; Tumulty to Cox, October 18, 1920; Tumulty MSS. For the details of the O'Leary telegram incident see Arthur Link, *Woodrow Wilson and the Progressive Era* (1954), 245-47.

Harding's candidacy, including "the Italian party whose members place a futile Italian imperialism over the interests of our nation." At Akron, Ohio, he spoke along the same lines and charged, "Every traitor in America will vote tomorrow for Warren G. Harding." Other Democratic spokesmen followed this line. The vice-presidential candidate, Franklin D. Roosevelt, described the Italian-Americans as people with "half-consciences" and "fifty-fifty citizens."[53]

In the wake of such sentiments, it is not surprising that the Italian language press no longer extended sympathy to the Democratic candidates as the unwilling handmaidens of Wilsonism. Cox and Roosevelt were denounced for raising the "bugaboo of Italianism or foreignism." Italian-Americans were advised to answer the "defamers of their patriotism at the polls." In final pre-election editorials, *Il Progresso Italo-Americano* called upon its readers to consider November 2, 1920 "a day of sacred and impressive revenge," while the *Gazzetta del Massachusetts* exulted, "Finally the day of reckoning for the administration of President Wilson and his pro-consuls has arrived. The united Italians in all the cities and villages of America will redeem Italian honor."[54]

Although Harding's election surprised very few people, his enormous plurality called forth such descriptions as "thundering protest," "an overwhelming repudiation," and "irresistible demand for change." Political observers throughout the country agreed that a desire for "normalcy" had combined with disillusionment over the war and the peace, and a reaction against eight years of Wilsonian idealism, to make a Republican victory inevitable. Still, even these factors did not explain why Harding should have achieved the greatest victory in the history of presidential elections.

[53] *New York Times,* October 15, November 2, 1920; *Bolletino della Sera,* October 28, 1920.
[54] *Bolletino della Sera,* October 28, 1920; *Il Progresso Italo-Americano,* October 28, 1920; *Gazzetta del Massachusetts,* October 20, 1920.

Political analysts of a wide variety of persuasions agreed
in their interpretations of the election: it was clear that
thousands of Americans of German, Irish, and Italian stock
had registered a vigorous protest against Wilson's foreign
policy by voting Republican. The nation's press concluded
that the Republicans had succeeded admirably in rounding
up the hyphenates. Ray Stannard Baker wrote disgustedly
that Harding had behind him all the disaffected and bitter
groups, "the pro-German, pro-Irish, pro-Italians and ne-
groes." Cox himself believed that the issue had been settled
when "the three large racial groups, German, Irish, and
Italian, had gone over to the Republican side."[55]

Italian-Americans joined their Irish and German counter-
parts in claiming a great share in the Democratic debacle.
In an article entitled "Do you understand now, Mr. Wilson?"
the *Gazzetta del Massachusetts* analyzed election returns in
Boston and New York, and claimed that the Italian vote
had turned en masse to Harding. Later research has confirmed its conclusions. A breakdown of voting patterns on
the national, state, and local level reveals a close relation
between the decline in Democratic voters and centers of
Italian-American population.[56]

The repudiation of the Democratic party in 1920 buried
the League of Nations as far as the United States was
concerned; few politicians afterward cared to challenge a
seven-million-vote plurality.

Some interpreters argue that this decision made another
world war inevitable within a generation. Although modern

[55] *Literary Digest,* November 13, 1920; *Baker Notebook,* November 4,
1920, Baker MSS; James M. Cox, *Journey Through My Years* (1946), 272-73.
[56] Irving Fisher, "Explaining the Nation's Vote," *New York Times,* March
6, 1921; Wesley M. Bagby, *Road to Normalcy* (1962), 159; Huthmacher,
Massachusetts People and Politics, 41-42; Burner, "The Breakup of the Wilson Coalition of 1916," 32; Samuel Lubell, *The Future of American Politics*
(1952), 135; *Gazzetta del Massachusetts,* November 6, 1920.

historiography rejects such narrow concepts of causation, it is true that without the participation of the United States the League was impotent. In retrospect, one feels a sense of remorse at America's abstention. For this missed opportunity for world leadership the Italian-Americans must bear their share of the blame.

THE MAGYARS

GEORGE BARANY

In the last days of December, 1917, "Congressman La
Guardia, Captain, Signal Corps," then on the Italian front,
suggested a conference with Count Michael Károlyi in
Switzerland "with the view of obtaining exact information
about internal conditions in Hungary and the possibility of
carrying out the aims of the party of 1848 for complete
separation from Austria and the establishment of a Hungarian Republic by means of revolution."[1] On January 5, 1918,
one week after the receipt of the cable from Thomas Nelson
Page, United States Ambassador in Italy, Secretary of State
Robert Lansing sent a wire to Rome advising the ambassador
that the "Department disapproves plan proposed by La
Guardia . . . as the Department does not deem it desirable
that anyone connected with this Government should be in
any way whatsoever associated with efforts to bring about
revolution in Hungary."

Behind the exchange of telegrams lay an effort that failed
and a peace feeler by Count Michael Károlyi that was
ignored by Washington. Before we examine the implications
of these two abortive efforts, a brief sketch of Hungarian-
American connections prior to World War I may serve as a
useful introduction to the problem of Magyar-Americans
and Woodrow Wilson's peacemaking policies.

From the time it established diplomatic and trade relations with the Austrian Empire in the early nineteenth
century, the United States was interested in Hungary chiefly
for economic reasons.[2] Many Hungarian politicians and
writers, including Széchenyi and Kossuth,[3] returned this
interest, which developed into such active political sympathy

that almost amounted to official recognition of an independent Hungary during the revolution of 1848-1849. Official American interest in the Hungarian cause, which for a while continued to defy Austrian protests,[4] all but disappeared after the eighteen-sixties. American preoccupation with domestic problems—and perhaps also the Compromise of 1867, which marked the opening of a new era in Austro-Hungarian relations—diminished its importance.

The establishment of the first United States consulate in Budapest in December, 1878, coincided with the beginning of the "new immigration" to America. When Frank Dyer Chester arrived in Budapest at the end of the century, the consulate's inferior personnel were submerged in routine activities. Thanks to Chester's ambitions, to the increasing weight of Hungary in the affairs of the Dual Monarchy, and to growing Hungarian emigration to the United States, the consulate was raised to the rank of Consulate General in 1904.[5]

At the same time Hungarian emigration to the United States began to change. Late nineteenth century emigration from Hungary consisted mostly of Slovaks, who in 1899 accounted for 25.2 percent of the total emigration from the

[1] Thomas Nelson Page to Lansing, December 29, 1917, and Lansing to T. N. Page, January 5, 1918, *National Archives, Washington, D.C., Records of the Department of State*, Record Group 59, 1010-1929, Decimal Files, 864.00/20. (Hereafter cited as Exchange.) The two cables, as well as Wilson's opinion, were published in Arthur Mann, *La Guardia, A Fighter Against His Times, 1882-1933* (1959), I, 346, note 27.

[2] George Bárány, "The Interest of the United States in Central Europe: Appointment of the First American Consul to Hungary," *Papers of the Michigan Academy of Science, Arts, and Letters*, XLVII (1962), 275-98; "The Opening of the Hungarian Diet in 1843: A Contemporary American Account," *Journal of Central European Affairs*, XXII, 2 (1962), 153-60.

[3] Stephen Gál, *Hungary and the Anglo-Saxon World* (1944), 25.

[4] Andor Klay, *Daring Diplomacy, The Case of the First American Ultimatum* (1957).

[5] George Bárány, "American-Hungarian Connections," *Year Book of the American Philosophical Society*, 1962, 335-40.

Dual Monarchy compared to the Magyars' 7.8 percent; the turn of the century, however, witnessed a rapid increase in the proportion of Magyars. Magyars furnished the largest contingent from 1906 to 1909 and continued close to first place, occasionally alternating with Slovaks, until World War I. In the 1910 census, 495,609 residents of the United States listed Hungary as their country of birth; of these, 227,742— 46 percent—reported Magyar as their mother tongue.[6] From these figures and those for the immigration from and remigration to Hungary in the years 1911-1915,[7] one may conclude that the number of first-generation Magyars in the United States in 1915 was around 280,000. This figure, which allows for mortality, is comparable to the figure for 1920, when "there were 268,112 foreign-born people in the United States who gave Magyar as their mother tongue, and 518,750 native whites of Magyar stock."[8] Since there was no significant Magyar immigration or repatriation in the years 1916-1919, we may assume that the number of first- and second-generation Magyars in the United States during World War I was about half a million.[9]

The bulk of the Magyars in America were of peasant stock. Most of them worked as miners or unskilled laborers, although there was a sizable percentage of skilled craftsmen, small shopkeepers, and professional people. City dwellers and factory workers, the majority lived in New York, Ohio,

[6] *61st Congress, 3rd Session, Senate Documents, #748, Reports of the Immigration Commission. Emigration Conditions in Europe* (1911), 374; Carl Wittke, *We Who Built America* (1939), 430. Wittke erroneously gives the number of Hungarians in 1910 as 338,151, which was the number of Magyars admitted as immigrants during the twelve-year period ending in 1910.

[7] Walter F. Willcox, ed., *International Migrations* (1929), I, 483.

[8] Hannibal Gerald Duncan, *Immigration and Assimilation* (1933), 365; D. A. Souders, *The Magyars in America* (1922), 51.

[9] For the difficulties of evaluating Hungarian-American immigration statistics see Emil Lengyel, *Americans from Hungary* (1948), 123.

Pennsylvania, New Jersey, Illinois, Michigan, Connecticut, Wisconsin, Indiana—the first five containing about two thirds of all Magyar Americans.[10] It is noteworthy that a very large proportion regarded America only as a temporary place of residence and planned to return to Hungary.[11] Their assumed state of transiency undoubtedly retarded the process of americanization.[12] This, plus inadequate education and a number of religious and national prejudices brought along from the "old country," accounts for the fact that many Magyars were unable to rid themselves of the influence of the official representatives or unofficial agents of the Dual Monarchy in the United States.

In addition to the bickerings and rivalries customary in any diaspora, the Magyars' assumption that they were only temporarily in the United States also explains the ephemeral life of a great many American Magyar clubs, associations, and newspapers. In fact the Magyar immigrant press, the churches, and most social or political organizations had a vested interest in maintaining Magyar cultural and linguistic

[10] *61st Congress, 3rd Session, Senate Documents, #662, Reports of the Immigration Commission. Dictionary of Races of Peoples* (1911), 94; *Emigration Conditions in Europe*, 27; Souders, *Magyars in America*, 51; Willcox, *International Migrations*, 1, 720, 723, Tables XIV and XVIII; Wittke, *We Who Built America*, 432.

[11] It was estimated that approximately "one-third of all European immigrants who come to the United States eventually return to Europe" and that until World War I re-emigration was a permanent movement. But the rate of Magyar repatriation was almost twice as high; for every 100 Magyar arrivals in 1908-1910 there were 64 departures. *Emigration Conditions in Europe*, 41, 51.

[12] According to an estimate, 80 percent of the Hungarian immigrants were not citizens of the United States before the end of the World War. *66th Congress, 1st Session, Senate Documents, #62, Brewing and Liquor Interests and German and Bolshevik Propaganda*, 3 vols. (1919), I, 712 (Konta testimony). The figures published in Souders, *Magyars in America*, 64, suggest that 11 percent of the Magyars were naturalized citizens whereas 16 percent had their first papers. While the latter figure corresponded to the national average for all foreign-born residents, the number of Magyar citizens was only one third of the average.

traditions and a "Magyar outlook" in the United States, in order to justify their existence. Artificial stimulation of "loyalty to the sweet Fatherland" by émigré organizations was not without its dangers; the editors of the most influential Magyar papers and even the priests of Magyar communities did not refrain from catering to the class and race prejudices and idiosyncrasies of their readers or listeners. Magyar chauvinism frequently combined, as in the case of the Cleveland-Hungarian paper *Szabadság* (Liberty) rabid anti-Habsburg slogans with violent Slovak-baiting or outcries against the Panslav menace.[13]

It would, of course, be erroneous to stress only the negative aspects of the Magyar immigration or to ignore the liberating experience of the New World that was ultimately to prevail. But in the decade preceding the first World War, the loyalty of the majority of Magyar immigrants was apparently divided between the old country and their adopted new fatherland. With the outbreak of the war, a conflict of loyalties was bound to arise.

In order to be realistic, one more word has to be said about the political and economic influences from Hungary that were directed at the Magyar newcomers. Official Hungary, as shown by numerous American reports, lamented the mass emigration to the United States and did its best, short of outright prohibiting, to slow it down through restrictive legislation and anti-American propaganda.[14]

The Hungarian authorities and public thus failed to grasp the political and economic significance of the presence of Hungarian masses in the United States. When they finally recognized it, the impetus appears to have come from the

[13] Robert E. Park, *The Immigrant Press and Its Control* (1922), 75, 345-52; Lengyel, *Americans From Hungary*, 170, 180-90.

[14] Report No. 63 of Consul-General E. Jussen, Vienna (February 10, 1886), *Consular Reports*, XIX, 4; Lengyel, *Americans From Hungary*, 124.

Hungarian-Americans, who were moved by the Austro-Hungarian political crisis that set in after the turn of the century. The struggle between crown and opposition served as a unifying force among Hungarians in America, where the nationalistic and republican legacy of Louis Kossuth was particularly strong. The Magyar-American organizations and the press enthusiastically supported the nationwide resistance to Francis Joseph, and a fund-raising campaign was started with the purpose of sending an army to fight for Hungary's independence. When, however, the Hungarian domestic crisis turned out to be a tempest in a teapot, there was disillusionment among Hungarian-Americans. But the statues of Louis Kossuth and George Washington, raised with the money collected by Hungarian-Americans and unveiled in the presence of United States officials during the revival of interest in common ideals, continued to be a symbolic reminder of the potentialities of Hungarian-American contacts.

A sign of this incipient political interest in America was the large delegation sent to the conference of the Interparliamentary Union at the 1904 World's Fair in St. Louis. After the session, the leader of the delegation, Count Albert Apponyi, who was a prominent figure of the Hungarian opposition and a friend of Theodore Roosevelt, along with other Hungarian parliamentarians, visited the most important Magyar colonies in the United States. Seven years later, Apponyi returned to America, this time upon the invitation of the New York Peace Society and Civic Forum. Widely publicized, Apponyi's second visit was made conspicuous by his fifteen-minute address delivered in Congress on February 9, 1911. Yet it was only on the eve of World War I that the leader of a new opposition party in Hungary, Count Michael Károlyi, arrived in the United States with the admitted purpose of organizing political and financial support for his party in the forthcoming elections.[15]

Károlyi's trip was sponsored by the more radical and leftist wing of the Magyar immigration. The progress of the radical element before the war was largely due to the strongfisted policy of Prime Minister Stephen Tisza, which resulted in a certain polarization of Hungarian political life. While mistrusting the political temper of Hungarian-Americans, Tisza was interested in stimulating the flow of American money to Hungary. With his—and his government's— strong support, Hungarian financial institutions established the Transatlantic Trust Company in New York at the beginning of 1912. The main task of the company was to siphon the savings, investments, and contributions to charity of Hungarian-Americans into the Hungarian economy through government-controlled channels. Capitalizing on the Hungarian immigrant's land hunger, his desire to help his family in the old country, and his fear of financial insecurity should old age overtake him in the United States, the Transatlantic Company succeeded—with the help of the Austro-Hungarian diplomatic and consular service, numerous agents, skillful advertising in the immigrant press, and the subsidized clergy—in building up a multimillion-dollar business within relatively short time. Although the war interfered, the company continued its activities on a limited scale until America's entrance. These activities included, in addition to floating Austro-Hungarian war loans, a certain amount of economic espionage directed by German and Austro-Hungarian representatives in the United States.[16]

[15] Géza Kende, *Magyarok Amerikában, Az amerikai magyarság története* 1926), 2 vols. (1927), II, 213-29, 253-57, 444-97; *New York Times*, February 10, 1911; *Congressional Record, 61st Congress, 3rd Session*, Part 3, 2222.

[16] *Brewing and Liquor Interests*, I, 649-732; II, 1464-84, 1513, 1548-63,

As a post-war congressional investigation showed, efforts aimed at organizing economic espionage and industrial sabotage among the Hungarian workers of the industrial and mining centers hoped to benefit from the spontaneous sympathies of most Magyar immigrants. In the words of Alexander Konta, Chairman of the American-Hungarian Loyalty League, which was founded under the auspices of the Committee on Public Information (Creel Committee) after the United States' declaration of war on Austria-Hungary in December, 1917, "During the early days of the war, when the United States was not involved, my sympathies were with Hungary. If they were against any one, they were against Russia, Hungary's historic oppressor."

With the increase of pro-Entente sentiment in the United States, and especially after the collapse of the tsarist regime and America's entrance into the war, Magyar Russophobia, anti-Slavism and pro-Germanism began to be regarded by many American officials and the public at large as a sign not of split loyalty but of disloyalty. Attacked by anti-Magyar groups, Magyar Hungarians tried to demonstrate their loyalty to the United States. A Magyar mass meeting, held in New York at the Madison Square Garden in January, 1916, pledged in a resolution addressed to the President the "unwavering loyalty" of the "American citizenry of Hungarian origin" and protested against "the constant systematic

2807-23, 2823-39, 2866-99. The total of the savings exported to Austria-Hungary in the years 1914-1917 was close to 145 million kronen or $29.3 million on the pre-war parity of exchange. According to Louis Steiner, "Hungary received about a hundred million dollars during the past, in normal years," but it is of course impossible to reach any completely reliable figure, let alone establish the share of Magyar immigrants in it. In any case, the yearly influx of American dollars represented a very considerable boost to the economy of Hungary, a fact ignored by Hungarian historians but not by politicians at the time. For a more realistic appraisal see George Bárány, "Hungary: The Uncompromising Compromise," *Austrian History Yearbook*, III (1967).

and increasing campaign of vilification" and against the "present groundless and unjust attitude of suspicion and antagonism." Wilson, who was touring the middle west with the slogan of "America first" and stressing the necessity for preparedness, sent a message to the meeting in which he expressed his "very deep and sincere confidence in the entire loyalty and patriotism of the naturalized citizens of the United States." Upon receiving the resolution of the meeting in the White House a month later, he made a similar declaration before members of a committee of Magyar-Americans.[17]

The Wilson administration's policy, which refrained from condemning all Hungarians in the United States for their alleged pro-Central-Power sympathies, proved to be judicious when the declaration of war against the Dual Monarchy technically added 1,700,000 alien enemies (all non-citizens from Austria-Hungary) to the 2,500,000 designated by the declaration of war against Germany. Actually a large proportion of the residents or naturalized citizens born in Austria-Hungary, particularly those of Slavic blood, were known to be pro-Ally; of the Magyars there was some doubt, in spite of their collective and individual expressions of loyalty.[18]

These doubts were kept alive by attacks on Hungarians in the press, despite the fact that during the war there was no trouble in workers' districts that were overwhelmingly Magyar, and that the controversial Hungarian-American Loyalty League succeeded in recruiting 23,000 members within a few months after it began its work in early January, 1918. Continued opposition to the League by Hungarian groups may be attributed only in part to personal rivalries; even after the American war declaration against Austria-

[17] *Ibid.*, I, 648, 718; *New York Times*, January 24 and 31, February 24, 1916.

[18] *New York Times*, April 15, December 5, 6, 9, 16, 25, 1917.

Hungary, Magyars in the United States were unable to unite in a nationwide organization similar to the Bohemian National Alliance or the Jugo-Slavic League, both of which were on record as being hostile toward the governments in Vienna and Budapest. As late as April, 1917, prominent Magyars like Dr. Arpad Gerster, former president of the American Surgical Association, endeavored to justify Hungary's participation in the war on the grounds that "Hungary had to choose between going in with Austria and Germany and being swallowed up by Russia" and that "Pan-Slavic propaganda in Serbia . . . threatened the territorial integrity of Hungary." Yet American officials and large segments of the public could not be won over simply by being reminded of the love of liberty allegedly common to Americans and Hungarians since the times of Washington and Kossuth; nor could they be convinced by such statements as that "of all the governments in Central Europe, none, except Switzerland, is so liberal in its political ideas and institutions as Hungary's." Indeed, such allegations could only help those who suggested that Magyars, like Germans, were hostile to the Allies and America, and that they were the dominating factor rather than an oppressed nation in the Dual Monarchy.[19] This is why La Guardia's proposal, if accepted, might have resulted in a complete reevaluation of Hungarian-American relations. Even if given a chance, however, the plan would have had to overcome great political and psychological obstacles to succeed either in the United States or in Hungary, let alone in both.

La Guardia proposed to arrange a conference with Hungarian politicians in Switzerland "with the view of obtaining

[19] *New York Times,* April 15, December 9, 1917, March 17, June 30, September 19, 26, 27, October 15, 19, 1918. *Brewing and Liquor Interests,* I, 650-54, 712, 717-23, 726-32; II, 2829; George Creel, *How We Advertised America* (1920), 187, 192, 199, 425, 459.

exact information about internal conditions [in] Hungary and [the] possibility of carrying out the aims of the party of 1848," which La Guardia interpreted as "complete separation from Austria and [the] establishment [of a] Hungarian Republic by means or revolution."[20]

La Guardia, who served in the American consulates at Budapest, Trieste, and Fiume during the years 1901-1906, had a thorough knowledge of the old Monarchy's social, economic, and nationality problems.[21] Since he also spoke Italian and Croatian, he was able to refresh his memory with firsthand accounts of prisoners of war and refugees, while stationed in Italy in the autumn of 1917. One of these refugees, a former Italian deputy to the Hungarian Parliament, Zanella, offered his good services as mediator between La Guardia, Károlyi, and other Hungarians then on neutral Swiss soil. Italian officials seem to have approved the plan —a natural response in the critical situation after Caporetto, when no opportunity to create a diversion in the hinterland of the invading enemy could possibly have been ignored.[22] This is probably why Ambassador Page, who frequently used La Guardia as a popular orator to bolster Italian military and moral resistance,[23] recommended the serious

[20] Page to Lansing, *Exchange*.

[21] Fiorello H. La Guardia, *The Making of An Insurgent. An Autobiography: 1882-1919* (1948), 34-61 (hereafter cited as *Autobiography*); Mann, *La Guardia*, I, 35-41.

[22] Before Italy's entrance into the war, Italian politicians, including foreign minister Sonnino, were repeatedly sought out by Károlyi and other leaders of the Hungarian parliamentary opposition. See Michael Károlyi, *Memoirs* (1957), 71. In addition, Italy was the only country besides Russia that held a large number of Austro-Hungarian prisoners of war. According to Ambassador Page, Italians did not exclude the possibility of enlisting Hungarian help in the movement aimed at breaking up the Dual Monarchy through the emancipation of her subject peoples. Thomas Nelson Page, *Italy and the World War* (1920), 343; S. Harrison Thomson, *Czechoslovakia in European History*, 2nd ed. (1953), 304.

[23] La Guardia, *Autobiography*, 184; Mann, *La Guardia*, I, 89; Florence C. Speranza, ed., *The Diary of Geno Speranza*, 2 vols. (1941), II, iii; *New York Times*, February 19, 1918.

consideration of La Guardia's proposal by the Department of State.

Although prompted by Italy's desperate need and his own desire for action, La Guardia's proposal was more than the result of a sudden impulse. In July, 1917, La Guardia supported a petition from his Hungarian-American constituents of New York's fourteenth district that asked for permission "to have an exchange of personal family news" with their relatives in Hungary. Submitting this petition to Congress, La Guardia mentioned that he was "somewhat familiar with local conditions and the situation in Hungary" since he had served "in the American Consular Service in that country for a period of over five years." He also added:

> I know that the sympathies of the true Hungarian people are entirely with our cause. They are a liberty-loving people with a glorious history. There is no people in this world that could do more to bring this conflict to an end than the Hungarian people. Their enemy is our enemy. It is advisable and prudent that we give them all the moral support we can, because if the Hungarian people knew [sic] that they have the support of the American people they may soon repeat the efforts of 1848 and wrest themselves from the Hapsburg domination. I am sure the lesson of Kossuth, the great Hungarian liberator, is not forgotten. [Applause.][24]

On another occasion, La Guardia expressed the hope that "perhaps the Hungarian people after all will play a great part in the speedy termination of this conflict and for the great cause of democracy."[25] More important, he strongly supported a memorandum submitted by Marcus Braun,

[24] La Guardia's speech of July 23, 1917, *Congressional Record, 65th Congress, 1st Session,* Part 5, 5406.

[25] Cited from *Amerikai Magyar Népszava,* July 23, 1917, in Howard Zinn, *La Guardia in Congress* (1959), 21, note 16.

Chairman of the Executive Committee of the Hungarian Republican Club in New York, to Secretary of State Lansing. In a letter dated May 31, 1917, La Guardia emphasized that he had read Braun's memorandum "and talked it over with him thoroughly" and assured Lansing that "Braun's plans are feasible and his purpose no dream."[26]

In the first part of his four-page confidential memorandum,[27] Braun stressed the traditional friendship of Magyars toward England and France and their dislike for Germany and Austria. Of Hungarian participation in the war he wrote, "The whole people, with the exception of a comparatively small number of hidebound Slavophiles, rose like one man to defend Hungary against the Russian Tyrant," adding that one and a half million Hungarians in the United States also supported the war effort by purchasing hundreds of millions of Hungarian war loan bonds and by sending other hundreds of millions to their families, for war relief and kindred charities in Hungary. This feeling of solidarity among Hungarians at home and in America, according to Braun, had undergone a radical change because of recent events in Russia and the United States, since "a Democratic Russia is no further peril" and the entry of the United States on the side of the foes of Germany must serve as a warning for Hungarians to withdraw from the struggle. In Braun's opinion, Hungary was ready to withdraw from the war, to declare her independence and to dethrone the Habsburgs, "but her people do not know the real conditions existing

[26] La Guardia to Lansing, May 31, 1917, *National Archives, Records of the Dept. of State,* RD 59, 1910-1929, Decimal Files, 763.72/6945. Hereafter referred to as *Braun Memorandum.* In April, 1919, the Hungarian Republican Club's stationery listed Theodore Roosevelt, W. H. Taft and Fiorello La Guardia among the honorary members of its executive committee.

[27] Marcus Braun, a naturalized citizen of Hungarian-Jewish extraction, was immigration inspector and visited his native country in this capacity at the time La Guardia was in the consular service. Like La Guardia, Braun, too, came into conflict with authorities of the monarchy. Despite this clash, there is evidence that Braun visited Hungary again in 1914.

today and she must be enlightened and helped from without." The Hungarians of the United States, who "for the last twenty-five years . . . sent to Hungary over twelve billions," were destined to give that help, since their brethren in Hungary would follow their advice.

In the second half of the memorandum, Braun proposed to organize an "Independent Hungary" movement in the United States, to issue a manifesto, the rough draft of which he attached to the memorandum, and to send people to Hungary "to spread the gospel of democracy and organize together with such men as Count Károlyi, Count Apponyi, Deputies Varsonyi [Vázsonyi], Holló and Madarász the independence of Hungary." Hungarian patriots, suggested Braun, should carry the declaration to the front trenches and spread it among the civilian population in Hungary; some should stay in neutral countries to extend help and keep up communications. Braun also proposed the publication of a Hungarian weekly entitled "Independent Hungary" and the recruitment of Hungarian social and ecclesiastic leaders in America as organizers; furthermore, he said, "clever agents" should be sent to Switzerland or Denmark to contact the representatives of the Hungarian Independence Party. Braun did not think it difficult to send emissaries to Hungary as "messengers from Hungarians in America sending money to their families;" he also intended to use "Siberian refugees who ostensibly want to go back to fight, but who in reality will carry the 'Independent Hungary' manifesto to the front and into the trenches."

In the draft of his "Manifesto to American Hungarians to their Brethren of Hungary," Braun urged Hungarians to consider their own interest and not to continue to shed their "life blood for emperors, kings and dynasties." Reminding his former compatriots of the revolutionary tradition of 1848 and of Kossuth, he warned them that Hungarian liberty had been lost because "the Russian Czar saved the Austrian

Emperor." Condemning the "damned reign of Francis
Joseph" during which "hundreds and hundreds of thousands
of Hungarians emigrated from our mother country and came
to America to find a new and better home," the manifesto
stated: "The 'great power' madness, the continuous maintenance of a giant army, the severe taxation of the poor people,
the three years military service, the reign of certain classes
and the exclusion of the general people from every constitutional and personal rights characterized the reign of Francis
Joseph and caused the emigration of us." [*sic!*] Scolding the
Habsburgs and the new Emperor-King Karl's right to the
throne ("the unexperienced young man, a through and
through Hapsburg"), the manifesto summoned Hungarians
to wake up and sacrifice their blood "for Hungarian liberty
and world-wide democracy" rather than for the interests of
the Habsburgs. Recalling that the Russian Czar was de-
throned "comparatively easily" and that the Russian people
liberated themselves, the manifesto suggested that Hungarians could do the same thing, that Hungarians had
nothing to do with the war, and that Hungary should "join
the democratic nations, like this new country of millions
of your brothers."

This brief summary must suffice to indicate that Braun's
proposed manifesto did not abstain from using inflammatory
language. And his memorandum, which La Guardia em-
phatically supported, resorted to the revolutionary means
referred to in the latter's proposal at the end of the same
year. Both the more elaborate memorandum and La Guardia's plan of December, 1917, relied heavily on the influence
and willingness to act of certain responsible leaders of the
Hungarian parliamentary opposition—a reliance that proved
misplaced. In addition, the memorandum reflected certain
traditional Hungarian constitutional concepts that completely ignored the anti-Habsburg movements of non-Magyar
peoples in the monarchy, nay, the whole question of nation-

ality. Still, the democratic republicanism that characterized Braun's plan might have assisted in bridging the gulf between Magyar and non-Magyar independence movements sponsored in America, had the plan been able to get off the ground. So far, no answer has been found to the Braun memorandum of May, 1917; the memorandum, the manifesto, and La Guardia's letter of May 31 were all filed, without comment, in September, 1917. In a letter written to Acting Secretary of State Frank L. Polk shortly after the establishment of a Hungarian Soviet Republic, Marcus Braun referred to his plan submitted to and turned down by the State Department two years previously.[28] But according to the cable sent by Ambassador Page in December, 1917, concerning La Guardia's proposal, "La Guardia states that he personally discussed this possibility before leaving Washington."[29] This may refer to the previous Braun plan supported by La Guardia.

Be this as it may, the revived project did not fare better than its abortive predecessor. Writing to Lansing on January 1, 1918, Wilson rejected La Guardia's offer as "very unwise and dangerous, and quite contrary to the attitude of *honour* which it has been our pride to maintain in international affairs." The President even added: "Too many irresponsible 'agents' are at large, and they are apt to do a

[28] Braun to Polk, April 2, 1919, *National Archives, Records of the Dept. of State*, RG 59, 1910-1929, Decimal Files, 864.01/9. It is possible that the Department of State ignored the Braun-La Guardia proposal because of the former's alleged pro-German sympathies and connections with the German embassy. See *New York Times*, February 28, 1921; *Brewing and Liquor Interests*, I, 702, 710; II, 1474-82. According to the evidence presented at the hearings of the Senate's Subcommittee of the Committee on the Judiciary, held in December 1918 and presided over by Senator Lee S. Overman, Braun was editor during the early years of the war of a magazine called *Fair Play*, for which he accepted contributions from the German embassy. One report indicated that Ambassador Count von Bernstorff seemed to have purchased $10,000 worth of stock in the paper, but Braun stated later that he had bought the stock back. To me, the affair does not look like an instance of sincere German sympathy.

[29] Page to Lansing, December 29, 1917, *Exchange*.

great deal of harm. This is worse than the Anderson case, about which there was at least nothing underhand and of the nature of intrigue."[30] There is no need to doubt the sincerity of the President's or some of his advisors' moral scruples, although they sometimes had strange effects on American diplomacy and even military planning.[31] One must keep in mind, however, the broader connotations of Wilson's decision. The President's "New Year's message" to Lansing was written but one week before he delivered the Fourteen Points address to Congress. At this time Wilson became increasingly concerned with the propaganda effects of the recent Bolshevik coup in Russia, with the peace negotiations in Brest Litovsk, and with the problem of giving moral leadership to the world.

Furthermore, the indignant repudiation of La Guardia's proposal coincided almost to the hour with the awakening of the President's interest in a peace feeler put out through the American legation in Bern by the prominent Viennese businessman, Julius Meinl.[32] One may recall that the American declaration of war on Austria-Hungary came only in December, 1917, eight months after war had been declared

[30] Wilson to Lansing, January 1, 1918, *Exchange*. In spite of instructions to the contrary, Frank E. Anderson, Special Agent of the Department of State in Europe, visited Vienna and Budapest after the United States' declaration of war on Austria-Hungary in early December, 1917, and engaged in unofficial peace conversations with Count Albert Apponyi and other officials of the monarchy. Page (London) to Lansing, October 23, 1917; Wilson (Bern) to Lansing, December 4, 7, and 19; Lansing to Wilson (Bern), December 7, 10 and 26, 1917, in *Papers Relating to the Foreign Relations of the United States, 1917, Supplement 2*, I (1932), 277, 454, 458, 461, 466, 478-82, 492; Memorandum of the Office of the Counselor to Lansing, December 11, 1917, *National Archives, Records of the Dept. of State*, RG 59, 1910-1929, Decimal Files, 763.72119/1025½.

[31] Mamatey, *The United States and East Central Europe*, 73, 88, 158.

[32] *Ibid.*, 171-75. For Meinl's negotiations in Switzerland, see Heinrich Benedikt, ed., *Die Friedensaktion der Meinlgruppe 1917/18* (1962), 192-217. For the possible impact of the Meinl feeler on the formulation of point ten in the Fourteen Points, see G. Bárány, "A Note on the Genesis of Wilson's Point Ten," *Journal of Central European Affairs*, XXIII/2 (July, 1963), 219-22.

against Germany. Actually, negotiations aimed at detaching the monarchy from her German ally went on throughout the better part of the year, in particular after the weakening of the Russian front. The collapse of the tsarist regime and the increasing awareness of the necessity of creating another military counterweight in East-Central Europe, first against Germany and then against Bolshevik Russia, tended to cause both the British and the French to be somewhat less eager to break up the Habsburg Empire. The Lloyd George speech of January 5, 1918, and the formulation of Point Ten in President Wilson's address three days later suggested that, departing from the Entente note of the previous January, the two preferred separating Austria-Hungary as a whole from Germany to turning her own nationalities against the Habsburg Empire. It was only after Brest Litovsk and the subsequent German-Austrian offensive on the Western front, after the Count Czernin-Clemenceau affair which resulted in the publication of the Sixtus letter, and after the Pact of Rome in April, 1918 (i.e., after the policy aimed at a separate peace with Austria-Hungary had failed) that the United States publicly announced, at the end of May, its "sympathy" toward the cause of the "oppressed nationalities" of the Habsburg Empire.[33]

Before this turning point in American foreign policy the cautious and pragmatic diplomacy of the United States "ruled out any direct liberating policy on the part of the United States towards the oppressed peoples of the Habsburg and Ottoman Empires and it neglected the potential aid that a revolution of these peoples might render to the Allied cause." One of the implications of this attitude was

[33] For the American attitude regarding a separate peace with Austria-Hungary and for Allied negotiations with representatives of the Monarchy in 1917, see Mamatey, *The United States and East Central Europe*, 56-71, 84, 88-95, 104, 108, 113-52, 156-64. For the genesis of parts of the Fourteen Points relevant to Central Europe and the Balkans, the reaction to the address, and subsequent changes in American policy: *ibid.*, 171-268.

that, despite the President's lofty aims, the influence of immigrant groups from Austria-Hungary on the Wilson administration remained limited.[34] As a consequence the Braun memorandum and La Guardia's proposal were given no serious consideration in the Department of State or White House. But in order to pass a valid judgment on these projects, one has to examine yet another side of the story.

Five weeks before the President's rejection of La Guardia's proposal, the American legation in Bern was approached by the same Count Michael Károlyi, whom both Braun and La Guardia regarded as the potential leader of a Hungarian anti-Habsburg revolution. In point of fact, Károlyi, who on the eve of the war visited the United States in order to solicit support from Hungarian-Americans, did not hide his pro-Entente sentiments during the war. A prominent member of the oppositional Independence Party, whose leaders were Counts Julius Andrássy the younger and Albert Apponyi, Károlyi and some twenty other deputies seceded in the summer of 1916. The group, henceforth known as the Károlyi Party, was in favor of breaking with the German alliance and of concluding a "peace of understanding."

During the summer and fall of 1917 Károlyi worked for a negotiated peace, and on November 23 he went to Switzerland to get in touch—as Baron Musulin, Austro-Hungarian minister at Geneva, put it—with the representatives of the Entente.[35] Three days later, Hugh R. Wilson, the American chargé, reported that Károlyi, who through a messenger had earlier expressed his desire to make a statement to him, called at the legation the night before. "Knowing Károlyi's

---

[34] *Ibid.*, 74, 117, 131.

[35] Musulin to Czernin, November 26, 1917, cited in L. Zsigmond, "Die Zerschlagung der Österreichisch-Ungarischen Monarchie und die internationalen Kräfteverhältnisse," *Etudes historiques publiées par la Commission Nationale des Historiens Hongrois*, 2 vols. (1960), II, 319 and note 61; for further information on the conference by Musulin, see page 345, note 195.

influence in Hungary, I felt the matter might be of such importance that I could not risk for the benefit of our Government refusing to see him."

The peculiar combination of expectation and suspicion, intensified by the romantic circumstances of the meetings between the belligerents, certainly did not contribute to the clarification of disputed issues and the elimination of misunderstandings. In the case of Károlyi we are fortunate to have, in addition to the official report, the American chargé's description of the blinding snowstorm raging during the midnight interview and Károlyi's own recollections of the conversation.[36] A careful reading of these documents yields some interesting results.

Károlyi, believing that Austria would be ruined whether Germany won, lost, or drew a stalemate, proposed a secret agreement between Austria-Hungary and the Entente. Austria-Hungary, he suggested, would force Germany to attend a peace conference to be proposed by the Entente "on the basis of the relinquishment of occupied territories and a discussion at the conference of debatable territories such as Italian claims, Alsace-Lorraine, Poland, etc." At the peace conference, Austria-Hungary would support the Entente claims; in return, she would not be heavily penalized territorially and the brunt of the penalties would fall on Germany.

Thus Károlyi was ready to go much further on the road leading toward peace with the Entente than any of the official or semiofficial Austrian emissaries, let alone Hungarian politicians. He also recognized the weakness and inconsistency of young Emperor Karl and suspected that

[36] Wilson (Bern) to Lansing, November 26, 1917, *Foreign Relations, 1917, Supplement 2*, I, 322-25. Unless indicated otherwise, references to the Károlyi interview are based on this report. Hugh R. Wilson, *Diplomat Between Wars* (1941), 39-43; Michael Károlyi, *Fighting the World: The Struggle for Peace* (1925), 219-26.

Czernin was playing a double game. Correctly emphasizing that the recent victory in Italy considerably strengthened the military parties in both empires, Károlyi thought a separate peace out of the question in view of Germany's military hold on the country and the fact that it had supplies sufficient for another year and a half. Furthermore, Károlyi's peace scheme depended upon his taking over the direction of the monarchy on his own terms, a condition that he hoped would soon materialize. Because of the adamant opposition of Tisza, Andrássy, and other leaders of Hungarian political life, however, Károlyi did not obtain a dominant influence in Hungary for another year, until the very collapse of the Habsburg Empire.

Anti-German and pro-Entente, Károlyi took a course that was neither antidynastic nor revolutionary. True, he stressed his close connections with extraparliamentary forces (labor, socialists and feminists), intimated his ability to cause a general strike, and arranged contacts with the Entente.[37] But since he did not suggest the breakup of the Dual Monarchy he could not be counted upon as the political leader of a Hungarian anti-Habsburg national revolution in 1917. Yet the La Guardia-Marcus Braun project submitted to Lansing and President Wilson had assumed precisely the opposite.[38]

Since Károlyi's peace plan had serious shortcomings,

---

[37] In addition to H. R. Wilson's report to Lansing, see Lammasch to Meinl, December 24, 1917, in Benedikt, *Die Friedensaktion der Meinlgruppe*, 216.

[38] For pro-Magyar propaganda in Great Britain, which magnified the allegedly anti-German attitude of Hungarians and also exaggerated the influence of Károlyi and the Independence Party, see Harry Hanak, *Great Britain and Austria-Hungary during the First World War* (1962), 167. Some of this information, apparently strengthened by American reports, might have encouraged those inclined to see in Károlyi the potential leader of an anti-Habsburg and democratic Hungarian uprising. "Peace Move in Hungary. Károlyi Party Declares for [Peace] Propaganda and Equal Suffrage," *New York Times*, May 12, 1917.

especially in regard to the "nationality question" of Hungary,[39] and since the entire plan depended on his coming into power, it is hard to see how the United States or the Allies could have given him any tangible assistance before the general collapse of the Habsburg Empire. In the end Károlyi was swept into a responsible position too late to realize his program.

When, on December 29, 1917, La Guardia's proposal arrived at the State Department, Károlyi had already gone back to Hungary. The majority of the former "Party of 1848," on whose support La Guardia and Marcus Braun counted, supported Andrássy and Apponyi, who were both in favor of the monarchy's "German" foreign policy. It is also questionable whether a conference between La Guardia and Károlyi, if it could have been arranged in time, would have turned the latter into a leader willing to bide his time in exile like Masaryk or trying to stir up a violent mass movement at home as La Guardia expected him to do.

In point of fact, such mass movements began to develop spontaneously both in Austria and Hungary shortly after Károlyi's return from Switzerland in January, 1918.[40] Social forces were brought into play that turned out to be beyond the control of any individual or single political group. Without overlooking the inconsistencies and shortcomings of Károlyi's political program before the outbreak of the October Revolution in Austria-Hungary, one must not ignore the moral courage with which he, almost alone among Hungarian parliamentarians, supported the causes of the

[39] Robert A. Kann, *The Multinational Empire*, 2 vols. (1950), I, 145-49, 317, 392, notes 95-97. The sketch of Beneš, which presents Károlyi as a cunning politician who had a great influence in Allied councils, seems to be overdrawn. Eduard Beneš, *My War Memoirs*, trans. Paul Selver (1928), 473-77.

[40] Rudolf Schlesinger, *Central European Democracy and Its Background* (1953), 136-39.

Entente and of peace in and outside parliament. The task he set for himself was the more formidable since it was almost impossible to understand the social changes latent in wartime[41] in a country whose political institutions and civil rights had for decades before the outbreak of hostilities lagged behind developments in the structure of society. Resentment against the strict censorship of the press, and against the abuses of a harsh military dictatorship that prevailed for nearly three years before the changes introduced under Emperor Karl; food and fuel shortages that made the monarchy increasingly dependent on Germany economically as well as militarily; ambiguities in the attitude of both the emperor and Foreign Minister Czernin; elation at the great military successes in both Russia and Italy that seemed to outweigh the multiplying signs of unrest among industrial workers and oppressed nationalities; naive hopes of Wilson's miracle-working pacifism and fears of quick German retaliation against any move to conclude a separate peace; news of the Bolshevik revolution and the prospect of using the resources of Eastern Europe to crush the Entente in one powerful spring offensive before American help could affect the situation on the Western front—all these factors contributed to a combination of confusion and war weariness that would have taxed the ingenuity and astuteness of any statesman. In addition, Károlyi was mistrusted and opposed by all influential Magyar politicians from Tisza to Apponyi, who with desperate blindness resisted any constitutional changes affecting the dual structure of the monarchy. Had it not been for this circumstance, which reflected the uneven development of Hungarian society since 1848, Károlyi might

[41] David Mitrany, *The Effect of the War in Southeastern Europe* (1936); Joseph Redlich, *Austrian War Government* (1929); Gustav Gratz and Richard Schüller, *The Economic Policy of Austria-Hungary During the War in Its External Relations,* trans. W. Alison Phillips (1928).

even have succeeded, given some time and good luck, in working out a *modus vivendi*. Unfortunately for him, the Hungarian people, and the monarchy, he had neither time nor luck.

In the light of what happened in 1918 and 1919, it would be easy to say, then, that La Guardia's proposals, so intimately connected with Károlyi's political fate, were foredoomed to failure. Still, one must hesitate to use even the term "premature" of the La Guardia plan. This plan, which was closely related to the emergency situation in northern Italy, was also a modified version of a proposal previously made by Hungarian émigrés in the United States. In addition, it reflected La Guardia's own ideas about the Habsburg Empire. In 1904, as a consular agent in Fiume, he reported that "the present antagonistic feeling toward anything Teutonic" could be used to promote direct trade between the United States and Hungary;[42] in 1917, as an American of Italian extraction aware of latent anti-German sentiment in Hungary, he wanted to exploit it for the benefit of the United States, Italy, and Hungary.

La Guardia's proposal came but two weeks after the United States had declared war on Austria-Hungary. The declaration of war was intended chiefly to bolster Italian morale[43] and to prevent Italy from dallying with the idea of a separate peace with the Central Powers. It was not meant, however, to terminate efforts aimed at concluding a separate peace between the Entente and Austria-Hungary.

[42] Chester to Loomis, November 20, 1904, including La Guardia's "Annual Report of the Navigation, Commerce & Industry at the Port of Fiume, Hungary, for the Year 1903," *National Archives, Records of the Foreign Service Posts of the Dept. of State*, RG 84, American Consulate General, Budapest, Despatches, 1904-1907, 85.

[43] Robert Lansing, *War Memoirs* (1935), 255-59; Page (Rome) to Lansing, October 27, 29, November 1, 3, 8 and 10, 1917; *Foreign Relations, 1917, Supplement 2*, I, 282, 286, 298 and 302; May, "Woodrow Wilson and Austria-Hungary," 230-34.

As an excellent recent study points out, the attempted detachment of Austria-Hungary from the war was an organic part of the American attempt to avert hostilities with Germany or at least to weaken her military potential.[44] This policy could hardly have been abandoned on the threshold of the feared great German offensive in the West. Consequently, Wilson's rejection of the La Guardia plan can be justified despite its moralistic overtones. Between one agent, Anderson, who let himself be duped by Apponyi and had to be disavowed by Washington in order to avoid embarrassment with the Allies, and another, La Guardia, whose dynamism might have compromised the hopes for a separate peace just aroused by the Meinl mission, the President endeavored to be doubly cautious. On January 2, 1918, Lansing, reporting on Bolshevik peace appeals, reminded Wilson of "the very real danger" of international anarchy; the same day, the President also received a report on the negotiations of General Smuts with Count Mensdorff in Switzerland. It was not without significance that, again on January 2, Wilson warned George Creel not to take any steps involving an unnecessary risk "in the midst of Peace intimations of every kind,"[45] and that the day before he took a personal stand on both the Meinl feeler and the La Guardia proposal.

Yet La Guardia's proposal was not without merit or vision. Lansing, to be sure, disapproved of it in his instruc-

[44] Daniel M. Smith, *Robert Lansing and American Neutrality, 1914-1917* (1958), 159-62.

[45] Ray Stannard Baker, ed., *Woodrow Wilson, Life and Letters*, 8 vols. (1927-1939), VII, 443. For the text of Lansing's memorandum of January 2 and its implications, see *Foreign Relations, The Lansing Papers, 1914-1920*, II, 346-49. In addition to Austro-Hungarian peace feelers, on December 28 Chargé Wilson cabled a feeler made by the Bulgarians; this report, received on the evening of December 30 in the Department of State, may have reached the President along with the Meinl offer. Wilson (Bern) to Lansing, December 28, 1917, and January 2, 1918, *Foreign Relations, 1917, Suppl. 2*, I, 514, and *Foreign Relations, 1918, Suppl. 1*, I, 3.

tions cabled to Rome on January 5, 1918. But unlike the President, he did not oppose the plan on moral grounds. Although he agreed with the Chief Executive that the involvement of La Guardia had to be avoided since he was associated with the government of the United States, Lansing also told Ambassador Page that he "should make use of other means rather than La Guardia . . . to bring about revolution in Hungary." Actually, La Guardia's proposal was very much in line with Lansing's own ideas concerning the necessity of breaking up the Habsburg Empire. He did not oppose, to be sure, the President's efforts to achieve a separate peace with Austria-Hungary, since he knew that "the necessity of centralizing national power for the efficient and successful conduct of war is manifest."[46] But privately he questioned the wisdom of preserving the monarchy, favored the dismemberment of the Habsburg Empire in order to erect new independent national states, and advocated the separation of Austria and Hungary. Lansing voiced this opinion, in connection with Wilson's Fourteen Points address, only five days after his official disapproval of the La Guardia plan. His memorandum was a forceful expression of his vision of "an insuperable barrier to German ambition." Since, however, Wilson intended to preserve the Dual Monarchy, the Secretary of State decided "to await an opportune time" to lay the question of nationalities in Austria-Hungary before the President.[47]

The opportune time seemed to have arrived with the publication of the Sixtus letter, which Lansing deplored, and the breakdown of Allied negotiations with Austria-

[46] "Responsibility for Official 'Red Tape' in Executive Departments," October 25, 1917, Private Memoranda, 114, Lansing Papers.

[47] See the comments on point ten in Lansing, *War Memoirs*, 261; "Memorandum on Subjects in the President's Statement of War Aims on January 8, 1918, Which Are Open to Debate," January 10, 1918, Private Memoranda, 124-28, Lansing Papers.

Hungary.[48] By the end of June, 1918, less than six months after his indignant rejection of the La Guardia plan, the President agreed with Lansing that the integrity of the "artificial Austrian Empire" ought not be respected any more. At that time, Wilson even expressed his doubts "if even Hungary is any more an integral part of it than Bohemia." Basing his judgment "in part upon a very interesting and illuminating conversation" he had "a month or two ago with a group of Magyar-Americans, who spoke very plainly to that point," the President suggested that "Hungary should also be definitely considered to be an independent nationality, no longer united with Austria."[49]

Thus even the President's moral scruples could have been overcome in due time if political necessity and circumstances had warranted. American foreign policy, furthermore, was not inspired by the anti-Magyar bias that even non-Magyar historians sometimes intimated.[50] Although it was of course meant to promote the military victory of the Allies, President Wilson would not have been deaf to justifiable Hungarian demands if they had been brought to his attention in time. The basic problem, however, was that there was no Hungarian political leadership in Europe or America adequate to the task. No consolation can be drawn from the fact that the weak efforts made in 1917 by Károlyi and Jászi to build bridges between a future democratic Hungary and the Entente were watched with but little sympathy or foresight by Czech and Yugoslav émigré circles. By establishing a Czechoslovak propaganda center in Switzerland under the direction of Stefan Osusky and by

[48] Mamatey, *The United States and East Central Europe*, 235-39.

[49] Wilson to Lansing, June 26, 1918, Private Memoranda, 155, Lansing Papers; Lansing, *War Memoirs*, 271. See also Mamatey's *The United States and East Central Europe*, 269, note 102; George Bárány, "Wilsonian Central Europe: Lansing's Contribution," *The Historian*, XXVIII (1966), 226-35.

[50] C. A. Macartney and A. W. Palmer, *Independent Eastern Europe: A History* (1962), 99.

vitriolic attacks on Károlyi and Jászi in *La Serbie* and the *Bulletin du Bureau de Presse Serbe à Genève*, both published under the auspices of the Yugoslav Committee in Switzerland, these circles endeavored to discredit *a priori* the Hungarian politicians participating in the pacifist conference of Bern in the fall of 1917.[51]

The absence of a timely agreement with the leaders of neighboring peoples sealed the fate of Károlyi's and Jászi's endeavors in 1917. Along with a lack of understanding in Entente policy toward Hungary, it spelled disaster for the ephemeral republic Károlyi proclaimed in October, 1918, when the disintegration of the Dual Monarchy was well under way. By that time, however, some of the most influential organs of the American press became suspicious of anything that came from Hungary; editorials commented sarcastically on the belated dissolution of the uneasy partnership between Austria and Hungary, and newspapers printed reports of Slav opposition to Károlyi.[55]

Yet, in its hour of need, the Károlyi regime looked to the United States, expressing through official and unofficial channels its trust in Wilson's Fourteen Points. According to the reports of the Coolidge mission, which visited Hungary in January, 1919, the Hungarian government, fearing the country's dismemberment, rested its case on the sense of justice of the United States; one minister declared, "Our only hope is in God and President Wilson," and the President of the

[51] Thomas G. Masaryk, *The Making of a State* (1927), 221, 305; Stefan Osusky, "The Secret Peace Negotiations between Vienna and Washington," *The Slavonic Review*, IV (1926), 658; Dodge (Corfu) to Lansing, December 15, 1917, *National Archives, Records of the Department of State*, R G 59, 1910-1929, Decimal Files, 763.72119/1137, enclosures (*La Serbie*, December 2, 1917, and *Bulletin du Bureau de Presse Serbe a Genève*, November 19, 1917). At the same time, Károlyi was described as "a dangerous fanatic" to Anderson by Apponyi: Wilson (Bern) to Lansing, December 19, 1917, *Foreign Relations 1917, Supplement 2*, I, 481; Anderson to Lansing, December, 1917, *The Lansing Papers*, II, 76.

[52] *New York Times*, October 15, 19, and 28, 1918.

new republic, Károlyi, claimed that Hungary's policy was "Wilson, Wilson, and again Wilson."[53] Professor George D. Herron, reputed to be the President's personal representative in Switzerland, was also contacted by several supporters of Károlyi who invited him to visit Hungary and collect the necessary information on the spot. But Herron, mindful of the "Hungarian danger," declined the offer; while faithfully reporting the overtures, he advised caution.[54] No doubt, Herron's reserved attitude regarding things Hungarian was motivated both by his sympathy for the cause of Czechoslovakia and by the letters of Professor Isidor Singer, former editor of the Viennese paper *Die Zeit*, who repeatedly warned him against Károlyi.[55]

True, Károlyi himself did not make matters easier for those who, in the words of a *New York Times* editorial, recognized that he was more realistic than "most of the other statesmen of the Central Powers." While complaining, with some justification, to an American correspondent about the "aggression" of Czechoslovaks, Jugoslavs, and Rumanians on Hungarian territory, he also stressed, in January, 1919, that "Hungary must be a geographical unit—"[56] a statement hardly palatable to any Allied leader.

Still, there was some sympathy toward the Hungarian Republic in the United States, perhaps because of the fear

[53] Francis Deák, *Hungary at the Paris Peace Conference* (1942), 16-22, note 24, 366; *New York Times*, December 19, 1918.

[54] *The Herron Papers*, Vol. V, Documents VI-VIII and XII, Hoover Institution on War, Revolution, and Peace, Stanford University, no. D613/H567.

[55] *Ibid.*, Documents I, IA, II, III. On Singer, at the time an exile in Switzerland, who had lectured in the United States before the war and knew Wilson from Princeton, see also Benedikt, ed., *Die Friedensaktion der Meinlgruppe*, 273. It is not without interest that before the war Herron was on friendly terms with some Hungarian socialists. J. Jemnitz, "The Relations of the American and the Americo-Hungarian Labour Movement as Revealed in the Correspondence of Ervin Szabo," *Acta Historica*, IX/1-2 (1963), Documents 3, 6, 7, 9, 20, 40, 42, on pages 189, 193, 198, 212, 214.

[56] *New York Times*, January 13, 1919.

that Károlyi's fiasco would result in complete chaos and bolshevism. Reports to this effect had reached the administration from members of the Coolidge mission, members of the Hoover Food Commission, and George Creel.[57] One may also point out that the official recommendations of the United States delegation to Paris were more favorable to Hungary than the decisions subsequently made by the Peace Conference. Although American representatives, including the President, endeavored to be fair to the former enemy, their efforts resulted in few concessions because the establishment of Béla Kun's Communist regime in the spring of 1919 provided the Magyars' opponents with additional arguments; by the time the bolshevik regime was overthrown, America was about ready to withdraw from the Peace Conference.[58]

Other aspects of this little-known chapter of American-Hungarian relations must also be considered. Since bolshevik dictatorship and military occupation of large segments of Hungary resulted in a rapid deterioration of the country's fuel and food supply, and since the restoration of the Hungarian economy was a precondition of the rehabilitation of the rest of Southeastern Europe, the American Relief Administration under Herbert Hoover extended its help to Hungary immediately upon the collapse of the Communist regime. In fact, the Hoover organization contributed, through economic pressure and its influence with the diplomatic representatives of the Allies, chiefly the British and the Italian, to the elimination of Béla Kun and his henchmen. Advising the establishment of a moderate government under

[57] Deák, *Hungary at the Paris Peace Conference*, 17, note 25, 364-67; Herbert Hoover, *Years of Adventure*, Vol. I of *Memoirs* (1951), 398; T. T. C. Gregory, "Stemming the Red Tide," *The World's Work*, XLII (May, 1921), 99; Creel, *How We Advertised America*, 423; "[G. Creel] Says Allies Failed to Help Karolyi," *New York Times*, March 25, 1919.

[58] For a detailed analysis of the American attitude toward Hungary, see Deák, *Hungary at the Paris Peace Conference*, 27, 33, 58, 67-74, 342-52, 385-88, 452. Alfred D. Low, *The Soviet Hungarian Republic and the Paris Peace Conference* (1963).

Social Democratic leadership, it also nipped in the bud an
attempt to restore the Habsburgs in Hungary through the
elevation of the Archduke Joseph, whose supporters over-
threw Julius Peidl's caretaker government one week after
Kun's disappearance. Along with other members of the
Interallied Military Mission in Hungary, the American Major
General Harry H. Bandholtz did his best to prevent the
merciless looting of Budapest and other parts of Hungary
by the occupying Rumanian forces.[59]

President Wilson, as his recommendation in early July,
1919, for the ratification of the Treaty of Versailles suggests, regarded Hungary as one of the "new nations" to
be created.[60] Outraged by a report of the unauthorized
Rumanian advance against Hungary, he asked Lansing
whether it might not be well "to authorize our representatives at Paris to notify the Rumanians that we shall not only
not support but shall oppose every claim of theirs to territory
or sovereignty anywhere if they continue their present course
of outlawry?"[61] The report in question, cabled by the Amer-

[59] Herbert Hoover, *Years of Adventure*, 350, 382, 398-407; T. T. C.
Gregory, "Overthrowing a Red Regime," *The World's Work*, XLII (June,
1921), 155-64; George Creel, *Rebel at Large* (1947), 212; Vilmos Böhm, *Két
forradalom tüzében* (In the Fire of Two Revolutions) 2d ed. (1946), 247,
268, 342-47, 360-67; H. H. Bandholtz, *An Undiplomatic Diary*, ed. Fritz-
Konrad Krüger (1933); Deák, *Hungary at the Paris Peace Conference*, 104,
108, 111, note 37. An interesting protocol of the session of the Council of
Ministers on August 6, 1919, pertinent to the Friedrich-Archduke Joseph
Putsch, is available in the Hungarian material of the Hoover Institution on
War, Revolution and Peace under Vw/Hung./Al.

[60] Ray S. Baker and William E. Dodd, eds., *The Public Papers of Woodrow Wilson*, 6 vols. (1925-1927), V, 542.

[61] Wilson to Lansing, August 8, 1919, *National Archives, Records of the
Department of State*, R. 59, 1910-1929, Decimal Files, 864.00/111½. See
also the reference to Captain Gregory's report to Hoover, dated August 7,
1919; Assistant Secretary of State F. L. Polk's letter of August 20, 1919, to
Clemenceau; and the "Memorandum by the American Representatives on the
Organization Committee of the Reparations Commission on the Hungarian
Situation and the Effect of Rumania's Appropriation of Values and Property
in Hungary on the other Allied and Associated Powers, September 23, 1919"
in Deák, *Hungary at the Paris Peace Conference*, 115, note 51, 488, 499-502.

ican Mission to the Department of State on April 23, 1919, contained a warning that the Rumanian advance might drive patriotic Hungarians into the arms of Béla Kun; it also mentioned a counterrevolutionary plot "being worked out in Vienna, Belgrade and Berne by *reactionary Hungarians of old school*" (italics added) who counted upon Szekler support and whose plans the Rumanians "probably thwarted."[62]

Thus the American attitude, while hostile to the Kun regime, was not, as has been suggested, friendly to the forces of reaction. In fact, the counterrevolutionary "white" regime of Admiral Horthy, faced with the necessity of accepting the harsh peace treaty imposed on Hungary by the Entente, endeavored to counteract the unwarranted blind trust in Wilson's magic power by putting the major blame on "the Wilsonian principle" and "the man who laid down the basic principles of peace and who was one of the framers of these treaties."[63]

Anti-Wilsonian and essentially anti-American, this Hungarian propaganda was part and parcel of the consolidation of an archconservative semifeudal regime that lasted until the end of World War II. This regime brought Hungary into the second World War again on the side of the foes of the United States thus defying the Wilsonian principle of a barrier of strong and independent national states that would support democracy and cooperate with each other economically and politically. It is well to remember, however, that the idea itself, urged upon the President by Secretary of State Lansing and others at the close of World War I,

[62] *National Archives, Records of the Department of State*, R. 59, 1910-1929, Decimal Files, 864.00/73. For the friendly attitude of the United States toward Hungary and the limitations of American sympathies, see also Piotr S. Wandycz, *France and Her Eastern Allies, 1919-1925* (1962), 66.

[63] See the interpretation of Eugene Karafiáth and Prime Minister Count Paul Teleki's answer in Francis Deák and Dezsö Ujváry, eds., *Papers and Documents Relating to the Foreign Relations of Hungary* (Royal Hungarian Ministry for Foreign Affairs, 1939), I, 1004.

was marred from the very beginning by the consolidation of a revisionist and socially backward Hungary.

Unfortunate as this situation was, it was but one of the many difficulties inherent in an effort to apply the principle of national selfdetermination—an idea which in Western open societies worked for a greater degree of individual freedom and civil liberty—to an area where the guarantees of constitutional life and democratic practices had no firmly established traditions.[64] At any rate, a politically "underdeveloped" Hungary was a crack on the surface of Wilsonian Central Europe that facilitated the penetration of the whole area by totalitarian trends after the establishment of a fascist regime in Italy, the oncoming of the world depression, and the restoration of German and Soviet strength. The consequences are well known.

[64] Hans Kohn, *Nationalism: Its Meaning and History* (1955), 81.

THE SOUTH SLAVS

GEORGE J. PRPIC

Between the two World Wars, in the Slavic capitals and cities all over East Central Europe, the most beautiful streets and squares were named after an American President. Woodrow Wilson was popular with all classes of the people, idealized and idolized by political leaders, writers, intellectuals, and historians to such an extent that it became difficult to distinguish between the legend and historical truth.

Wilson enjoyed particular popularity among the South Slavs, who, along with the Poles, Czechs, and Slovaks, hailed him as their liberator from the Habsburgs. And yet, it would be erroneous to believe that Wilson assumed the role of a liberator eagerly and enthusiastically. In the case of the South Slavs his role was especially difficult, for their problem was complex and confused. Wilson's Fourteen Points announced not the independence but rather the autonomy of the South Slavs under the Habsburgs. Toward the end of the war, when Wilson finally consented to the dissolution of the Dual Monarchy, he was still uncertain how precisely to solve the question of the Slovenes and Croats.

During World War I a clash of different national interests —transplanted from the Old Country—arose in America. While the feelings of some national groups coincided with the official American line, the strivings of others were contrary to American policy. In a maze of conflicting interests the position of Wilson was extremely difficult. He was exposed to the pressures of numerous groups ridden with nationalistic ideas, torn by feuds, rivalries, and hatred; often they lacked a clear and realistic picture of the situation in their old countries, and were disunited in action, leadership, and goals. No wonder that even the best American experts frequently could not grasp the politics and the problems raised by national groups among the heterogeneous Slavs of East Central Europe. This was especially true of the South Slavs.

On the eve of World War I the South Slavs in this country (including the second and third generation) numbered approximately 1,000,000. Among them were some 650,000 Croatians, most of whom had immigrated after the 1880s. They arrived from the Habsburg provinces of Croatia-Slavonia, Istria, Dalmatia, and Bosnia-Herzegovina. Some 250,000 Slovenian immigrants came from Carniola, Styria, Carinthia, Gorizzia, and Trieste. Of the 100,000 Serbian immigrants only a few were from the kingdom of Serbia, the great majority coming from the Croatian provinces. From the little kingdom of Montenegro there were about 20,000 immigrants. The Macedonian Bulgarians numbered about 10,000. Many of the Slavs from Austria-Hungary were wrongly classified by our immigration authorities as Austrians or Hungarians, while all South Slavs were grouped and counted under these confusing categories: 1) Croatians and Slovenians; 2) Montenegrins, Serbs, and Bulgarians; 3) Dalmatians, Bosnians, and Herzegovinians.[1]

Although a considerable number of these Croats, Slovenes, and Serbs were still loyal subjects of the old Francis Joseph, Emperor of Austria and King of Hungary, divisions existed. These three nationalities practiced three religions, spoke two or even three different languages, used two

---

[1] On South Slavic immigrants, see Emily Greene Balch, *Our Slavic Fellow Citizens* (1910); Gerald G. Govorchin, *Americans From Yugoslavia* (1961); George J. Prpić, "The Croats in America," unpublished doctoral dissertation, Georgetown University, 1959; Ante Tresić-Pavičić, *Od Atlantika do Pacifika: Život Hrvata u Sjevernoj Americi* (1907).

alphabets, and in America they had separate organizations, parishes, schools, and newspapers. The majority were laborers, and very few were prosperous. The largest South Slav organization was the National Croatian Society (Narodna Hrvatska Zajednica), a fraternal organization founded in 1894 in Pittsburgh, which in 1914 numbered some 34,000 members. The most significant political organization was the Croatian League (Hrvatski Savez), which was founded in Kansas City in September, 1912, by the leaders of the N.C.S. Reverend Niko Gršković of Cleveland became President, while Dr. Ante Biankini, a Chicago physician, served as vice-president. This organization was violently opposed to Austria, advocating an independent Croatian state that would eventually join Serbia, Slovenia, and Montenegro in a new South Slavic state.[2]

In the political movements of the American South Slavs their press played a most important role. The newspapers could be divided roughly into two groups, pro- and anti-Habsburg. *Domovina* (The Fatherland), and *Narodni List— The National Gazette* were pro-Habsburg. The last, a daily published in New York by a Croatian banker and steamship agent, Frank Zotti, had a circulation of 12,000 and was especially popular among the Croatians.[3] The influential anti-Habsburg daily, *Hrvatski Svijet* (The Croatian World, circulation 10,000) was also printed in New York, where the Serbs published their anti-Austrian *Srpski Dnevnik* (The Serbian Daily, circulation 10,000). *Glasnik* (The Messenger, circulation 12,000) was a Slovenian anti-Habsburg publication, as was *Hrvatska Zastava* (The Croatian Flag, circulation 5,000), published in Chicago by Dr. A. Biankini. *Cleve-*

[2] Hrvatska Bratska Zajednica, *Kratki Pregled Povijesti Hrvatske Bratske Zajednice* (1949), 33-48, 180; M. D. Krmpotić, "Hrvatski Savez—Croatian League," *Hrvatski Svijet*, December 17, 1913.

[3] R. E. Parks, *The Immigrant Press and Its Control* (1922), 341-42.

landska Amerika (Cleveland America), published every other day, was anti-Habsburg, as were *Srbobran* (The Serbian Defender) in New York, and *Srpski Glasnik* (The Serbian Messenger) in Chicago.[4]

In January, 1915, Franko Potočnjak, an exiled Croatian politician, arrived in New York. He was a member of a group of South Slav politicians from Austria, gathered in Rome under the leadership of Dr. Ante Trumbić, a Croatian patriot who was a former member of the Reischsrat in Vienna and of the Dalmatian Diet. Potočnjak came as a delegate of the group to stir up his compatriots in America and to organize a South Slav unification movement. His main supporters were Grśković, Biankini, and Josip Maro-hnić, then president of the N.C.S. The anti-Habsburg news-papers, including *Zajedničar*, the weekly organ of the N.C.S., proved very helpful in the propaganda activities.[5]

Potoćnjak's mission resulted in the calling of a great national congress of the American and Canadian representa-tives of many Slovenian, Serbian, and Croatian organizations. Five hundred sixty-three delegates, representing some 400 groups, gathered on March 10 at the La Salle Hotel in Chicago, where the strongest colony of Croatians existed. Dr. Paul Radosavljević, a scholar who brought the greetings of Nikola Tesla, the great inventor then living in New York, was the most prominent Serbian delegate. One of the lead-ing Slovenians in attendance was Franjo Sakser, a banker and owner of newspapers and steamship agencies. On that occasion a telegram was sent to President Wilson, and a resolution was adopted announcing as the goal of the move-ment the destruction of Austria-Hungary and creation of a democratic Serb-Croat-Slovene state. This resolution was

---

[4] Franko Potočnjak, *Iz Emigracije* (1926), IV, 56-58.
[5] Franko Potočnjak, *Iz Emigracije: U Americi* (1927), 27-61.

also sent to the authorities in Washington.[6] On the second day of the congress, a Yugoslav National Council of thirty-seven members was formed. Niko Grškovič became President with Dr. Radosavljević, Franjo Sakser, and Josip Marohnić serving as vice-presidents.

While the Chicago resolution presented a formal basis for cooperation between the South Slavs, it did not succeed in creating a united front among them. In fact, the first difficulties arose almost immediately. Only a few days after the congress the news came from Trumbić in Europe about the forthcoming secret treaty between the Allies (Britain, France, and Russia) and Italy. To buy Italy's entrance into the war on the Allied side, the Allies were now promising the Italians generous slices of Slovenian and Croatian territories. Alarmed by this news, the council contacted the Russian ambassador in Washington and urged him to have his government denounce the treaty.[7] On April 26, 1915, however, the secret Treaty of London was signed, and Italy soon entered the war on the side of the Allies. The fact that Russia, regarded by many of the South Slav politicians in exile as the protector of Slavdom, agreed to cede South Slav territories to Italy was a great blow to the morale of the South Slav movement. Paradoxical as it may seem, the Russian official policy at that time was opposed to the creation of a state of the Serbs, Croats, and Slovenes. Sazonov told this to Supilo, a close collaborator of Trumbić. (It was through Supilo who was visiting Petrograd in March,

[6] *Hrvatska Zastava*, March 3, 9, 10, and 11, 1915; Potočnjak, *U Americi*, 94-96; Ferdo Šišić, *Dokumenti o Postanku Kraljevine Srba, Hrvata i Slovenaca* (1920), 20-21, hereafter mentioned as *Dokumenti;* Victor S. Mamatey, *The United States and East Central Europe, 1914-1918: A Study in Wilsonian Diplomacy and Propaganda* (1957), 114-18. This includes an excellent discussion of South Slavic politics in America.

[7] Potočnjak, *U Americi*, 104, 115-25; Šišić, *Dokumenti*, 21-22. Ante Smith Pavelić, *Dr. Ante Trumbić* (1959), 46-48.

1915, that Trumbić learned about the forthcoming Treaty of London.) The Russians feared that Orthodox Serbia might become too exposed to what they considered as unfavorable influences of a union with Catholic Croatia and Slovenia. The written accounts of Ivan Meštrović, the famous Croatian sculptor (one of the most prominent members of the South Slav movement in exile), Frano Supilo, Count Carlo Sforza, and Milada Paulova (who wrote the best documentary history of the South Slav movement in exile), as well as Franko Potočnjak, who also spent some time in Russia, all testify to this fact.[8]

Even before the disclosure of this information, however, opposition to the unification movement had appeared among the South Slavs in America. For instance, Rev. M. D. Krmpotić of Kansas City, a member of the Croatian League and representative of four Croatian organizations at the Chicago Congress, immediately reacted against the resolution, denounced plans for a Yugoslav state and Pašić's Great-Serbia designs, and along with a group of Croatian and Slovenian priests later condemned the Italian territorial aspirations in the eastern Adriatic. He wrote a pamphlet in English stating that the Croatians and Slovenians "would much rather remain under the sovereignty of the Austrian Emperor than to become subjects of the Pan-Serbian illusions." Of Austria Krmpotić wrote, "A new policy of federation must be carried out."[9] This statement was still in accordance with American policy; Wilson himself advocated until May, 1918, the policy of federation within Austria.

[8] I. Meštrović, *Uspomene na Političke Ljude i Dogadjaja* (1961); M. Paulova, *Jugoslavenski Odbor* (1925), 77, 148-55, 169-79; Carlo Sforza. *Fifty Years of War and Diplomacy in the Balkans* (1940), 109; René Albrecht-Carrié, *Italy at the Paris Peace Conference* (1938), 31; Milan Marjanović, *Londonski Ugovor iz Godine 1915* (1960).

[9] M. D. Krmpotić, *Are Italy's Claims on Istria, Dalmatia and Islands Justified: On Great Serbia* (1915).

Also opposed to the activities of Potočnjak and his friends was the Slovenian Socialist leader, Etbin Kristan, who knew Potočnjak from the old country. In his weekly organ *Proletarec* Kristan constantly attacked the unification movement. The Socialists maintained that the future Yugoslavia should be a republic rather than a monarchy.[10]

When Potočnjak reached Paris (with ample funds collected in America, including $5,000 from the Croatian League alone) the Yugoslav Committee had just been founded. Dr. Trumbić became president and its membership included, among other exiled South Slavs from Austria-Hungary, Meštrović and Supilo. Shortly afterwards the committee moved to London, where, through the connections of H. Wickham Stead and R. W. Seton-Watson, good friends of the South Slavs who wrote a great deal about them, they found some interest and support in the Foreign Office.[11] For tactical reasons the committee had three members from America: Biankini, Gršković, and the Serbian scholar and inventor, Professor Mihajlo Pupin of Columbia University who also served as the Serbian consul in New York.[12]

In addition to serving as the representative of the South Slavs from Austria-Hungary, the committee had as its political goal the destruction of the Habsburg monarchy and establishment of the South Slav state; this was its mandate from the Chicago Congress. Its object was to be accomplished through Allied intervention and direct negotiations with the Serbian government. While Trumbić and his men envisaged the future unified state as a democratic

[10] Potočnjak, *U Americi*, 61-64; *Proletarec*, February 23, 1915, and many following issues.

[11] Seton-Watson, *The Southern Slav Question and the Habsburg Monarchy* (1911); *Absolutism in Croatia* (1912); and *The Rise of Nationality in the Balkans* (1917). See also H. Wickham Stead, *Through Thirty Years: 1892-1922* (1924), II, 53-65.

[12] Kosier, *Srbi, Hrvati i Slovenci*, 59-88.

union of equal partners, the Serbian Premier Nikola Pašić insisted that it would merely be an expanded Serbia. Thus the Yugoslav Committee had to deal with two major problems, Italian Irredentism and Pašić's Great-Serbian designs. Although financial contributions from the immigrants made the committee financially independent of both the Allies and the Serbian government, in spite of this close connection the Yugoslav National Council in America remained a distinct organization and it was not a part of the Yugoslav Committee in London.

In mid-July, 1915, another great congress of the South Slavs, attended by some 2,000 delegates, convened in Pittsburgh. They issued a resolution condemning Austria-Hungary and appealing to the South Slavs in the Austrian army to turn their arms against the Habsburgs. They also sent telegrams to President Wilson and Premier Pašić.[13]

In the meantime, the committee in London increased its political and propagandistic activities.[14] Trumbić was aware that a great number of the South Slavs in America opposed the destruction of Austria. To rally American public opinion and the immigrants themselves to the South Slav cause, the committee sent an able Croatian journalist and organizer, Milan Marjanović, to America in October, 1915. While in America Marjanović published several pamphlets in English and Croatian.[15]

In the same month Bulgaria joined the Central Powers, which by the end of the year occupied almost all of Serbia. After a tragic flight through Macedonia and Albania, the

[13] *Hrvatski Glasnik,* July 15 and 22, 1915; Šišić, *Dokumenti,* 40-41.

[14] Potočnjak, *U Americi,* 164, 169. "Yugo" means "south" in both Croatian and Slovenian; thus "Yugoslav" either as adjective or noun denotes a Southern Slav, implying rather a geographic distinction embracing also the Bulgarians and Macedonian Slavs.

[15] Paulova, *Jugoslavenski Odbor,* 236-47; *Zajedničar,* April 15, 1916. For more information see Paul D. Ostović, *The Truth About Yugoslavia* (1952), 56-62.

remnants of the Serbian army and the government, along with many civilians, were transported by the Allies to the Greek Island of Corfu, which served as a temporary seat of government. At that time Serbia's chances seemed so poor that the American ambassador in Vienna, Penfield, in his message to the Secretary of State on December 9, 1915, predicted that the future Serbia would be "decreased in area, and under a dynasty unrelated to the House of Karageorgevich." He further noted that "the greatest difficulty of governing Austria-Hungary . . . is the presence of many discordant races, with more trouble coming from the Southern Slavs than all other races combined."[16]

Throughout 1916 the major obstacle of the South Slav movement was the heated controversy over the secret Treaty of London. The South Slavs in America "did not possess sufficiently developed conscience for a revolt against the Habsburgs,"[17] and since America had not yet entered the war the pro-Habsburg elements were comparatively free in their propaganda activities. The latter accused Gršković and his group of having "sold" the Croatian and Slovenian territories to the Italians through the Allies. Violent brawls between the pro- and anti-Habsburg elements were frequent. Particularly pro-Austrian were many of the Dalmatian Croats, while the New York daily of Frank Zotti, *Narodni List*, actively argued against the unification movement.

The Treaty of London was publicized by the Austrian authorities in an effort to induce the Croatian and Slovenian units to fight against the Italians. These South Slavs felt that in fighting on the Isonzo River they were defending their own ethnic territory. As one of Wilson's biographers observed in commenting on the Treaty of London, "The Croats and Slovenes, . . . looking to the Allies as their friends,

[16] Department of State, *Papers Relating to the Foreign Relations of the United States: The Lansing Papers, 1914-1920* (1939), I, 649-50.
[17] Paulova, *Jugoslavenski Odbor*, 207.

saw Italy rewarded by being given territory and ports which they considered as belonging to them."[18]

The American authorities were well aware of the disunity among the South Slavs. Some senators, such as Senator Stone who had been briefed by Krmpotić, were under the impression that a majority of the immigrants were opposed to the destruction of the Habsburg monarchy. On the other hand, those opposing the Habsburgs sent telegrams to President Wilson demanding the destruction of Austria. Near the end of April, 1916, for instance, the Croatians of Pittsburgh held their traditional Zrinski-Frankopan commemoration, paying homage to the national heroes who were executed by the Habsburgs in 1671. The participants sent a telegram to the President, who replied to them on May 2, 1916.[19]

Such confusion and disunity was a legacy of the old-country politics. To create a greater Serbia, Pašić had to eliminate Montenegro; his efforts to do so reached as far as the United States. In order to obtain additional soldiers for his army, the Montenegrin King Nicholas in early 1915 sent two representatives to the Montenegrin colonies in America to recruit several thousand soldiers. Pašić sent one of his agents to prevent these activities. After the Serbian defeat at the end of 1915, Pašić decided to do the same thing the Montenegrins had attempted to do. He sent Colonel Milan Pribičević from Corfu to recruit volunteers for the badly depleted Serbian army that was then being organized.[20]

These activities in 1915 and 1916 of course raised the question of the South Slav vote in the election of 1916. Numerous South Slav political writers, including such visitors

---

[18] R. S. Baker, *Woodrow Wilson and World Settlement* (1922), I, 53.

[19] *Zajedničar,* May 10, 1916.

[20] Paulova, *Jugoslavenski Odbor,* 236; Ostović, *The Truth About Yugoslavia,* 62-68.

to America as Potočnjak, H. Hinković, and the Czech author Milada Paulova, claimed that thousands of the South Slav votes had given Wilson his small margin over Charles E. Hughes in the California election. After the bureau of the Yugoslav National Council in Washington received a telegram to this effect from its branch in California, the council in turn sent a congratulatory telegram to the President stating that he had been elected by the vote of the South Slavs. Wilson allegedly acknowledged and appreciated this support. The story even reached the American ambassador in Paris, William Sharp, who repeated it to some members of the Yugoslav Committee.[21]

In 1916 approximately 80,000 South Slav immigrants lived in California. A high percentage were American citizens who traditionally voted Democratic. A Croatian journalist who supported the South Slav movement, Franjo Akačić, stated that the South Slavs in California voted for Wilson because they hoped he would advocate the liberation of their countries from Austria. He of course accepted the theory that the South Slavs "elected Wilson."[22] Others carried the story a step further. Bogdan Raditsa, a Croatian writer and scholar in America, recently commented: "Legend has it that these Croats [in California] helped persuade Woodrow Wilson to back the Yugoslav idea, and that their votes supplied the narrow margin in California, by which he was re-elected in 1916."[23]

Although the interpretation can be neither proven nor disproven, the fact is that the Yugoslav National Council

[21] *Ibid.*, 245, 449.

[22] F. Akačić, "Jesu li iseljeni Hrvati jednoč izabrali Predsjednika Sjed. Drzava Amerike?" *Zajedničar*, October 17, 1956, p. 4.

[23] B. Raditsa, "Clash of Two Immigrant Generations," *Commentary*, XXI (January, 1958), 9-10. The margin was 3,773 votes; Wilson scored 277 electoral votes, and Hughes 254; 266 electoral votes were necessary for Wilson's election; the 13 electoral votes of California secured his victory. See Mark Sullivan, *Our Times* (1933), V, 239-40.

sent the congratulatory telegram to Wilson, reminding him in a polite way that the South Slavs had helped to elect him, because they wanted his help in the future.

The fact that many South Slav writers accepted this theory can be attributed to the efforts of the Yugoslav National Council in Washington, whose main purpose was to conduct propaganda activities and in a way to be the representative of the Yugoslav Committee. In this respect its leaders lobbied for the establishment of a South Slav state. Their office at 932 Southern Building was the first of its kind in Washington—an agency of a national group fighting for the establishment of an independent state in the old country. While Paulova maintained that "this work was quickly noted, recognized and supported by the American government,"[24] another observer of these activities found that the council's influence on American policy "appears to have been small, at least until the final months of the war, when American public opinion was aroused about the cause of subject nationalities in general." Wilson himself did not pay much attention to the propaganda activities of immigrant groups in behalf of their compatriots in Europe "until American public opinion as a whole created pressures in their favor."[25]

Partly to impress the Americans and arouse public opinion, another great congress of the South Slavs convened at Pittsburgh on November 29 and 30, 1916. Six hundred and fifteen delegates from the United States and Canada, and three from South America, claimed to speak in the name of more than 500,000 South Slavs. The congress, organized by Milan Marjanović, included representatives of the following South Slav organizations: the National Croatian Society with some 500 branches and 40,000 members; Croatian Society of Illinois with 110 branches and

---

[24] Paulova, *Jugoslavenski Odbor*, 246.
[25] Mamatey, *The United States and East Central Europe*, 117-18.

10,000 members; Croatian League of the Pacific with 10 local organizations; League of United Serbs "Unity" with 10,000 members; Serbian Orthodox League, "Srbobran," with 7,000 members; Croatian League with 110 chapters; Slovenian League with forty branches; and the Yugoslav Sokol League with forty organizations. Niko Gršković was elected chairman while Professor Pupin, Colonel Pribičević, and the Slovenian representative, Dr. Niko Županič, a member of the Yugoslav Committee in London, attended the sessions.[26] Among other actions, the congress issued a resolution recognizing the Yugoslav Committee in London as the spokesman for all South Slavs from Austria-Hungary, pledged full moral and financial support, drafted a constitution for the Yugoslav National Council in America, and sent telegrams both to the Serbian government at Corfu and to President Wilson, greeting him as "the defender of the rights of small nations."[27]

To counter such unification activities, a group of Slovenian and Croatian priests, meeting in Pittsburgh on November 19, composed a memorandum to President Wilson hailing him for his defense of the small nations. The *Narodni List* reported that "the Memorandum was written on parchment by an artistic hand and was signed by all the present priests." A delegation of three priests reportedly went to Washington to hand the memorandum to the President in person. These priest-opponents of the unification movement also issued a proclamation entitled "Our Declaration," which was later printed and distributed to leading American politicians and journalists. The signers appealed to the people of America to help the struggle for "a union of all Croatian and Slovenian lands in an independent and free state." On December 6, 1916, *Narodni List*, at the time the most widely read South

[26] *Hrvatski Glasnik* and *Hrvatska Zastava*, November 20-30, 1916.
[27] Šišić, *Dokumenti*, 74-80.

Slav paper in America, issued a "Proclamation to the Croatian People in America," while on the next day it carried the Croatian version of "Our Declaration," including the signatures of Krmpotić and thirteen Croatian and Slovenian priests. The declaration with comments was then printed in the form of a pamphlet addressed to the Croatian and Slovenian immigrants.[28]

Although these divisions continued throughout the winter of 1916-1917, the American declaration of war on Germany on April 6, 1917, considerably strengthened the position of the Yugoslav movement in America. Many South Slav organizations reacted to this news as did the Croatians of Joliet, Illinois; gathered for the annual commemoration of Zrinski and Frankopan, they sent a telegram to Wilson expressing their loyalty and declaring themselves willing "to sacrifice their lives and their fortunes on the altar of Liberty, trusting that American victory will deliver their brothers in Croatia from tyrannical Austrian oppression and bring them full unity, independence and liberty."[29]

Meanwhile, the new Serbian minister in Washington, Ljuba Mihajlović, emerged as an important force in the unification movement. In a note to Secretary Lansing in May, 1917, he tried to convince the American Government that it should pay great attention to the Balkans and the Serbian question. "The noble expressions of President Wilson," stated Mihajlović, "have recently caused great hostile outbursts of feeling in the Croatian Diet in Agram [Zagreb], notwithstanding the oppression of the Austrian military regime."[30] Through the intervention of Mihajlović, Colonel Pribičević was able to open in Washington a special recruiting office for volunteers for the Serbian army at Corfu. By

[28] *Narodni List*, December 6, 1916; *Naša Izjava i k Našoj Izjavi* (1916).
[29] *Hrvatska Zastava*, May 8, 1917.
[30] *Foreign Relations of the United States: 1917, Supplement II* (1932), I, 590; Meštrović, *Uspomene*, 44-47.

June, 1917, some 2,000 South Slavs had left America for Europe to swell that meager force.[31] With the combined efforts of Mihajlović and the National Council, the unification movement now intensified its activities across the country. It organized numerous meetings, conventions, parades, and anti-Habsburg demonstrations, most of which sent telegrams to President Wilson.

In July, 1917, Dr. Ante Trumbić, President of the Yugoslav Committee in London, went with several of his collaborators to Corfu to negotiate with the Serbian Premier N. Pašić. Meanwhile, a serious crisis had broken out in the ranks of the Yugoslav movement in America. Many of the anti-Habsburg immigrants were republicans by conviction and as such opposed a monarchy for future Yugoslavia. Among the antimonarchists were numerous Slovenian and Croatian Socialists, whose centers were then Chicago and Cleveland. The threat was discussed at the meeting of the Yugoslav National Council in Washington on July 14 and 15, 1917, which Mihajlović and Pribičević attended. The council sent an urgent appeal to the Reverend Niko Gršković in Cleveland to quit his parish, go to Washington, and work for unity in the desperately split movement. With his abundant energies, excellent pen, great anti-Habsburg zeal, and a reputation among the immigrants, with whom he was popular, he was highly qualified for such a job.[32] On July 20, 1917, Trumbić and Pašić signed the Declaration of Corfu, an agreement that the future democratic South Slav state, the Kingdom of the Serbs, Croats, and Slovenes, would be a union of equal partners under the Karageorgevich dynasty.[33] Its publication caused a further deterioration of

[31] Paulova, *Jugoslavenski Odbor*, 247, 368.
[32] *Ibid.*, 367-68.
[33] Šišić, *Dokumenti*, 96-99; Paulova, *Jugoslavenski Odbor*, 331-45; Ivan Meštrović, "The Yugoslav Committee in London and the Declaration of Corfu," in *The Croatian Nation* (1955), 171-91.

hope for a unified movement; the republicans and, notably, the socialists denounced the monarchist and antidemocratic attitude of Pašić.

On the other side, the nationalistic opponents of the movement attacked any union of the South Slavs and Pašić's Great-Serbia idea, for which he was well known among the Allies. H. Wickham Stead later had a hard time convincing Pašić that Slovenia and Croatia were not like Macedonia and that the British and American governments would never tolerate a Yugoslavia created as an expansion of Serbia. Pašić bluntly told him that he had agreed to the Declaration of Corfu only for tactical reasons, in order "to deceive the Yugoslav Committee."[34] To make things worse, Mihajlo Pupin, a great friend of Pašić and an opponent of Minister Mihajlović's pro-Yugoslav tendencies, vigorously attacked through *Srpski Dnevnik* and *Srobran* the Croatian and Slovenian opponents of the monarchy as "separatists" and pro-Austrian elements. As a result of his criticism, a number of leading South Slavs came to the United States to strengthen the position of the monarchists. The Serbian government unofficially sent Dr. Hinko Hinković, a Croatian politician and member of the Yugoslav Committee who spoke fluent English, with the hope that he would engage in pro-monarchistic activities. (Little did Pašić know at that time that Hinković, influenced partly by the democratic climate of America and considerably by the immigrant opposition to the monarchy, would later denounce the Pact of Corfu and the monarchy, and leave the Yugoslav Committee.)[35] Since Hinković came without the authorization of the Yugoslav Committee, a few weeks later it sent one of its members, Bogumil Vošnjak, to attract the Slovenian immigrants. Vošnjak's father, Mihael, an old Slovenian politician and a former

---

[34] H. Wickham Stead, *Through Thirty Years*, II, 236-37.
[35] F. Potočnjak, *Iz Emigracije: Nadiranje Italije na Nas* (1919), 12-13.

deputy in the Reichsrat, at the end of 1917 sent an emotional appeal to the American Slovenes from his exile in Switzerland to join the unification movement.[36]

Meanwhile, learning from P. Dodge, the American special agent at Corfu, of the Serbian desire to send an official military mission to the United States, and having received similar reports from Ambassador Sharp in Paris, the American government agreed to receive such a mission. It was to be headed by the Serbian Minister in Paris, Dr. Milenko Vesnić. A problem arose, however, when the members of the Yugoslav Committee wanted to go along. Dodge telegraphed from Corfu that the five members of the committee, "all Austro-Hungarian subjects," wanted to go to Washington "to present to the President a memorial embodying views of committee and also thank him for expressions regarding small nations." At the end of September the State Department informed Dodge that, while the American government would gladly receive a Serbian mission, it could not receive the delegates of the Yugoslav Committee since it was "representative or partially representative of a body of Austro-Hungarians who are opposed to their Government with which the United States is not formally at war."[37]

Finally, on December 7, 1917, when America declared war on Austria-Hungary, it seemed that American policy would change. In the name of the Yugoslav Committee Dr. Trumbić on December 9 sent a telegram to Wilson hailing the historical step. "America can be sure," said Trumbić, "that our people, under Austro-Hungarian yoke, shall receive at our territory the American troops as our defenders and liberators."[38] The Serbian Military Mission, headed by Dr. Vesnić, arrived in Washington in the second half of Decem-

[36] Kosier, *Srbi, Hrvati i Slovenci*, 82.
[37] *Foreign Relations: 1917, Supplement II*, I, 147, 208, 223-24, 278.
[38] Šišić, *Dokumenti*, 106.

ber. The President received the members on December 21, and on the same day he and his wife gave a dinner in their honor.[39] Early in January of 1918, the President received a report of the Inquiry on "War Aims and Peace Terms" prepared by S. E. Mezes, D. H. Miller, and Walter Lippmann, which he used to formulate six of his Fourteen Points. Of the Habsburg Empire the report explicitly recommended: "Our policy must therefore consist first in a stirring up of nationalist discontent, and then in refusing to accept the extreme logic of this discontent which would be the dismemberment of Austria-Hungary."[40] The report distinctly mentioned that "no dismemberment of the Empire is intended." America's objective would be merely "to encourage the present movement towards federalism in Austria, a movement which, if it is successful will break the German-Magyar ascendancy."[41]

These recommendations agreed with the President's plan to preserve Austria and if possible to make a separate peace with her—a plan contrary to the hopes of both the Yugoslav Committee and the Serbian government. In drafting Point XI, Wilson attempted to obtain an opinion from the outside. As Wilson described it, his draft provided that "Rumania, Serbia, and Montenegro [were] to be evacuated; occupied territories restored; Serbia accorded free and secure access to the sea." When House submitted this draft to Vesnić for his opinion, Vesnić objected that what had been written would not satisfy Serbia. On the bottom margin of the President's original text Vesnić noted, "There will and there cannot be in Europe any lasting peace with the conservation of actual Austria-Hungary." Immediately after meeting Vesnić House went to see the President, who was "rather

[39] R. S. Baker, *Woodrow Wilson: Life and Letters* (1939), VII, 424; R. Lansing, *War Memoirs* (1938), 279.
[40] Baker, *Woodrow Wilson and World Settlement*, II, 28.
[41] *Ibid.*, 38.

depressed" by Vesnić's remarks. House advised Wilson to make no change in the paragraph but to go ahead as if no objection had been made. Wilson followed his advice. House, Wilson's closest collaborator, later remarked that Wilson at that time did not want to give "assistance to a revolution that might end in the Balkanization of the Danube regions."[42]

Wilson's well-known Point X did not threaten the integrity of the Habsburg Empire but said simply: "The peoples of Austria-Hungary, whose place among the nations we wish to see safeguarded and assured, should be accorded the freest opportunity of autonomous development."[43] It is obvious from a careful analysis of the Fourteen Points that "any hint at the dismemberment of Austria-Hungary was carefully avoided."[44] In Lansing's judgment, Point X "did not advocate the independence of the several nationalities, but gave the impression that they ought to be autonomous states within the Empire."[45] On the historic day of January 8, 1918, the members of the Yugoslav National Council (including Dr. Hinković) and the members of the Serbian Military Mission sat in the galleries of Congress to hear the President's speech. They were disappointed and "shocked beyond all limits" after hearing the Fourteen Points, as Hinković later reported in his recollections.[46]

The speech itself created a wide range of reactions. The Croats and Slovenes in the Dual Monarchy greeted the message enthusiastically. Wilson's ideas became very popular in Zagreb and Ljubljana, and in 1918 the whole course of Croatian and Slovenian politics was directed and influenced

[42] House, *Intimate Papers*, III, 334-36.
[43] *Ibid.*, 336-37; IV, 199. *Foreign Relations: 1918, Supplement I*, I, 12-17.
[44] Charles Seymour, *Woodrow Wilson and the World War* (1921), 341.
[45] Lansing, *War Memoirs*, 261.
[46] H. Hinković, *Jugoslavija u Americi* (1922), 3-23.

by them. Although the South Slavs now started an effective
political offensive, they did not necessarily at this moment
want complete independence, which the Yugoslav Committee sought.[47] On the day after Wilson's message Lloyd
George, speaking in Parliament, expressed his hope for
federalism in Austria. Two days later *The Times* of London
published the protest of the Yugoslav Committee denouncing
the Prime Minister's views.[48] On January 10 Secretary
Lansing expressed his dissatisfaction with Point X in a
memorandum addressed to the President, in which he recommended "a union of Croatia, Slavonia, Dalmatia, Bosnia,
Herzegovina, Montenegro and Serbia under one sovereignty." Apparently, Mr. Lansing forgot to mention Slovenia.[49]

When the Allied negotiations for a separate peace with
Austria failed in February, Lansing's stand on the destruction
of Austria-Hungary gained support. The idea gradually
prevailed in the intimate circle around Wilson that "there
could be no stable peace in Southeastern Europe so long
as the Slavs remained under Austrian domination."[50] Accordingly, the acting Secretary of State, Frank Polk, instructed
Dodge to inform the Serbian government at Corfu that if
the Allies won the war "they would meet Serbo-Croat
national aspirations as far as possible."[51] This did not, however, mean complete independence for the South Slavs in
Austria.

In the beginning of May the American ambassador in
Rome, speaking of the Allied propaganda among the Slovenian and Croatian troops fighting for Austria on the Isonzo

[47] Josip Horvat, *Politička Povijest Hrvatske* (1938), 9-18. Joso Kljaković,
U Suvremenom Kaosu (1958), 109-19.

[48] Šišić, *Dokumenti*, 112.

[49] Lansing, *War Memoirs*, 262.

[50] House, *Intimate Papers*, III, 379.

[51] *Foreign Relations: 1918, Supplement I*, I, 793-94.

Front, suggested that a propaganda drive be launched at once among the South Slavs in the United States, and recommended the "formation . . . of special legions of these nationalities and sending these legions to join the Czech forces now being organized on this front."[52]

In the same month the problem of Montenegro arose. On May 6, 1918, in Rome, old King Nicholas (the father of the Queen of Italy) handed Ambassador Page a document expressing the aspirations of Montenegro. Nicholas declared that his hope, and the hope of his people, was "in America, the champion of Liberty and Democracy"; the King also expressed his fear that the Serbs wanted to absorb his country. He was about to send a minister to Washington, but he knew that this would arouse great opposition on the part of the Serbian legation and the Yugoslav National Council.[53] In Europe as in America the Montenegrins had split into two factions: those who wanted an independent Montenegro, or at the most a South Slav confederation, and those who advocated a union of Montenegro and other South Slav countries in a Yugoslav state under the rival Karageorgevich dynasty. In August, 1918, the latter group, represented by the Montenegrin Committee for National Unification which was centered in New York, sent President Wilson a memorandum signed by 126 leading American Montenegrins. It demanded a South Slav state, recognized the Montenegrin National Committee in Paris, and repudiated King Nicholas' government in exile, located then at Neuilly near Paris.[54]

It was not until May 29, 1918, however, after the repeated insistence of Secretary Lansing and American ambassadors

[52] *Ibid.*, 801.

[53] *Lansing Papers*, II, 122-24; Ambassador Page to Wilson, May 7, 1918. For a Montenegrin comment see Sekula Drljevic, *Balkanski Sukobi* (1944), 75-104.

[54] Šišić, *Dokumenti*, 136-37. On the Montenegrin problem see also Temperley, *Paris Peace Conference*, I, 201-203.

in Western Europe, and interventions from the Serbian minister, Ljuba Mihajlović, that America committed herself to a policy of the total dismemberment of Austria and the promise of full independence to the South Slavs. As early as May 10, in a letter to the President, Lansing again urged the dissolution of the Empire. On the 29th, Lansing sent to Ambassador Page in Rome and to all important American embassies a statement recognizing the ultimate aspirations of the South Slavs and Czechs. This was motivated by Lansing's desire, as he described it, "to give great encouragement" to the American South Slavs and to encourage the same nationalities in Austria-Hungary. Lansing's statement thus marked a radical change in the Wilsonian policy toward the South Slav question. Wilson and America were now committed to the dismemberment of Austria and independence for its South Slav subjects. The decision was accepted with deep appreciation by Trumbić and the Yugoslav National Council in America, and the British and French hastened to confirm it.[55] On June 24, 1918, Lansing issued another statement, addressed to Mihajlović, confirming that "the position of the United States Government is that all branches of the Slav race should be completely freed from German and Austrian rule."[56]

On July 4 the American authorities invited many South Slavs, Dr. Ante Biankini among them, for a special celebration of Independence Day in Washington. Many South Slav organizations sent delegations, and thousands of them—many dressed in colorful national costumes—participated in festivities and marched in a parade reviewed by the President in front of the Capitol. It was a unique and historical event;

[55] *Foreign Relations: 1918, Supplement I*, I, 803-809; *Lansing Papers*, II, 126-30; see also V. C. Mamatey, "The United States and the Dissolution of Austria-Hungary," *Journal of Central European Affairs*, X (October, 1950), 256-70.

[56] *Foreign Relations: 1918, Supplement I*, I, 815-16.

never before had so many South Slavs gathered in the capital, and they would never repeat the occasion.[57]

This manifestation may have given the impression that the Yugoslav movement, encouraged by the new American policy toward Austria, was strong and united. The truth was that a great crisis had arisen as a result of Pašić's continued insistence that Yugoslavia should be an expanded Serbia, and in particular of his recall of Minister L. Mihajlović because of the latter's sympathies with the democratic tendencies of the Yugoslav movement. On August 25, the Yugoslav National Council prepared a farewell dinner in honor of Mihajlović. Wickham Stead, who as a friend of the South Slav movement was in constant touch with official Washington, was of the opinion that Pašić's dismissal of Mihajlović "on account of his Southern Slav sympathies" caused "much harm in Washington."[58]

Dr. Hinko Hinković, who had originally come to America as an emissary of Pašić, now denounced Pašić's policy and the Declaration of Corfu in lectures and speeches throughout the country. On September 20, shortly after his tour in the West, Hinković was received by Wilson together with T. G. Masaryk and J. Paderewski. Wilson assured them of his personal convictions that Austria should be dissolved. A convinced federalist and republican, Hinković now joined the Croatian and Slovenian opponents of the monarchy (some of whom were members of the Yugoslav National Council), and withdrew from the Yugoslav Committee in London.[59]

[57] *Hrvatski Glasnik* on July 6, 1918, published a message from President Wilson to the Yugoslav National Council inviting the South Slavs to Washington; the issue of July 20 bears a long description of the historic day.

[58] H. Wickham Stead, *Thirty Years*, II, 238.

[59] Hinković, *Iz Velikog Doba*, 121-22. On September 8, 1918, *The Denver Post*, one of many newspapers reporting on his lectures, printed an extensive report on Hinković under the title, "America Means Slavic Freedom, Croat Declares."

On September 21, 1918, Secretary Lansing prepared a new memorandum. In Point VIII he recommended: "The territories . . . Croatia, Slavonia, Dalmatia, Bosnia, and Herzegovina should be united with Serbia and Montenegro forming a single or federal state." At the same time, our ambassadors in Paris and Rome and the special agent at Corfu were reminding Mr. Lansing that the Montenegrin government firmly opposed the absorption of Montenegro by Serbia and that many people in Slovenia and Croatia also opposed any union with Serbia.[60]

In the meantime the South Slav republican movement in America, known as the Yugo-Slav Republican Alliance, was growing stronger especially among the Slovenians, who in 1917 organized the Slovenian Republican Alliance. These republicans wanted a Yugoslav federal republic. In October, 1918, they delivered to the authorities in Washington a memorandum claiming that the Yugoslav Committee in London was undemocratic and was working to impose a monarchy against the will of the people, thus violating the Wilsonian principles of selfdetermination.[61] Later in 1919 the Slovenian republican leader, Socialist Etbin Kristan, appeared before the Senate Foreign Relations Committee and denounced the Italian territorial claims.[62]

The desperate situation of the unification movement created by these divisions led Niko Gršković to inform Trumbić, in the name of the National Council, that "from day to day we are losing the support of the people and are in danger to be overcome by the force of the people."[63]

Meanwhile, both Gršković and Hinković, because of their close relations with the Department of State, and under the

[60] R. Lansing, *The Peace Negotiations* (1921), 199; *Foreign Relations: 1918, Supplement 1*, I, 828-31, 853.
[61] Paulova, *Jugoslavenski Odbor*, 523.
[62] *Slovenian Review*, I (October 15, 1917), 4.
[63] Hinković, *Jugoslavija u Americi*, 24.

promptings of Trumbić, tried to induce Secretary Lansing to recognize the Yugoslav Committee of London as the de facto revolutionary government of the South Slavs under Austria. On September 3, 1918, the American government had given such recognition to the Czecho-Slovak Council under Professor T. G. Masaryk. The government, however, refused to recognize the South Slavs because of the Italian and Serbian opposition as well as the serious dissensions in the ranks of the South Slav movement.[64]

The failure of the Yugoslav Committee to obtain American recognition seriously undermined the prestige of the Yugoslav National Council in America and seemed to imply, as the Italians urged, that the Slovenes and Croats, being Austrian subjects, might be treated as enemies of the Allies. It is questionable that even Trumbić, if he had come to Washington before September, 1918, could have helped the situation.

The Habsburg monarchy was by early October virtually in a state of dissolution. A National Council (Narodno Vijece) of all Slovenes, Croats, and Serbs living in the territories of the Dual Monarchy was formed in Zagreb on October 8, 1918.[65] A week later, on October 19, Secretary Lansing answered an Austro-Hungarian note of October 7, in which Austria asked for peace under the provisions of the Fourteen Points. Referring to the South Slavs, the Secretary of State stated: "The President is . . . no longer at liberty to accept the mere 'autonomy' of these peoples as a basis of peace, but is obliged to insist that they, and not he, shall be judges of what action on the part of the Austro-Hungarian Government will satisfy their aspirations."[66] This American note was in fact the death sentence of the Dual Monarchy. In Zagreb, the Croatian Diet (Sabor) enthusiastically ac-

---

[64] *Lansing Papers*, II, 139-40; Hinković, *Jugoslavija u Americi*, 25, 38.
[65] Šišić, *Dokumenti*, 171-76; Horvat, *Politička Povijest Hrvatske*, 9-31.
[66] *Foreign Relations: 1918, Supplement I*, I, 368.

claimed Lansing's statement. Stjepan Radić, the leader of the rising republican Croatian Peasant Party, praised his idol Wilson in a speech, exclaiming, "Militarism is crushed. . . . Wilsonian principles are victorious all over the world."[67]

In the historical session of the Sabor on October 29, the Croats proclaimed their independence from Austria-Hungary. There were tremendous ovations for Wilson, and the president of the Sabor declared, "What did Wilson say in his last message to the . . . Monarchy? He said that he can count us now, too, among the cultural peoples who for themselves should decide their destiny. He declared us a mature nation which no longer needs guardians and protectors."[68] To the South Slav leaders and to the people Wilson was more than a politician and leader of a great nation, to them Wilson was a philosopher. They called his philosophy and his message of selfdetermination "Ex Occidente Lux"—"The Light from the West."[69]

Across this enthusiasm, however, lay the shadow of the secret Treaty of London. On October 30, Ante Trumbić and his English friends, Wickham Stead and Sir Arthur Evans, sent an urgent telegram to Washington's Yugoslav National Council to intervene with the State Department to save the eastern Adriatic from Italian occupation. It was especially emphasized that American troops should occupy the "chief points in Dalmatia, Istria, Carniola and Croatia-Slavonia. The important matter is that neither Italian nor Serbian troops be used."[70]

Disappointed and alarmed with the Italian and Serbian occupation of Slovenian and Croatian lands, Gršković and

---

[67] Horvat, *Politička Povijest Hrvatske*, 102; on revolution in Slovenia and Croatia, see Temperley, *Paris Peace Conference*, IV, 192-93; 197-201.

[68] Horvat, *Politička Povijest Hrvatske*, 102.

[69] *Ibid.*, 9; *Narodni List* on October 29 announced in big headlines, "Croatia with enthusiasm and confidence greeted the note of President Wilson."

[70] Mamatey, *The United States and East Central Europe*, 363.

Hinković addressed a proclamation to all Croatian and Slovenian immigrants, printed in *Jugoslovenski Svijet* in New York on November 3, 1918. They denounced the Italian and Serbian occupation, Pašić's policy, and the monarchy imposed on the new state. The Yugoslav National Council then met for four days (November 13-16) in Washington. A majority of its members were now in favor of a democratic federal South Slav state, a "republic after the model of the United States."[71] On November 4, the National Council of Zagreb sent a telegram to President Wilson asking protection against the Italian occupation and hailing Wilson "as the representative of justice and freedom of all small and oppressed peoples, as a protagonist of the principle of self-determination."[72]

All the telegrams, protests and appeals to the American President could not, however, prevent the Italian occupation of the Eastern Adriatic territories. While Wilson was preparing for his departure to Europe to fight for his principles at the Paris Peace Conference, a group of some twenty prominent Croatian and Slovenian leaders, gathered in Pittsburgh on November 19, wrote a memorandum asking the President, in the name of all their compatriots in America, to protect their homelands from Italian and Serbian occupation. A special delegation was sent to Washington to submit this document.[73]

At Paris the Adriatic Question almost wrecked the peace conference. The question was considered "one of the most important struggles from the point of view of principle and of result."[74] Colonel House regarded it as "the most difficult territorial question, discussed between the Allies."[75] Thus

[71] Hinković, *Jugoslavija u Americi*, 40-51.
[72] Šišić, *Dokumenti*, 227.
[73] *Narodni List*, November 20, December 6-7, 1918.
[74] Temperley, *Paris Peace Conference*, IV, 296.
[75] House, *Intimate Papers*, IV, 233.

the South Slavs created one of the greatest problems at
Paris, one which caused Wilson much worry and eventually
his friendship with House. The crux of the problem was the
fact that the Italians, despite the promise of the Treaty of
London to grant Fiume (Rieka) to the future Croatian state,
insisted on possession of this important port in the upper
Adriatic.[76] Thus the shadow of this secret treaty, a product
of the secret diplomacy that Wilson abhorred and denounced
in his Points, loomed constantly over the conference. Baker
called the Treaty of London "the chief obstacle of the Peace
Conference."[77]

Although on February 6, 1919, America recognized the
Kingdom of Serbs, Croats, and Slovenes, Wilson had his
doubts about the new state. As he was looking into the
position of Montenegro,[78] a memorandum from Stjepan Radić
signed by 157,669 Croatians, asking for a Croatian Republic,
reached him from Zagreb.[79] As Baker noted, the "hope lay
in America. . . . Especially was he [Wilson] the hope of the
weak countries of Central Europe, for in him they saw also
the good-will of America."[80] An American observer in
Zagreb, Lieutenant LeRoy King, stated in March, 1919, in
his report to the American Delegation on the situation in
Zagreb, that "the Americans are very popular" and that all
Croats "look upon America as their last hope."[81]

In the first week of April the Adriatic Question became
an acute issue at the conference; on April 15 Colonel House

[76] *Ibid.*, IV, 433-34.

[77] Baker, *Woodrow Wilson and World Settlement*, I, 52.

[78] *Foreign Relations, The Paris Peace Conference* (1943-1947), XI, 8, 50;
also V, 681; D. H. Miller, *My Diary at the Conference of Paris* (1925), IV,
Document 268.

[79] Mirko Glojnarić, *Borba Hrvata* (1940), 388.

[80] Baker, *Woodrow Wilson and World Settlement*, I, 3.

[81] *Paris Peace Conference*, XII, 486-90; Jerome Jareb, "LeRoy King's
Reports from Croatia, March to May, 1919," *Journal of Croatian Studies*, I
(1960), 75-168.

noted that "Fiume was the main difficulty."[82] On May 1 the allied and associated powers recognized the new South Slav state, which became one of the original members of the League of Nations and a signatory of the Treaty of Versailles. Before the treaty was signed on June 28, 1919, Wilson tried to save Fiume for the new state. Of his proposed line, a compromise between the Italian and Yugoslav claims, the Italians thought he gave them too little, and Trumbić (now the new Yugoslav Foreign Minister) considered it too much.[83]

The Adriatic Question was not resolved in Paris. Italy and the Kingdom of Serbs, Croats, and Slovenes made a final agreement at Rapallo on November 12, 1920, whereby Istria and Fiume—considerably more than Wilson was willing to concede—were given to Italy.[84] All the protests of the South Slavs in America and in their new state could not save the territories inhabited by more than 600,000 of their countrymen.

By the summer of 1919 the South Slav movement in America was dead, and a new movement opposing the new state was arising. Grškovic̆ and Marjanović, who had already left America for Europe in February, 1919, expressed their disgust with the new conditions in their homeland.[85]

It seems that everyone was disappointed. The opponents of Yugoslavia (still strong in many parts of America) lamented the passing of the old Austrian Empire. The advo-

[82] House, *Intimate Papers*, IV, 441.

[83] A. E. Moodie, *The Italo-Yugoslav Boundary* (1945), 168-78. Albrecht-Carrié, *Italy at the Paris Peace Conference* (1938), has been a standard work on these problems. One of the most recent scholarly and comprehensive discussions, using many unpublished sources, is Ivo Lederer, *Yugoslavia at the Paris Peace Conference* (1963).

[84] Smith Pavelić, *Dr. Ante Trumbić*, 268-88.

[85] *Jugoslovenski Svijet*, July 1, 1919; Jugoslovansko Republikansko Zdruzenje, *An Appeal to the President and the People of the United States* (1920).

cates of the South Slav union were disappointed about the
territorial losses to Italy, the establishment of monarchy,
and the victory of Pašić's idea of an enlarged Serbia. The
masses of the immigrants, disgusted with old-country politics
and politicians, started to pay more attention to America,
giving up their intention of returning to their homeland.
Wilson himself must have been disappointed by the dissension among the South Slavs and weary of the constant
outpour of protests, telegrams, and memoranda. Although
the South Slavs, after all his efforts, were of the opinion that
his principle of selfdetermination was not adequately enforced, he nevertheless helped create—although reluctantly
—what the Yugoslav movement had begged him to create.
Now the same people who had advocated creation of the
state were against it, while the old opponents of unification
were shouting in protest meetings all over this country that
they had been right in their prediction about Italian occupation and Pašić's Greater Serbia.

Most of the American South Slavs failed in their efforts
to influence the final settlement, except for those around
Mihajlo Pupin in New York, the friend of Pašić, who was
now premier of the first Yugoslav government in Belgrade.
The son-in-law of King Nicholas of Montenegro, Peter
Karageorgevich, was now the King of all Serbs, Croats, and
Slovenes, including the Montenegrins. The old King Nicholas
died brokenhearted in the spring of 1921, exiled in France.

In spite of all disappointments, however, Wilson's name
and legend survived among the South Slavs for a long time
after Wilson had become a forgotten man in his own country.
When Wilson died, most South Slav papers in America and
in the old country paid him great tribute. One of the leading
Croatian journalists of that time, Ivan Krešić, wrote on this
occasion a warm necrological tribute under the title "Thank
You—For Good Will." "His famous Fourteen Points re-

sounded through the whole world, and every enslaved and oppressed people expected that Wilsonian principles would be generally accepted. . . . Unfortunately Wilson's principles remained only on paper. . . . Wilson wanted to help us Croats, as all other peoples, announcing selfdetermination and liberty. Croatia is laying a wreath of flowers upon his tomb thanking for—his good will."[86]

On June 29, 1919, when a tired and disappointed American President was sailing from Brest aboard the "George Washington," Colonel House made a fitting entry in his diary: "How splendid it would have been had we blazed a new and better trail."[87]

[86] I. Krešić, *Danica Koledar za 1924* (1923), 61-62.

[87] House, *Intimate Papers*, IV, 487. While this essay was in the proof-reading stage, the following study appeared in Zagreb: Franjo Tudjman, "Jugoslavenski Odbor i stvaranje zajedničke Države južnoslavenskih naroda," [Jugoslavenska Akademija Znanosti i Umjetnosti] *Zbornik* (1966), 369-447, with a two-page summary in English; it represents the most recent discussion of the Yugoslav Committee and the creation of the South Slav state written from a Marxist standpoint.

THE CZECHS

OTAKAR ODLOZILIK

In the tenth of his Fourteen Points President Woodrow Wilson declared that "the peoples of Austria-Hungary, whose place we wish to see safeguarded and assured, should be accorded the freest opportunity of autonomous development." Announced several weeks after the United States declared war on Austria-Hungary, it promised less than the Entente message submitted to President Wilson on January 10, 1917, that called for "the liberation of Italians, of Slavs, of Rumanians, and of Czechoslovaks from foreign domination." Was the President offering to protect the Dual Monarchy or its inhabitants? Did he have in mind primarily the subject nationalities or all ethnic groups, including the Germans in Austria and the Magyars in Hungary? The foreign ministries of Italy, Rumania, and Serbia reacted unfavorably to the tenth point, sensing danger for their countries in the President's vague advocacy of autonomous development. The leaders of the Czech groups in the United States met on February 6, 1918, and after a lively discussion of the tenth point expressed their dissatisfaction in a letter to the chairman of the Senate Committee on Foreign Affairs, Senator William Stone, hoping that echoes of their conversations would reach the White House.[1] The political exiles in Europe, led by the triumvirate of Thomas Garrigue Masaryk, Edward Beneš, and Milan Rastislav Štefánik, representing the Czechs and Slovaks, did not issue a formal statement since they did not reside in the same country and could not exchange ideas quickly. When constituted in February, 1916, as the Czechoslovak National Council, they made Paris their headquarters and designated Beneš as their secretary.

In the winter of 1917–1918 the chairman, Masaryk, was occupied with the organization of Czechoslovak military units in Russia and in the Ukraine, and communications with him were hindered not only by technical difficulties but also by the struggles between the Bolsheviks and their opponents. At the end of January, 1918, according to his own account, Masaryk cabled from Kiev to Washington an exhaustive analysis of the Fourteen Points.[2] Knowing full well the necessity of gaining American support for Czech claims, on March 7, 1918, his sixty-eighth birthday, he set out on his long journey from Moscow to the United States, traveling across Siberia to Vladivostok, and from there through Japan to the western coast of Canada. From Vancouver he proceeded by train across the mountains and the great plains, reaching Chicago on May 5, 1918.

Masaryk's arrival in Chicago symbolized the union of two groups in America behind the Czech struggle for freedom—the political exiles from Austria-Hungary, of whom he was the recognized leader, and the organizations of people of Czech ancestry living in the United States. The former he knew well; the latter constituted a new world with an experience all its own. It was this world he would have to know better if his mission was to be a success.

Part of the trouble with the study of the Czechs—or, for that matter, of any immigrant group from Central Europe—starts with the offical terminology of the United States Census Bureau. In the early and middle nineteenth century the United States authorities in dealing with immigrants from the Habsburg empire paid little attention to

[1] Charles Pergler, *America in the Struggle for Czechoslovak Independence* (1926), 107-11.

[2] Masaryk referred to it in his war memoirs, *The Making of a State* 1927), 273; yet Mamatey, *The United States and East Central Europe, 1914-918* (1957), 215, note 174, writes that he "searched in vain for this message n the Wilson Papers and the State Department files."

language differences. When they began to distinguish, they respected the provincial boundaries more than ethnic divisions. Thus in the census of 1870 Bohemia appeared as distinct from Austria proper, and under it were included the immigrants from both Bohemia and Moravia.[3] Other official documents were more specific; after 1899 the Commissioner General of Immigration referred in his reports to three distinct races, the Bohemian, Moravian, and Slovak. In 1909 he added the word Czech in parentheses after Moravian.[4] The use of these names creates problems for the student of the Czechs and their influence on Wilson, since the Czechs in America continued to call themselves Bohemians even after the start of the war, while the political exiles in Europe used the term Czech. This practice also calls into question the accuracy of the statistics released by the Census Bureau. In the thirteenth census, 1910, one finds that 539,392 persons of Bohemian (Moravian) stock lived in the United States.[5] By 1914 this figure was probably higher; after 1910 the influx of immigrants from Central Europe continued as a result of the obvious drift toward war after Austria-Hungary annexed Bosnia-Herzegovina in 1908. Unfortunately, although these figures may be a little more accurate than those for other Central European groups, one cannot take them at face value.

An effective pressure group, however, requires more than sheer numbers. Much depends upon the original motivation for emigrating, as well as the geographic distribution in the United States. Although some Bohemian and Moravian

[3] *Compendium of the Ninth Census* (June 1, 1870), Part 1 (1872), 392.

[4] *Annual Report of the Commissioner General of Immigration* (1899), 6, Table III; *Annual Report of the Commissioner General of Immigration* (1909), 38, Table IX.

[5] The total figures were subdivided as follows: Bohemia and Moravia, foreign-born, 228,738; native of mixed parentage, 310,654; see *Thirteenth Census of the U.S.* (1910), vol. I, 963, Table 3, "Mother Tongue of the Foreign White Stock."

Czechs came in the nineteenth century as political emigrants, the majority chose America for economic reasons. The rapidly expanding cities along the seacoast and the great lakes attracted many people, but most Czech immigrants looked toward the boundless plains of the middle west and Texas. In her novel *My Ántonia* Willa Cather presented more vividly than any historical account could do both the hard conditions of life among the Czech pioneers in the prairies of Nebraska and their mingling with other ethnic elements settled there. Of the cities, Chicago was recognized long before 1914 as the main stronghold of the Czechs, having supplanted the earlier centers, Milwaukee, St. Louis, and St. Paul. Although a keen competition for primacy developed between Chicago, Cleveland, and New York in the late nineteenth century, Chicago retained its prominence, since it offered opportunity to newcomers seeking employment in business, trades, and professions, and could be reached by railroad from the farming districts in Illinois, Wisconsin, Iowa, Nebraska, Minnesota, and Texas,

The Czechs engaged in little political activity before 1914. Since no detailed analysis of their political affiliations is available, one can only assume that the urban communities sided more often with the Democrats and that the rural regions were more receptive to the Republicans. One reason for the lack of information is that their newspapers are not available in a central location, and many are missing.[6] Of those that are available, the local Czech weeklies and the dailies appearing in Chicago, New York, and Cleveland stressed the interests of the Czech community more strongly than political allegiance; during the election struggles, they became more outspoken following the political orientations of the owners or chief editors. Even toward the old country

[6] Tomáš Čapek, *Padesát let českého tisku v Americe* (1911), is a comprehensive survey of the early period, 1860-1910.

the Czechs took a moderate political attitude. Before 1914 neither the Czech press in America nor their organizations and societies campaigned systematically for political liberation of the homeland. Although they seldom missed an opportunity to expose the Habsburg misrule, only in a few cases did they advocate a disruption of the Dual Monarchy and establishment of an independent Bohemia. Such a scheme emerged from conferences held in the early stage of the war and continued after Masaryk's arrival in Geneva in 1915.[7]

Religious differences, as well as political indifference and the scattered settlements, had hindered the creation of a national political organization before 1914. But the war so accelerated the exchange of ideas and speeded up organization that all differences eventually disappeared. The first national alliance was founded in Chicago only weeks after the outbreak of hostilities in Europe. New York, Omaha, Detroit, and Cleveland soon followed, and at a congress of delegates, held in Cleveland in March, 1915, the local alliances were merged in a national organization, known henceforth as the Bohemian National Alliance,[8] with headquarters in Chicago. This alliance included Democrats, Republicans, and Socialists. While it proved comparatively easy to allay political passions, ideological differences between the Catholic parishes and the freethinkers caused a temporary abstention of the Catholics from the alliance. The mutual distrust was dispelled early in 1917. In February of that year the National Alliance of Bohemian Catholics was organized, and it soon adopted the political program of the older body. A formal agreement concerning close cooperation of the two alliances was signed in Chicago on

[7] Vojta Beneš, *Československá Amerika v odboji*, I (1931). This work covers the period from June, 1914, to August, 1915. The second volume was never published.

[8] Vojta Beneš, *Československá Amerika*, 273ff.

July 4, 1917. At that time the Bohemian National Alliance had over 200 branches, the Catholic more than sixty.[9] Contacts were also established with the Slovak League, which had its headquarters in Pittsburgh.

By this time the Czechs in America were catching up with their comrades at home in the terminology they used. The settlers of Czech origin, when writing or speaking in English, liked to use the adjective Bohemian, because of the strong emotional appeal in its reference to the medieval kingdom of Bohemia and because it conformed to official usage. On the other hand, the political exiles operating under Masaryk's guidance in the allied countries preferred the adjective Czech, which they later combined with the name of the second group they represented, the Slovaks. Thus emerged the compound Czechoslovakia. The American Czechs followed rather slowly and reluctantly, but eventually agreed.

The work of these organizers, who rallied the immigrants behind a slogan, prepared the day for Masaryk's arrival. Chicago had already played a part in Masaryk's life before the war, although it was not as significant as Brooklyn, the home of his wife Charlotte Garrigue. He had lectured at the University of Chicago in the summer of 1902, and had revisited the city in August and September, 1907. The announcement, in the spring of 1918, that he was coming from war-torn Russia electrified the community, and he was greeted with enthusiasm. From the Northwestern Station to the Blackstone Hotel there was a huge procession. According to some estimates—most likely exaggerated—200,000 people appeared in the streets. The city was decorated with American, Czech, and other friendly flags. During the procession English and Czech speeches were made in the streets. At the entrance in the Blackstone the

[9] *Bohemian Review*, I (August, 1917), 15; (October, 1917), 14.

president of the University of Chicago, Harry Pratt Judson, welcomed Masaryk in the name of the American people.[10]

The parade, prepared by the Bohemian National Alliance in close cooperation with the Catholics and the Slovaks, manifested the identity of Masaryk's efforts with the aspirations of the American Czechs. Although not agreed in all details, they were at one in the conviction that no internal reform of the dual system could satisfy the Czechs and other subject nationalities. The program was *Austria est delenda,* and both wanted a clarification of the tenth point. There immediately arose the practical questions of how the roles should be distributed, what actions should be undertaken, and whose help should be sought to reach the ultimate goal, a straight and unequivocal declaration by President Wilson for an independent Czechoslovakia.

Historical truth, sober and cold as it often is, has a dangerous rival, popular mythology, uncurbed by any rules or commandments. What could be simpler and more appealing than a picture of friendly sessions in which Masaryk, a professor of the ancient Charles University, convinced the former professor and president of Princeton of the necessity to smash the Habsburg Empire to pieces? In accepting this idyllic hope, Masaryk's uncritical admirers exaggerated just as grossly as did his foes in Vienna and in Budapest, substituting faint appearances for solid facts. Before his journey from Russia to the United States, Masaryk had not met the President, and the memoranda that he had occasionally sent to Washington were treated just as other similar mail. Little, if anything, was done to facilitate personal contacts and confidential talks on the major issues of American foreign policy.

Masaryk was anxious to see President Wilson as soon as

[10] *Bohemian Review,* II, 5 (May, 1918), 77; Masaryk, *The Making of a State,* 206-207.

possible. He had two great problems to discuss with him, the ultimate fate of Austria-Hungary and the position of the Czechoslovak army in Russia. Masaryk did not spend much time in Chicago, and on May 9, 1918, he reached Washington. There are indications that he had originally no intention of stopping in the United States, thinking of England or France as his final destination. But soon after his arrival in Washington he realized that a good deal more time would be needed to gain access to both the Department of State and the White House. Accepting a prolonged stay as a necessity, he adjusted his program to the strategy which some personal friends and the officers of the Bohemian National Alliance worked out.

As soon as reliable reports of Masaryk's journey across the Pacific reached the Chicago headquarters of the Bohemian Alliance, the executive committee designated its vice-president, Charles Pergler, to act as Masaryk's secretary. A Czech by birth and lawyer by training, Pergler had a prominent part in the work of the Czech organizations. After the entry of the United States into the war, he gave up his practice at Cresco, Iowa, and served as director general of the Czech-Slav Press Bureau in New York, where he was successful in making contacts among journalists, political leaders, and scholars. Before Masaryk's arrival, Pergler delivered several speeches in support of the Czech national program. He made Masaryk's acquaintance during the latter's sojourn in Chicago, in 1907, and enjoyed his confidence. To assist Masaryk on his long trip, Pergler met him in Vancouver and accompanied him in Chicago and in Washington, "working indefatigably."[11]

There was in the sixty-fifth Congress no distinct group committed to the support of the Czechoslovak cause. Since the voters of Czech and Slovak origin were widely scattered,

[11] Masaryk, *The Making of a State,* 206.

only certain areas felt their influence. Although individual members of Congress spoke favorably of their aims either in the Congress or in public meetings, they did not belong to a single party and did not act as a team. Senator William S. Kenyon and Congressman Adolph J. Sabath as early as May, 1917, introduced resolutions in favor of an independent Bohemian-Slovak state; the former represented the state of Iowa, which had a high percentage of Czech immigrants, and the latter practiced law in Chicago. Charles Pergler had personal contacts with both.[12] Sabath, a native of Southern Bohemia, formed a group of twenty-seven congressmen who went early on May 9 to the railroad station to greet the leader of the free Czechoslovaks.[13]

More familiar with the traditional practices of American public life, the leaders of the Czech and Slovak colonies not only searched for contacts in Congress but also endeavored to awaken American public opinion. When no invitation came from the White House, they prepared public meetings, at which Masaryk was the guest of honor and the principal speaker, in the cities where Czech and Slovak immigrants were concentrated. In Boston Masaryk addressed the annual meeting of the American Unitarians.[14] From there he proceeded to New York and was introduced to a large audience in Carnegie Hall by the president of Columbia University, Nicholas Murray Butler. Revisiting Chicago, he spoke at the University of Chicago at the invitation of its president, Harry Pratt Judson.

The parade held in Pittsburgh on Decoration Day was followed on May 31, 1918, by Masaryk's conference with the

---

[12] *Congressional Record, 65th Congress, 1st Session* (May 5, 1917), 1889, 2856.

[13] Pergler, *America in the Struggle*, 75-76.

[14] "Freedom and Fellowship in Religion," *Proceedings and Papers of the Fourth International Congress of Religious Liberals* (1907), 142-52. It is very likely that Masaryk's wife, Charlotte Garrigue, a native of Brooklyn and a Unitarian, helped to establish connections with Boston Unitarians.

spokesmen of the Bohemian National Alliance, the National Alliance of Bohemian Catholics, and the Slovak League. Out of the session emerged an agreement on the future political organization of Czechoslovakia. Known henceforth as the Pittsburgh Convention or Pact, the document was destined to become, after the war, one of the most controversial issues in Czech-Slovak relations.[15] Its immediate effect, however, was to enable Masaryk to speak in interviews and conferences in the name of both the Czechs and the Slovaks.

Back in Washington, Masaryk met such prominent Congressmen as Senator Gilbert M. Hitchcock, Chairman of the Foreign Relations Committee, and the leading Republican Senator Henry Cabot Lodge. No introduction to Senator Elihu Root of New York was needed, since they had become acquainted in Petrograd when Root visited the residence of the provisional Russian government on a goodwill mission. Masaryk deliberately maintained connections with individual members of the two parties instead of attaching himself to one bloc.

Although Masaryk did not underestimate his contacts in Congress, he seems to have put more trust in his personal friends—especially Charles R. Crane, whose son Richard served in the Department of State directly under Robert Lansing. In Masaryk's opinion the elder Crane was "an admirable auxiliary for he knew nearly everybody whom Masaryk wanted to meet and was 'close to' President Wilson."[16] "My work obliged me to visit the principal cities, to get into personal touch with people and to look up old acquaintances; and, in Washington, to cultivate the society of the Senators and Congressmen of the two chief parties and of all shades of political opinion—including, of course,

---

[15] Mamatey, *The United States and East Central Europe*, 282-84.
[16] See Masaryk, *The Making of a State*, 221, for a condensed account.

Mr. Hitchcock, Chairman of the Foreign Relations Committee of the Senate and Republicans like Senator Lodge whom I sought to inform. Senator Root I had already met in Russia. I had, too, the advantage of knowing the Preparatory Committee which, under the Chairmanship of Professor Mezes, was working upon material and memoranda in view of the peace negotiations and for the President."[17]

Since Masaryk's departure from Russia a great many changes had occurred both in the European territories and in Siberia, about which official Washington lacked detailed information. The Czechoslovak armed units, which Masaryk and his chief assistants, Beneš and Štefánik, wanted to transfer to France, became involved in Russian internal problems that followed the Bolshevik revolution. As a result of local clashes with both Bolshevik and anti-Bolshevik forces, a conflict developed in May, 1918, which led the Czechs to occupy the Siberian railroad. Their advance along the line eastward, though not easy, was steady, ending on June 29, 1918, in Vladivostok on the Pacific coast. As the administration, Congress, the press, and the public became interested in the campaign, the question of Allied intervention in Russia—which many statesmen and army leaders had considered since the Bolshevik revolution in November, 1917—took on new significance. The Czechoslovak troops were regarded as an Allied army; they were on the spot, and their use for purposes other than the control of the Siberian railroad—such as the overthrow of the Bolsheviks—came to be regarded as lesser evil than intervention by either Japan or another major Ally.

Masaryk believed that "through the good offices of Charles Crane he came into touch with Colonel House and President Wilson."[18] Indeed, Crane obtained for Masaryk

[17] *Ibid.*
[18] *Ibid.*

an invitation to Colonel House's home in Massachusetts, but the President consented to receive the Czech leader only after an exchange of letters with Mr. Sabath. On June 16, 1918, the congressman from Illinois urged that it would be of some advantage if the President granted Masaryk an opportunity to present his ideas concerning the future collaboration of the Slavic peoples.[19] Three days later, on June 19, Masaryk was introduced to the President, and their conversation lasted forty-five minutes.

The story of Masaryk's effort to gain access to the White House was obscured by tendentious accounts that were circulated before the war was over. The initiative did not come from the President but from Masaryk's sponsors, who applied a good deal of pressure to get the appointment. The main topics of the discussion were not Czechoslovak aspirations but the Russian civil war and the chances of an Allied intervention.[20] Nothing could be more misleading than the assumption that President Wilson hoped by granting an audience to Masaryk to increase his own popularity among the potential voters of Czech or Slovak ancestry. If this had been true, the course of the conference would have been different and the Siberian imbroglio would have taken less time than it actually did.

The future of the Czechs and Slovaks in Central Europe could not be treated as an isolated case. There could be no serious discussion of their independence and political union before the President had adopted the program of dismembering Austria-Hungary. His departure from the tenth

[19] Antonin S. Kalina, *Krví a železem* (1938), 305, 307. In an appendix, a collection of documents, Kalina published a Czech translation of a letter from Representative Sabath to President Wilson, June 16, 1918, and the President's reply of June 18, 1918. This exchange of letters shows that the grant of audience was a friendly gesture to the representative from a largely Czech constituency.

[20] Mamatey, *The United States and East Central Europe*, 285-86.

point did not occur abruptly, under some external influence, but gradually. Anyone attempting to detect its origin and trace its development from January to November, 1918, would have to study the progress of the war in Europe, the diplomatic contacts among the Allies, the political and economic troubles ravaging Austria-Hungary, and above all the mounting discontent among the subject nationalities. More and more information concerning the rise of revolutionary spirit reached Washington through such channels as the reports from Professor George Herron. Such startling events as Clemenceau's breaking off the secret negotiations with Vienna, the Congress of Oppressed Nationalities in Rome, and the journey of Emperor Charles to the German military headquarters in Spa, likened by the Allied press to "Canossa," played their part.

Although the American press and the public reacted more strongly to these events than did official Washington, no cleavage developed between the administration and the public. In the Czechoslovak affair, the existence of armed forces operating in Siberia under their own banners and recognizing the Czechoslovak National Council as their political authority exercised the decisive influence. On May 29, 1918, the Secretary of State, after consultation with the President, announced that "the proceedings of the Congress of Oppressed Races of Austria-Hungary, which was held in Rome in April, have been followed with great interest by the government of the United States and that the Nationalistic aspirations of the Czecho-Slovaks and Jugo-Slavs for freedom have the earnest sympathy of this Government."[21] Lansing's declaration expressed agreement in principle with the resolutions, adopted by the congress in Rome, that envisaged the breakup of the Habsburg monarchy.

[21] *Papers Relating to the Foreign Relations of the United States, 1918, Supplement 1*, I, 809.

As far as the Czechs and Slovaks were concerned, the most urgent task was the coordination of military with political affairs. Armed units, using the name Czechoslovak, existed not only in Russia but also in Europe. Those fighting on the western front were recognized by the French government on December 16, 1917, as an autonomous army. A similar body in Italy was in the process of formation; late in April, 1918, Štefánik obtained official sanction for it. Although in their training and use in battle the Czechoslovak forces were subordinated to the French and Italian supreme commands, they owed political allegiance to the Czechoslovak National Council and, in particular, to its chairman, T. G. Masaryk, who told F. L. Polk, "I dispose of three armies [in Russia, France and Italy], I am, as a wit said, the master of Siberia and half Russia, and yet I am in the United States formally a private man."[22]

To facilitate the contacts between the Allied governments and the Czechoslovak National Council, the French felt that formal recognition of the Czechoslovak political leaders was desirable. On June 28, 1918, the French Minister of Foreign Affairs, Etienne Pichon, transmitted to Edward Beneš a note in which the French government recognized the council as the supreme organ administering all Czechoslovak national affairs and as the first basis of a future Czechoslovak government. Several weeks later, on August 9, British Foreign Secretary Arthur James Balfour recognized "the Czechoslovaks as an allied nation, their legions in France, Italy, and Siberia as a united Allied and belligerent army waging regular warfare against Austria-Hungary and Germany, and the National Council as the trustee for the future Czechoslovak government."

The French and British notes were well ahead of any

[22] T. G. Masaryk to F. L. Polk, July 20, 1918, *Foreign Relations, 1918,* Supplement 1, I, 818.

official statement made by the United States government. The obvious discrepancy embarrassed not only Masaryk and his friends but also the Allied diplomats. The French ambassador to the United States, Jean Jusserand, who exercised considerable influence in the highest circles, was impressed by Masaryk's honest efforts and helped him "everywhere, and in every way even with the President."[23] In the Senate William Henry King, a Democrat from Utah, presented a resolution similar to the one introduced in May, 1917, by Senator Kenyon demanding the liberation of the Czechs and Slovaks as one of the principal conditions of peace.[24] Czechoslovak political aspirations were discussed in Congress in connection with such broader questions as the amendment of the immigration law to allow American volunteers in Allied armies to return to the United States, and Senator Hitchcock's plan for organization of a Slavic legion.[25]

Diplomatic interventions, debates in the Congress, resolutions adopted at public meetings, letters and telegrams, and press campaigns had no noticeable effect on President Wilson's deliberations. Although he authorized Lansing to announce on June 28, 1918, that the United States government wished "that all branches of the Slav race should be completely freed from the German and Austrian rule,"[26] this was as far as he would go, whether pressed by the advocates of the Polish cause, asked to make a statement favorable to the Southern Slavs, or prompted to follow France and Great Britain in their acceptance of the Paris

[23] Masaryk, *The Making of a State*, 235, 274.

[24] *Congressional Record, 65th Congress, 2nd Session* (May 31, 1918), 7231. Senator King recommended that it be "resolved that the nationalistic aspirations of the Bohemian people for freedom and self government have the earnest sympathy of the United States."

[25] Pergler, *America in the Struggle*, 69-75. See *Congressional Record, 65th Congress, 2nd Session*, 8227.

[26] *Foreign Relations, 1918, Supplement 1*, I, 816.

National Council as the supreme organ of the Czechoslovak movement abroad.

The transfer of the army from Siberia to France, which proved to be a much harder task than was originally anticipated, was never achieved. Although its size was respectable it was not large enough to protect itself in the vast territories of Siberia. When interviewed in Chicago, Masaryk spoke of 50,000 men and expressed the hope that in a short time 50,000 more would join them. Effective control of the Siberian railroad and of strategic points in its vicinity, however, was a tougher proposition than its simple occupation. Preparations for transport from Vladivostok to France were slow and inadequate, and before any concrete progress had been made the army became deeply involved in the Russian civil war. In view of the events in Russia and the more hopeful situation on the western front, the Allied military authorities resolved in July, 1918, that the Czechoslovak units should be kept in Siberia as the advance guard of the Allied armies. Some consideration was given to a reopening of the eastern front, to tie down German and Austro-Hungarian forces that would otherwise be used in the west. This change of plan immediately created an urgent need for reinforcements. The United States and Japan were assigned the task of landing 7,000 men each at Vladivostok and of supplying all Allied units in the northern plains of Asia.[27]

Armed intervention conflicted with the sixth of the Fourteen Points, which claimed for Russia an "opportunity for the independent determination of her own political development and national policy." President Wilson and some of his intimate advisers, at first tenaciously opposed to intervention, changed their line under steady pressure from the European Allies. When it was described as an

[27] Mamatey, *The United States and East Central Europe,* 291-92.

auxiliary expedition, the landing of troops in Vladivostok seemed to be less objectionable than an intervention on behalf of one Russian party against another. The vision of America rescuing the Czechoslovak legions from disaster was taken up enthusiastically by the press, by some members of the Congress, and by numerous speakers all over the country, especially in areas inhabited by recent immigrants.[28] On August 16, 1918, the first American troopship reached Vladivostok.

The sanction of military assistance did not relieve the President of another, no less perplexing, problem—the recognition of the Czechoslovaks as partners in the Allied bloc. His reluctance to join the European Allies in this matter disturbed Masaryk and his circle as well as the press, which carried front-page reports of the movements of the Czechoslovak forces. The election campaign was to open in September, and the Republicans, not the Democrats, were to assume the role of protectors of the unredeemed peoples. In his long speech on problems of war and peace on August 23, 1918, Senator Henry Cabot Lodge declared, "If we are to make the world safe in the way we mean it to be safe, the great Slav populations now under the Government of Austria, the Jugo-Slavs and the Czecho-Slovaks—who have been used to aid the Germans whom they loathe—must be established as independent states."[29]

Lansing's note, prepared after thorough discussion with the President and published on September 3, 1918, was the first formal commitment to support the idea of an independent Czechoslovakia. Worded cautiously to avoid references to boundaries or systems of government, it stressed the state

[28] *Congressional Record, 65th Congress, 2nd Session* (June 19, 1918), 7995; Mamatey, *The United States and East Central Europe,* 290.

[29] *Congressional Record, 65th Congress, 2nd Session* (August 23, 1918), 9393.

of belligerency between the Czechoslovaks and the German and Austro-Hungarian empires and recognized the Czechoslovak National Council as "a de facto belligerent government clothed with proper authority to direct the military and political affairs of the Czech-Slovaks."[30] On the latter point it was more generous than either the French or British documents.

In the early fall of 1918 the roles of the Allies underwent a gradual change. France, Great Britain, and Italy, continuing the policies adopted while the President was "investigating in the stratosphere,"[31] supplemented recognition in principle by more specific actions. In September, 1918, Japan and China also recognized the Czechoslovak army in Siberia as a regular belligerent force. The atmosphere of Paris, pervaded by the feeling of victory over the invaders, was particularly stimulating. It was in the French capital, not in Washington, that the Czechoslovak Provisional Government was set up on September 26, 1918, to replace the National Council. When news of its formal recognition by the French on October 15 reached Washington, Masaryk took the final step and issued the Declaration of Czechoslovak Independence. Drafted by Masaryk, it was put into good English by Professor Herbert Adolphus Miller of Bryn Mawr and transmitted to the White House by Masaryk's private secretary, Mr. Jaroslav Císar.[32] The document, dated October 18, 1918, was released at approximately the same hour by the headquarters of the Provisional Government in Paris and in Washington.

Although pressed by high-ranking officials, members of

[30] *Foreign Relations, 1918, Supplement 1,* I, 824.
[31] R. W. Seton-Watson, *History of the Czechs and Slovaks,* 305.
[32] Its text is in *Foreign Relations, 1918, Supplement 1,* I, 847-51. A special edition was printed immediately (1918) for the Czechoslovak Art Club in New York in an arrangement by Rudolph Ruzicka.

the Congress, Masaryk and his personal friends, and the public to substitute an open endorsement of the Czech and Slovak aims for a vague assurance "of the freest opportunity of an autonomous development," President Wilson was slow to respond. The readers of newspapers and magazines soon forgot the slow pace of political deliberations and confidential talks in the White House and the Department of State. They projected into the past the role President Wilson played in September, and particularly in October, 1918, when not only the Allies and the exiled leaders but also Berlin and Vienna recognized his primacy. Less attention was given to official transactions emanating from the Paris headquarters of the Provisional Government than to statements issued by T. G. Masaryk from Washington, to his interviews with American journalists, to speeches made in the capital, in Philadelphia, and in New York in the final period of the war and immediately after the armistice. The public in his homeland, among the Allies, and in the defeated countries insisted on interpreting the Czechoslovak struggle for independence as the moving story of two professors debating the principles of democracy and of selfdetermination, and thereafter digging the grave for the corrupt and wicked Austria-Hungary.

On November 15, 1918, Masaryk paid his fourth and last visit to President Wilson and said goodbye to Secretary Lansing and Ambassador Jusserand.[33] On November 20, he sailed from New York, hastening to reach liberated Czechoslovakia, where on November 14 he had been elected president. With no other Allied statesman was he so closely

[33] Masaryk, *The Making of a State*, 285. Charles Pergler, an American citizen, was appointed, after the publication of Lansing's note of September 3, "Commissioner of the Czecho-Slovak Provisional Government." He represented Czechoslovakia after T. G. Masaryk's departure. Regular diplomatic representation was established in 1919.

associated by his countrymen as with the American President, whose portraits soon were to be seen not only in public buildings along with those of Masaryk but also in private homes—evidence of the belief that President Wilson was the best friend of Czechoslovakia, the chief promoter among the Allies of its interests and aims.

THE SLOVAKS AND
CARPATHO-RUTHENIANS

Victor S. Mamatey

In 1918 a band of relatively small national states arose in East Central Europe[1] on the ruins of the multinational Austrian and Russian empires and, to a smaller extent, of Germany. This constituted the most drastic revision of the political map of Europe since the Congress of Vienna, a century earlier, and represented a projection of the principle of national selfdetermination and of national states from Western Europe, where these ideas were born, to Eastern Europe.

The name of President Woodrow Wilson is intimately associated with the propagation of the principle of national selfdetermination, and he is regarded as the principal architect of the Paris peace settlement of 1919, which sanctioned the erection of the new national states in East Central Europe. As early as May 27, 1916, in an address before the "League to Enforce Peace" in Washington, he postulated as the foremost principle of an equitable peace "first, that every people has a right to choose the sovereignty under which they shall live."[2] The principle of government by consent of the governed, or national selfdetermination, which the founding fathers had invoked to justify the American Revolution, was for Wilson a selfevident truth, a natural right, an indispensable corollary of democracy but not yet a principle of action. At that time he appears to have been either unaware of its revolutionary implications if applied to multinational empires or reluctant to accept its logical conclusion, namely, their dismemberment. A year later, in August, 1917, in declining the peace proposal of Pope Benedict XV, he wrote that "dismemberment of empires . . . we deem inexpedient."³ When he in his memorable address of April 2, 1917, recommended that Congress declare war on Germany, he counselled it at the same time not to declare war on Austria-Hungary and Germany's other allies, Bulgaria and the Ottoman Empire. And when recommending to Congress a declaration of war against Austria-Hungary on December 4, 1917, he hastened to give Vienna assurances against dismemberment: "We owe it, however, to ourselves to say that we do not wish in any way to impair or to rearrange the Austro-Hungarian Empire. It is no affair of ours what they do with their own life, either industrially or politically. We do not purpose or desire to dictate to them in any way."⁴ Finally, on January 8, 1918, in his celebrated Fourteen Points address, he called for "the freest opportunity of autonomous development" for "the peoples of Austria-Hungary" (point ten)⁵ but not for their independence. It was not until May, 1918, that he accepted—quite reluctantly at first, it appears—the necessity to dismember the Austro-Hungarian Empire.⁶ And it may be added *en passant* that he always upheld the territorial integrity of the Russian empire—with the exception of Poland, whose claim to independence was recognized in one form or another by all Russian governments, Tsarist, Provisional, and Soviet.

To what extent did the Slovak and Carpatho-Ruthenian⁷

¹ The term "East Central Europe" refers to the area of Europe between Germany and Russia. Specialists prefer it to the older term "Central Europe," which included Germany, or the newer term "Eastern Europe," which includes Russia.

² *The Messages and Papers of Woodrow Wilson*, 2 vols. (1924), I, 274.

³ *Ibid.*, 424.   ⁴ *Ibid.*, 447.   ⁵ *Ibid.*, 469.

⁶ On Wilson's reversal of policy toward Austria-Hungary, see this author's *The United States and East Central Europe, 1914-1918: a Study in Wilsonian Diplomacy and Propaganda* (1957), 252.

⁷ There is considerable confusion concerning the name of the Carpatho-Ruthenians. The term "Ruthenian" derives from Latin "Ruthenus" and it in turn from "Rusin"—the name officially and colloquially used in reference to the Ukrainians of the Austro-Hungarian Empire. "Carpathian" was used, somewhat arbitrarily, to refer only to the Ruthenians living on the

immigrants influence the evolution of President Wilson's thought and policies? Specifically, to what extent did they influence American policy to favor the breakup of Austria-Hungary and the establishment of Czechoslovakia, in which the Slovaks and Carpatho-Ruthenians found a new home?

In 1914, the Slovak and the Carpatho-Ruthenian communities in the United States were too small and too new to be able to constitute pressure groups and influence the foreign policies of the United States government through the machinery of American domestic politics—as, let us say, Irish-American, Italo-American, and Polish-American communities endeavored to do. The Slovak and Carpatho-Ruthenian immigration to the United States, a part of the socalled new or post-Civil-War immigration, was not political but economic and sociological in character. Although individual Slovak and Carpatho-Ruthenian immigrants began to arrive in the United States after the Civil War, it was not until the 1890s and early 1900s, when Royal Hungary experienced the first unsettling impact of the Industrial Revolution, that the Slovak and Carpatho-Ruthenian emigration began to assume the proportions of a mass flight that left northern Hungary seriously depopulated. In the single year of 1907, 203,000 Hungarian immigrants arrived in the United States; from 1890 to 1910 the total was more than 1,500,000.[8] Just how many of these were

---

southern slopes of the Carpathian Mountains in Royal Hungary, not those of Galicia and Bukovina in the Austrian portion of the Austro-Hungarian Empire. Until 1918 Carpathian Ruthenia was an integral part of Hungary; from 1919 to 1939 it was an autonomous province in the first Czechoslovak Republic under the name "Subcarpathian Russia" ("Podkarpatska Rus"); in March, 1939, it became for one day an independent state under the name "Carpathian Ukraine" ("Karpatska Ukraina") before reverting to Hungarian rule (1939-1945); finally, in 1945, it became an integral part of the Ukrainian SSR of the Soviet Union and is informally referred to by Soviet writers as "Transcarpathian Ukraine" ("Zakarpatskaia Ukraina" in the Russian language or "Zakarpatska Ukraina" in the Ukrainian language).

[8] Arthur J. May, *The Hapsburg Monarchy, 1867-1914* (1951), 235.

Slovaks and Carpatho-Ruthenians is not known. Available statistics are not accurate. The United States census for 1910 puts the figure of Slovak immigrants and their children born in the United States at 284,444. The analogous figure for the Carpatho-Ruthenian immigrants and their children is 6,616.[9] These figures appear to be unreliable, not only because in those days the American authorities were imperfectly informed on the ethnic composition of European immigration, but also because the Slovak and Carpatho-Ruthenian immigrants were often unable to give the American authorities accurate information about themselves. This was particularly true of the Carpatho-Ruthenians, who were at that time an inchoate people, without a precisely defined sense of nationality. The United States census for 1920 puts the number of Slovak immigrants and their children born in the United States at 619,458, and the Carpatho-Ruthenians and their children at 6,299.[10] According to these figures, the number of Slovaks in the United States more than doubled in a decade when because of the European war and its aftermath European immigration to the United States generally declined. At the same time, according to the same source, the number of Carpatho-Ruthenians in the United States inexplicably declined. Slovak writers usually put the number of Slovak immigrants in the United States in the period after World War I at 700,000,[11] and the Carpatho-Ruthenian writers number their compatriots in

[9] U. S. Department of Commerce, *The Thirteenth Census of the United States: 1910*, 11 vols. (1913), I, 963, 965.

[10] U. S. Department of Commerce, *The Fourteenth Census of the United States: 1920*, 11 vols. (1921-1922), II, 973.

[11] Konstantin Čulen, *Dejiny Slovákov v Amerike* [History of the Slovaks in America], 2 vols. (1942), I, 45, Čulen, the principal historian of Slovak emigration to the United States, made an exhaustive study of Hungarian and Czechoslovak statistics on emigration. However, he was unable to arrive at a definite global figure, because the statistics, while registering the number of emigrants, gave no indication of their ultimate destination or of the number of re-emigrants, i.e., of those who returned to their homeland.

the United States at 500,000.[12] But these figures, particularly for the Carpatho-Ruthenians, also appear to be unreliable. Frustrating though this may be, there are no accurate statistics on how many Slovaks and Carpatho-Ruthenians— or, indeed, many other ethnic groups—have come to the United States.

To understand the character of the Slovak and Carpatho-Ruthenian immigrants in the United States it is necessary to keep in mind the character of the Slovak and Carpatho-Ruthenian peoples. Socio-economically, the Slovaks and Carpatho-Ruthenians were before World War I what is now euphemistically called "underdeveloped," and in former days more frankly "backward," peoples. On the eve of World War I Hungary was only on the threshold of the Industrial Revolution. Most Slovaks and Carpatho-Ruthenians were peasants, deriving a living from the resource most directly available to man—land—either as farmers or as rural laborers. Neither people possessed a substantial urban industrial working class or a middle class in the West European sense. The modest commercial enterprise in Slovakia and Carpathian Ruthenia was almost exclusively in the hands of the Hungarian Jewish community, of Germans, or of other nonindigenous elements. The Slovak and Carpatho-Ruthenian middle classes were, therefore, limited to the "intelligentsia," a handful of village priests and parochial school teachers and a sprinkling of small-town lawyers and country doctors. Neither the Slovaks nor the Carpatho-Ruthenians possessed an upper class.

Culturally, the Slovaks and Carpatho-Ruthenians were likewise retarded by the singularly unenlightened cultural and social policies of the Royal Hungarian Government, which sought to "Magyarize"—that is, culturally and linguis-

[12] Augustin Vološin, "Carpathian Ruthenia," *Slavonic and East European Review* (1935), XIII, 370.

tically to assimilate the non-Magyar ethnic minorities, about half the population—and generally to keep the peasant masses, including the Magyar peasants, ignorant and obedient. As a result of these policies, the majority of the Carpatho-Ruthenians and the Slovaks in the eastern districts of Slovakia were illiterate and possessed no clearcut national consciousness. The Carpatho-Ruthenians derived a sense of cultural unity from their religion—the Greek Catholic or Uniate faith—rather than from their nationality. The politically and nationally conscious and articulate element among them was very small. This element, moreover, was divided among those who had succumbed to the official policy of Magyarization; those who sought to preserve the Ruthenian language and culture by leaning on the larger Ruthenian community in Austrian Galicia and Bukovina; and finally those who looked to Imperial Russia for help and wanted to merge with the Great Russian people.

The Slovaks, who were largely Roman Catholic in faith, possessed a clearer-cut sense of nationality, at least in the western and central districts of Slovakia. This was particularly true of the Slovak Protestant minority, which—perhaps because it was a religious as well as an ethnic minority in the "Apostolic" Kingdom of Hungary—clung tenaciously to its Slovak culture and language and was traditionally Czechophil and Russophil in sentiment. In fact, it was the Slovak Protestant intellectuals in the nineteenth century rather than the Czechs who first suggested the idea of Czechoslovak unity, and it was Slovak Protestant intellectuals in the nineteenth century rather than Russians who first began to propagate the idea of Pan-Slavic solidarity. Both represented attempts by a beleaguered minority to find strength by leaning on stronger peoples.

This background explains why the Slovak and Carpatho-Ruthenian immigrants in the United States were unable before 1914 to imitate Irish, Italian, or Polish immigrants by entering ward politics, forming lobbies, and in other characteristically American ways seek to influence American foreign policy. The average Slovak and Carpatho-Ruthenian immigrant was socially retarded, culturally unsophisticated, and politically inarticulate. He was bewildered at first by the complexities of American urban and industrial life. Of peasant stock, he would have liked to settle on the land as other immigrants before him, but by the time he arrived in America free land was gone, and he lacked the capital to buy and operate a farm. He was thus drawn to the industrial Northeast, particularly to the coal mines and steel mills of Pennsylvania and Ohio, where there was a demand for unskilled labor. Pittsburgh and Cleveland were the principal centers of the Slovak and Carpatho-Ruthenian immigrants. This environment, while often harsh and bewildering, was nevertheless stimulating; it offered opportunities for relatively rapid social and cultural advancement. After the initially painful adjustment from a rural-agrarian to an urban-industrial environment, the Slovaks and Carpatho-Ruthenians learned fast. Daily contact with half a dozen other immigrant groups stimulated in them a national and political consciousness keener than that of their compatriots in the "old country." They began to form cultural and fraternal organizations and publish newspapers and books. This effort, it should be noted, sought to promote their interests and welfare here in America rather than to propagate any political or revolutionary ideas among their countrymen in Europe. It was only the outbreak of the European war in 1914 that led them to formulate political programs in behalf of their compatriots in Hungary.

The Slovaks were the first to formulate a political program. This effort was sparked by a visit to the United

States of Count Michael Károlyi, in the spring of 1914,[13] to rally the Hungarian immigrant community behind the program of the opposition Hungarian Independence (Kossuth) Party, which opposed the Austro-Hungarian *Ausgleich* of 1867 and sought greater (possibly full) independence of Hungary from Austria. In 1917 Count Károlyi and his followers seceded from the Independence Party and formed, with the middleclass Radical Party of Professor Oscar Jaszi and a wing of the Social Democratic Party led by Sigmund Kunfi, an "electoral bloc" that agitated against the war and the German alliance, and for universal suffrage and a democratic peace. This made Károlyi the logical choice for president of the shortlived liberal Hungarian Republic of 1918-1919. Later, in exile, he became a radical socialist and pacifist. In 1914, however, he held conventionally Magyar nationalist and moderately democratic views. In an interview with a group of Slovak immigrant newspapermen on April 6, 1914, shortly after his arrival in New York, he declared that he personally favored universal manhood suffrage in Hungary (not all leaders of his party did) but insisted on the unitary nature of the Hungarian state and the exclusive use of the Magyar language in the state administration, courts, and schools.[14] To the Slovaks, who were suspicious of him because of his social position as a Hungarian magnate and landowner, there seemed little difference between his views and those of Count Stephen Tisza, the Hungarian premier and redoubtable foe of the ethnic minorities. As Count Károlyi toured American cities to address meetings of Hungarian organizations, the Slovaks summoned

---

[13] Michael Károlyi, *Faith Without Illusion: Memoirs* (1957), 51. Count Károlyi states that when he boarded a ship in Cherbourg bound for the United States, he was informed of the assassination of the Archduke Francis Ferdinand (June 28, 1914). But according to contemporary Slovak accounts he was in the United States already in April.

[14] Čulen, *Dejiny Slovákov*, II, 189-90.

counter-meetings at which they denounced him in innumerable resolutions and open letters.[15]

Károlyi's visit engendered a debate in the Slovak immigrant press on the nature of Slovak political aspirations, which was further stimulated by the outbreak of the European war in July, 1914. On the initiative of the Slovak League of America (formed in 1907 to speak for the Slovak-American community as a whole) several conferences were held between May and September, at which the "Memorandum of the Slovak League of America, issued in the name of the American Slovaks in behalf of the Slovaks in Hungary," was drafted and agreed upon. The memorandum marked the beginning of the political activity of the American Slovaks in behalf of their compatriots in Europe. It envisioned only Slovak administrative and cultural autonomy in Hungary, not independence or unity with the Czechs in a Czechoslovak state.[16] Published in September, 1914, it was translated into English, French, Russian, German, and Hungarian and printed in a handsome brochure, which was sent to the belligerent governments through their embassies in Washington as well as to the State Department.

The initiative toward political cooperation between the American Slovaks and Czechs came from the Czech side in December, 1914. Before the war, while relations between individual Czech and Slovak immigrants were often cordial because of their linguistic proximity (Czechs and Slovaks can converse in their respective languages and understand each other), relations between the two communities as a whole were not especially close. In the American social scale Czech immigrants ranked much higher than Slovak immigrants. The Kingdom of Bohemia, unlike the Kingdom of

[15] *Ibid.*, 191.
[16] Konstantin Čulen, *Pittsburghská Dohoda, 1918-1938* (1937), 42.

Hungary, was heavily industrialized and urbanized, comprising in fact 82 percent of all the industries of the Austro-Hungarian Empire. In their social, economic, and cultural development the Czech people had achieved by 1914 a level as high as any people in Europe. They had a large, well-educated, and often wealthy middle class; a large, politically and nationally conscious industrial working class; and a progressive, literate peasantry. Illiteracy had been reduced to a minimum in Bohemia. Czech immigration to the United States began earlier than Slovak immigration and comprised a large number of urban elements possessing high skills.

The contingency of war, however, overcame these differences and in October, 1915, at a conference in Cleveland, the Bohemian National Alliance and the Slovak League of America agreed upon the "Cleveland Pact," which envisioned the establishment of "independence" and "union of the Czech and Slovak peoples in a federal union of states with full national autonomy for Slovakia."[17] Thereafter, cooperation between the Bohemian National Alliance and the Slovak League of America and between them and the Czechoslovak National Council in Paris, under the presidency of Professor Thomas G. Masaryk, was very close. Funds raised by Czech and Slovak organizations in the United States made the Czech-Slovak National Council independent of the Allied governments and enabled it to pursue the objective of achieving Czechoslovak independence without regard to the vacillations of Allied policy.[18] The Czech and Slovak organizations in the United States also maintained jointly the Czech-Slav Press Bureau in New York, under Charles Pergler, an Iowa lawyer of Czech origin,

[17] *Ibid.*, 78.
[18] Thomas G. Masaryk, *The Making of a State: Memories and Observations, 1914-1918* (1927), 94.

which carried on a lively propaganda and lobbying activity in behalf of Czechoslovak independence.[19]

Such activities, however, could be of only limited service to the Czechoslovak cause as long as the United States remained neutral. Until 1917 President Wilson was a strong proponent of neutrality ("He kept us out of war") and frowned on activities of "hyphenated Americans" that tended to prejudice this neutrality. In May, 1917, after the American declaration of war on Germany, Charles Pergler scored a minor success with the Sabath and King resolutions in Congress.[20] The resolutions never came to a vote and evoked only a modest amount of comment in the press. The State Department found such resolutions embarrassing, for the United States was then at war with Germany but not yet with Austria-Hungary.

In June, 1917, Milan Štefánik, vice-president of the Czechoslovak National Council in Paris, the third member of the liberating triumvirate of Czechoslovakia (Masaryk-Beneš-Štefánik), and at the time a major in the French Army air force, arrived in the United States to solicit permission from the United States government to recruit volunteers among Czech and Slovak immigrants for the Czechoslovak legion in France. He asked immigrant organizations to prepare his entry into American government circles. Dr. J. L. Fisher and Albert P. Mamatey, presidents of the Bohemian National Alliance and the Slovak League of America re-

---

[19] Charles Pergler, *America in the Struggle for Czechoslovak Independence* (1926), 15ff.; Vojta Beneš, *Československá Amerika vodboji* [Czechoslovak America in our resistance movement] (1930). Czechoslovak propaganda in the United States used as its battle cry a quotation from Woodrow Wilson, *The State: Elements of Historical and Practical Politics* (1903), 336: "No lapse of time, no defeat of hopes, seems sufficient to reconcile the Czechs of Bohemia to incorporation with Austria." See Pergler, *America in the Struggle*, 36.

[20] Pergler, *America in the Struggle*, 61. For the resolutions see *Congressional Record, 65th Congress, 1st Session*, Vol. 55, Part 2, 1889 (May 5, 1917); Part 3, 2856 (May 25, 1917).

spectively, obtained an interview with Secretary of State Robert Lansing on June 3 and read him a statement which they had prepared together with Štefánik. They expressed the loyalty of Czech and Slovak immigrants to the United States, spoke of the desire of their compatriots in the Austrian empire for independence, and called Lansing's attention to the presence of Štefánik in Washington and the purpose of his mission to the United States. In reply, Lansing thanked them for their expressions of loyalty to the United States but did not react to the rest of the message.[21]

The fate of the resolutions in Congress and the result of the interview with Lansing showed the limitations of the influence of Czech and Slovak immigrant groups on the Wilson administration and on American public opinion. At best they could push the American government and public opinion a little further in a direction in which they were already predisposed to move. At the time, however, the United States government intended to maintain the Austrian empire essentially intact, and American public opinion was not only uninterested in the fate of the Czechs and Slovaks but, with rare exceptions, completely unaware of their existence. The pleas of the immigrant groups, therefore, went unheeded. Although Štefánik gained entry into official American circles by using his status as a French officer and eventually completed his military mission successfully, he left the United States disillusioned and a bitter critic of President Wilson.[22]

When Masaryk arrived in the United States a year later, in May, 1918, the situation had completely changed. President Wilson had reversed his policy on Austria-Hungary and had authorized the State Department to hold out the hope of independence to its subject nationalities. This

[21] Mamatey, *The United States and East Central Europe,* 130.
[22] *Ibid.,* 133.

policy, which it was hoped would result in the revolt of the subject people of the Austrian empire, enjoyed the support of significant segments of American public opinion.[23] The outbreak of conflict in Siberia in May, 1918, between the Czechoslovak legion and the Soviet government, against which the Allies were then preparing to intervene, further improved Masaryk's position in the United States. It was thus in much more propitious circumstances that Masaryk launched his campaign to gain American support for Czechoslovak aspirations to independence and his reaction to the American democracy and President Wilson was much more favorable than Štefánik's a year earlier. His efforts were crowned with success on September 3, when the United States Government officially recognized the Czechoslovak National Council in Paris as "a *de facto* belligerent Government, clothed with proper authority to direct the military and political affairs of the Czecho-Slovaks" and declared that it was prepared "to enter formally into relations with the *de facto* Government thus recognized."[24] Six days later, the President received the first "diplomatic agent" of the Czechoslovak National Council accredited to the United States government, Charles Pergler, in the White House. "By your conduct throughout the war," the President told him, "especially by your armies, you have demonstrated that you insist upon complete independence. We have merely recognized an accomplished fact."[25] By its recognition of the Czechoslovak National Council the United States government committed itself to support Czechoslovak independence at the future peace conference.

[23] *Ibid.*, 264, notes 86 and 87.

[24] For the text of recognition see U. S. Department of State, *Papers Relating to the Foreign Relations of the United States: the World War, 1918, Supplement 1,* 2 vols. (1933), 379. For the genesis of recognition see Mamatey, *The United States and East Central Europe,* 300.

[25] Pergler, *America in the Struggle,* 55-56.

Meanwhile, Masaryk took part in the formulation of the famous "Czecho-Slovak Convention" of Pittsburgh. During his tour of Chicago, Cleveland, Pittsburgh, and other centers of Czech and Slovak immigration, great parades and ovations organized by Czech and Slovak organizations in his honor did much to attract the attention of the broad American public to the Czechoslovak cause.

On May 31, the morrow of a great public meeting in Pittsburgh, representatives of the Bohemian National Alliance, the Federation of Czech Catholics, and the Slovak League of America met in private with Masaryk to discuss the future organization of Czechoslovakia. To allay the fears of Slovak spokesmen lest their compatriots in the new state be assimilated ("Czechified") by the much stronger Czech element, Masaryk drafted a program of common aims for the Czech and Slovak organizations in the United States to follow. The program envisaged that Slovakia would have her own administration and courts, for which Slovak would be the official language; that Czechoslovakia would be a democratic republic; and that detailed provisions regarding the organization of the future state should be left to the elected representatives of the Czechs and Slovaks in the liberated country. As some Slovak representatives were still apprehensive, Albert Mamatey of the Slovak League inserted in Masaryk's draft, among the Slovak desiderata, a claim to a "Diet." Masaryk agreed and signed the program, as did other Czech and Slovak representatives.[26]

A calligraphic copy of the Pittsburgh Convention was later made and signed by the participants in the conference. Masaryk signed it in Washington on November 14, 1918,

[26] For the drafting of the Pittsburgh Convention see Mamatey, *The United States and East Central Europe*, 282, and Čulen, *Pittsburghská Dohoda*, 177. For text see Čulen, 182. English translations may be found in Joseph M. Kirschbaum, *Slovakia: Nation at the Crossroads of Central Europe* (1960), 235; and Jozef Lettrich, *History of Modern Slovakia* (1955), 289.

the day of his election to the presidency of Czechoslovakia by the Czechoslovak National Assembly in Prague.[27]

The Pittsburgh program, though primarily a document in Czechoslovak political history, deserves notice, for it was in part designed to influence American policy. At the time of its drafting Masaryk was about to approach the United States government to support the Czechoslovak cause. The assumption that President Wilson based his support of nationalist causes on the principle of selfdetermination presented an embarrassing problem for Masaryk; while several statements by Czech political leaders at home claiming independence for the Czech people and union with the Slovaks were known in the United States, no Slovak expression of a desire for independence and union with the Czechs was known abroad. As a matter of fact, such a declaration had been made on May 1, 1918 (International Labor Day), at a public meeting in Liptovský Svätý Mikuláš, sponsored by the Slovak Social Democrats but attended by Slovak political spokesmen without regard for party affiliation. The meeting passed a resolution demanding the right of self-determination for the "Hungarian branch of the Czechoslovak nation."[28] But the news of this declaration did not reach the United States until the middle of June. In the absence of any mandate from the Slovaks at home, Masaryk was glad to have an expression of support from the Slovaks in the United States who, the Slovak leaders estimated, made up one third of the Slovak people. There was a possibility, moreover, that if he had not reassured the American

---

[27] Čulen, *Pittsburghská Dohoda*, 200. A facsimile of the ornate document is dated May 30, the day of the public demonstration, rather than May 31, the day of the private conference at which the convention was drafted. The date of June 30 given in Masaryk, *The Making of a State*, 208, and in innumerable works drawing on Masaryk's memoirs, is erroneous.

[28] See the English translation of the resolution in Lettrich, *Modern Slovakia*, 287.

Slovaks with the Pittsburgh program some of them, at least, might have embarrassed him before the American public by repudiating his leadership. As it was, however, they lined up solidly behind him and enthusiastically backed both his activities in Washington and, after his departure in November, the efforts of the astute Foreign Minister Edward Beneš, who represented Czechoslovakia at the Paris Peace Conference.[29] Whether or not it was due to the support of the American Slovaks, American officials never questioned Masaryk's and Beneš's right to speak for the Slovaks.

After the war a bitter controversy broke out in Czechoslovakia when the Czechoslovak Constituent Assembly disregarded the Pittsburgh Convention and proceeded to draft a highly centralist constitution, in harmony with the general trend toward centralism in the new states of East Central Europe. The American Slovaks became aware of this trend in the fall of 1919, and in December the Slovak League sent Albert Mamatey to Paris and Prague to make inquiries concerning the fate of the convention, but the mission proved a failure.[30] However, it would be beyond the scope of this work to discuss the controversy. In November, 1919, the United States Senate failed to ratify the Peace of Versailles and the League of Nations' Covenant, and America turned her back on Europe.

Meanwhile, the Carpatho-Ruthenian immigrants in the United States secured international guarantees of the autonomy of their native land. This success was all the more astonishing in that they had begun only late in the war to

[29] Pergler, *America in the Struggle*, 28, testifies: "The Slovak League . . . loyally co-operated with the Czechs and furnished conclusive evidence that Czechs and Slovaks sought not only liberty, but unity." On November 14, 1918, the day Masaryk signed the copy of the Pittsburgh Convention in Washington, the Slovak League gave him a check for $200,000. See Masaryk, *The Making of a State*, 94.

[30] On Mamatey's mission and its failure see Čulen, *Pittsburghská Dohoda*, 279; on the ensuing controversy, 305.

exert themselves in behalf of their kinsmen. The reason for this delay was that the Carpatho-Ruthenian immigrants in the United States were, like their compatriots at home, deeply divided over the question of what the future of Carpathian Ruthenia should be. Generally speaking, there were three principal groups among them. First, there was a Russophil faction, best but not exclusively represented by the American-Russian National Defense organization under the presidency of Ivan Pachuta. This faction looked forward to the absorption of Carpathian Ruthenia by Imperial Russia as indicated in the manifesto of the Russian commander-in-chief, the Grand Duke Nicholas, in August, 1914, which promised to bring the Ruthenians of Austria-Hungary "into the bosom of Mother Russia."[31] Second, there was a Ukrainophil faction, in part represented by the Ukrainian Federation of the United States and led by Bishop Ortinsky, a native of Galicia, which favored uniting the Ruthenians of Galicia, Bukovina, and Carpathian Ruthenia into a single autonomous province, either in the Habsburg empire or possibly in federation with the Ukraine. Third, there was an autochthonous faction, best but not exclusively represented by the American Greek Catholic Union, which insisted on the preservation of the special national character of the Carpatho-Ruthenians but was not clear about how or in what political framework this was to be done.

The battles of factions swayed in a confused fashion with the tides of the war. The Russophil faction waxed strong in 1914 and early 1915 when the Russian "steamroller" rolled into Galicia and Cossack patrols appeared in the Carpathian Mountains. It waned after the great retreat of the Russian army from Poland in May-September, 1915, but gained new strength after the outbreak of the Russian Revolution in March, 1917. It was stimulated by the sym-

[31] C. Jay Smith, *The Russian Struggle for Power, 1914-1917* (1956), 12.

pathetic interest of the American public in Russia when the fall of the Russian monarchy and the rise of the liberal Provisional Government seemingly transformed Russia from an autocratic monarchy into a democratic republic, as well as by growing socialist propaganda. On July 13, 1917, on the initiative of Peter Hatalak, a Carpatho-Ruthenian exile, a "Russian Congress" convened in New York, attended by Ruthenians from both parts of the Austro-Hungarian empire as well as by Ukrainians from the Russian empire and even some Great Russians. The Congress passed a resolution favoring union of the Carpatho-Ruthenians with Russia: "The Carpatho-Russian people want to live in close union with other Russian people, want to lead with them a single common life and share their happiness and grief."[32] Subsequently, a delegation led by Hatalak presented a memorandum embodying this resolution to Boris Bakhmetev, the Russian ambassador in Washington, to Allied embassies, and to the State Department.

The Bolshevik coup d'état in November, 1917, the proclamation of Ukrainian independence in January, 1918, and the ignominious peace of Brest-Litovsk in March, 1918, under which the Soviet government recognized the independence of the Ukraine, stimulated the Ukrainophil faction.[33] Finally,

[32] See the text of the "Memorandum of the Russian Congress in America, convoked by the 'Union for the Liberation of Carpathian Russia,' dedicated to the free people of Russia, the Russian Constituent Assembly, and the Russian Government," July, 1917, in Zdenék Peška, and Josef Markov, "Příspěvek k ústavním dějinám Podkarpatské Rusi" [Contribution to constitutional history of Subcarpathian Russia], *Bratislava* (1931), V, 511. For a discussion of the congress see Petr Hatalak, *Jak vznikla myšlenka připojit Podkarpatskou Rus k Československu* [How the idea originated to join Subcarpathian Russia to Czechoslovakia] (1935). The latter is a reprinting of an article in *Podkarpatské Hlasy*, Nos. 192-203.

[33] See the Memorandum of the Ukrainian Federation of the United States to President Wilson, June 29, 1918, State Department files (National Archives, Washington), 763.72119/1775. On April 10, 1918, Lansing noted in his desk diary: "Mrs. Annie Chapin with 7 Carpathian Russians presenting petition." (Manuscripts Division, Library of Congress.) It is not clear which faction this delegation represented.

the switch of the United States government from a policy of maintaining the Austrian empire essentially intact to support of the Austrian Slavs' aspirations to freedom stimulated the autochthonous faction. Secretary of State Lansing announced the new policy in declarations on May 29 and June 28. The latter, more explicit, took the position that "all branches of the Slav race should be completely freed from German and Austrian rule."[34] Beginning late, the autochthonous faction was ultimately the most influential, because the American government and public were at last ready to listen to Carpatho-Ruthenian pleas and because this faction found a superior leader in Gregory I. Zatkovich, a Pittsburgh lawyer who because of his American training became their most influential spokesman.

In the summer of 1918 the Austrian Slavs became one of the great questions of the day in the United States. The American people, who were virtually unaware of their existence until the spring of 1918, now, in their generous ambition to act the part of liberators of oppressed peoples, embraced them as their special wards.

On July 23, at a gathering of clerical and lay delegates of the Greek Catholic Union and the United Societies at Homestead, Pennsylvania, a new organization, the American National Council of Uhro-Rusins (Hungarian Ruthenians), was founded, which passed a resolution that: "(1) The Carpatho-Ruthenians should have full independence. If this should prove impossible, that (2) the Carpatho-Ruthenians should unite with their brethren in Galicia and Bukovina. If this should be impossible, then they should get (3) autonomy."[35] The "Homestead resolution," however, did not indi-

[34] See the text in U. S. Department of State, *Papers Relating to the Foreign Relations of the United States: the World War, 1918,* Supplement 1, I, 816. For discussion see Mamatey, *The United States and East Central Europe,* 265.

[35] See the text in G. I. Zatkovich, *Otkrytie—Exposé* (1921), I.

cate in what state the Carpatho-Ruthenians should or would seek autonomy.

In October, when the dissolution of the Austrian empire was in the air and was discussed in the American press as a foregone conclusion, Zatkovich developed a feverish activity. First, he solicited an interview with President Wilson to lay before him the Homestead program of the Carpatho-Ruthenians. To be received by the President was an honor eagerly sought by numerous suppliants from East Central Europe, but it was granted only to a few of them. The reception of a Carpatho-Ruthenian delegation by the President in the White House on October 21, which had been arranged by Representative Guy E. Campbell (D.-Pa.),[36] indicated how much importance Wilson attached to Slav questions at the time. During the conference, according to Zatkovich's account, the President told the delegation that the Allied powers would not look with favor on the first or the second solution of the Carpatho-Ruthenian question proposed in the Homestead program and advised them to seek the third one—autonomy.[37] It was probably also the President who advised them to seek admission to and work through the Mid-European Democratic Union, an energetic organization of exiles from East Central Europe under the presidency of Masaryk. Two days later, on October 23, when the Union opened a well-publicized meeting at Independence Hall in Philadelphia, the Carpatho-Ruthenians were admitted as an ethnic group distinct from the Ukrainians, who were already represented in the organization by Miroslav Sichinsky, a

[36] Ray Stannard Baker, *Woodrow Wilson: Life and Letters*, 8 vols. (1927-1929), VIII, 494. Congressman Campbell had no personal interest in the Ruthenian cause, but with the general interest in Slav questions at the time and with congressional elections coming up in November, 1918, he found it politically expedient to assist his Ruthenian constituents from Pittsburgh.

[37] Zatkovich, *Otkrytie*, 1; Walter K. Hanak, *The Subcarpathian-Ruthenian Question: 1918-1945* (1962), 8.

Ruthenian from Galicia. Along with Sichinsky, Zatkovich signed the "Declaration of Common Aims of the Independent Mid-European Nations" in the solemn ceremony that concluded the conference on October 26.[38]

On the previous day, in a conference with Masaryk, the Carpatho-Ruthenians suggested the possibility of federation with Czechoslovakia. Masaryk, who had not originally envisaged the inclusion of Carpathian Ruthenia in Czechoslovakia,[39] now welcomed it. According to Zatkovich, he assured the delegation: "If the Ruthenians decide to join the Czechoslovak Republic they shall constitute a fully autonomous state." And in reply to the Ruthenian query about the future boundaries of Carpathian Ruthenia, he assured them: "The frontiers will be so determined that the Ruthenians will be satisfied."[40] With these assurances, the American National Council of Uhro-Rusins, at a conference at Scranton on November 12, passed the following resolution: "That the Uhro-Rusins, with the broadest autonomous rights as a state, join on the federative basis the Czechoslovak

[38] Zatkovich, *Otkrytie*, 1. Misled by a poor translation of Zatkovich's account, the British historian C. A. Macartney, *Hungary and Her Successors: the Treaty of Trianon and its Consequences, 1919-1937* (1937), 215, wrote: "(On October 26, 1918) the so-called 'Philadelphia agreement' was signed by Masaryk and Zatkovich guaranteeing the Ruthenes autonomy if they would join Czechoslovakia." In fact, no agreement was signed by Masaryk and Zatkovich guaranteeing autonomy to Carpathian Ruthenia. What Zatkovich wrote about was the "Declaration of Common Aims of the Independent Mid-European Nations," which was signed by Masaryk, Zatkovich, and ten other representatives of the oppressed nationalities and was a general statement of principles, not an agreement on any specific issues. See the facsimile in Hanak, *The Subcarpathian-Ruthenian Question*, 10. Two recent writers, relying on Macartney's erroneous account, have perpetuated the myth of the existence of a Czechoslovak-Ruthenian "Philadelphia agreement": Hanak, *The Subcarpathian-Ruthenian Question*, 9, and Dagmar Perman, *The Shaping of the Czechoslovak State: Diplomatic History of the Boundaries of Czechoslovakia, 1914-1920* (1962), 26.

[39] See Masaryk's memorandum "Independent Bohemia" presented in April, 1915, to the British government in R. W. Seton-Watson, *Masaryk in England* (1943), 116.

[40] Zatkovich, *Otkrytie*, 2.

democratic republic, on condition that there should belong to our country all the original Uhro-Rusin counties: Spis, Saris, Zemplin, Abauj, Borsod, Ung, Ugoca, Bereg, and Maramoros."[41]

Zatkovich then hastened to Washington to communicate the Scranton resolution, through Congressman Campbell, to Wilson, Lansing,[42] and Masaryk. The President replied that he had received the resolution "with utmost interest" and congratulated Zatkovich "on the progress made towards satisfactory relations."[43] Lansing requested the opinion of the Near Eastern Division of the State Department about the resolution. In a memorandum dated November 21 the Near Eastern Division, headed by Albert H. Putney, a strong supporter of Masaryk, replied that the "Uhro-Rusins . . . while not being Czechoslovaks . . . are of Slav origin and, therefore, would naturally fall into such a confederation (i.e., with Czechoslovakia) from racial, territorial and political considerations."[44] When a delegation of the Ukrainophil faction led by Bishop Alexander called at the State Department on November 30 to protest the Scranton resolution, it met with polite evasions on the part of Basil Miles of the Russian desk.[45] Masaryk received the resolution "with great joy," but warned Zatkovich that it represented only a decision of the National Council and might be, for that reason, ignored by the peace conference. To gain greater authority for the resolution Zatkovich thought of submitting it to a "plebiscite" of the Carpatho-Ruthenians in the United States,

[41] *Ibid.*, 5.
[42] Zatkovich to Lansing, November 15, 1918, State Department files 763.72119/2691.
[43] Wilson to Zatkovich, November 19, 1918, The Woodrow Wilson Papers (Manuscripts Division, Library of Congress).
[44] Richard Crane (Lansing's secretary) to Albert H. Putney (chief of the Near Eastern Division), November 18, 1918, and Putney to Crane, November 21, 1918, State Department files, 763.72119/2691.
[45] Memorandum for the Secretary of State, December 1, 1918, and enclosed petition, State Department files, 763.72119/3129.

which, he assured Masaryk, would "without doubt confirm the decision and recommendation of the National Council."[46]

The "plebiscite," held in Carpatho-Ruthenian Greek Catholic parishes during November and December, resulted, according to Zatkovich, in the following vote: for union with Czechoslovakia, 67 percent; for union with the Ukraine, 28 percent; for union with Russia, less than 1 percent; for union with Hungary, less than 1 percent; and for complete independence, less than 2 percent.[47] The National Council communicated the results of the plebiscite to the State Department[48] and, through Charles Pergler, to the Czechoslovak government in Prague and the Czechoslovak peace delegation in Paris.[49] It also appointed Zatkovich and Julius G. Gardoš its delegates to lay the Scranton resolution and the result of the plebiscite before the Paris Conference and before the Carpatho-Ruthenians at home.

The Czechoslovak government sent Captain Josef Písecký, armed with the Scranton resolution and the result of the plebiscite, on a mission to Carpathian Ruthenia, which was then in a state of chaos. No less than three national councils had sprung up (at Prešov, Užhorod, and Hust), each demanding autonomy for the Carpatho-Ruthenians but each in a different state: the Prešov Council in Czechoslovakia, the Užhorod Council in Hungary, and the Hust Council in Galicia.[50]

[46] Zatkovich, *Otkrytie*, 3.

[47] *Ibid.* At this point also Pachuta's Russophil faction rallied to the Czechoslovak solution of the Carpatho-Ruthenian question. See "Memorandum of the American-Russian National Defense dedicated to Professor Masaryk, the Illustrious Tireless Worker for the Emancipation of the Slavic Nations," in Peška and Markov, "Příspěvek," 127.

[48] The American National Council of Uhro-Rusins to the Secretary of State, January 13, 1919, State Department files, 860F.01/47.

[49] Zatkovich, *Otkrytie*, 4.

[50] On the developments in Carpathian Ruthenia, which do not properly come within the purview of this article, see Hanak, *The Subcarpathian-Ruthenian Question*, 4; Kamil Krofta, "Ruthenes, Czechs and Slovaks,"

Since the Russian National Council at Prešov favored union with Czechoslovakia, the Czechoslovak government sent its head, Dr. Anton Beskid, to Paris to assist Beneš. In presenting the Czechoslovak claims to the Council of Ten (heads of state and foreign ministers of the Allied powers) at the Paris Peace Conference on February 4, 1919, Beneš included the incorporation of Carpathian Ruthenia, with guarantees of autonomy.[51] His hand was strengthened by the arrival in Paris on February 13 of Zatkovich and Gardoš from the United States. Together with Beskid, they cooperated closely with the Czechoslovak peace delegation. Their memorandum, formulating in detail the claims of the Carpatho-Ruthenians, was presented by Beneš to the Peace Conference as the Czechoslovak "Mémoire No. 6."[52] Through the intervention of Beneš the Carpatho-Ruthenian delegation, with Zatkovich acting as spokesman, was received by Colonel Edward Mandel House, then acting as the chairman of the American peace delegation in the absence of the President, who had returned briefly to the United States to be present at the final sessions of Congress. On February 24 they were received by André Tardieu, a member of the French peace delegation and secretary of the Council of Five (foreign ministers). Neither statesman appeared to have any objection to the inclusion of Carpathian Ruthenia in Czechoslovakia. With the exception of Italy, which sought to protect Hungary as a counterweight to Yugoslavia, the Allied powers were disposed to award Carpathian Ruthenia to Czechoslovakia. The Commission on Czecho-

---

Slavonic and East European Review (1935), XIII, 620; Jaszi, "The Problem of Sub-Carpathian Ruthenia," 202; Volosin, "Carpathian Ruthenia." For texts of the resolutions of these councils see Peška and Markov, "Příspěvek."

[51] U. S. Department of State, *Papers Relating to the Foreign Relations of the United States: the Paris Peace Conference, 1919*, 13 vols. (1942-1947), IV, 886.

[52] Zatkovich, *Otkrytie*, 4.

slovak Affairs of the Peace Conference sanctioned inclusion of
Carpathian Ruthenia in Czechoslovakia, in principle, as
early as March 12,[53] and definitely (with provisions for
autonomy suggested by Beneš, but not for federation) on
May 20, 1919.[54] Its report was approved by the Council of
Five on May 23,[55] and the new boundaries of Hungary,
leaving Carpathian Ruthenia to Czechoslovakia, were laid
down by the Big Four on June 12.[56] The provisions for Carpatho-Ruthenian autonomy, originally suggested by Beneš,
became articles 10 to 13 of the treaty signed between the
Allied powers and Czechoslovakia at Saint-Germain on
September 10, 1919.[57]

Meanwhile, on March 4, 1919, assured of favorable action
on their decision to join Czechoslovakia, Zatkovich and
Gardoš left Paris and hastened, via Prague, to Carpathian
Ruthenia to rally their compatriots in support of union with
Czechoslovakia. They brought with them the aura of rich
and powerful America—funds collected by immigrants in
America for the relief of their compatriots. Partly as a
result of their pleas, on May 8, 1919, the three councils
were merged into the Central Russian National Council at
Užhorod, which elected Zatkovich (a United States citizen)
as its president. On May 14 the new council formally approved the program of the American National Council,[58] and
on May 23 a great Carpatho-Ruthenian delegation arrived
in Prague to lay their resolution before President Masaryk
and the Czechoslovak government.[59] Zatkovich was appointed by the latter first governor of Carpathian Ruthenia,

[53] Perman, *The Shaping of the Czechoslovak State*, 153.
[54] *The Paris Peace Conference*, IV, 758.
[55] *Ibid.*, 751.
[56] *Ibid.*, VI, 351.
[57] *Ibid.*, XIII, 888.
[58] Zatkovich, *Otkrytie*, 7; Hanak, *The Subcarpathian-Ruthenian Question*,
13.
[59] *Ibid.*, 14; Zatkovich, *Otkrytie*, 9.

or Subcarpathian Russia, as it was officially designated in the Czechoslovak Republic. However, the international guarantee of Carpatho-Ruthenian autonomy in the Treaty of Saint Germain was not fully implemented by the Czechoslovak government. The Carpatho-Ruthenians were also deeply disappointed with the delimitation of the administrative boundary between Carpathian Ruthenia and Slovakia, which left many Carpatho-Ruthenians on the Slovak side. In May, 1921, Zatkovich in protest resigned as governor and returned to his law practice in Pittsburgh. But these events, like the unfulfilled promise of Slovak autonomy, are another story.

In conclusion it may be said that while the Slovak immigrants in the United States affected Wilson's peace policies only indirectly (as a part of the Czechoslovak movement under Professor Masaryk), the Carpatho-Ruthenian immigrants did so directly. Of the meeting of the Mid-European Democratic Union, Elmer Davis wrote: "The tail cannot wag the dog. Emigrant colonies cannot control the course of the people left at home."[60] In the case of the Carpatho-Ruthenians, however, the tail did wag the dog. The Carpatho-Ruthenian immigrants in America did determine the fate of their compatriots at home—a unique case, it appears, of the influence of an immigrant group in America on the political history of Europe.

[60] Elmer Davis, "America's Contribution to Central Europe," *The New Europe* (1918), 180.

THE MID-EUROPEAN UNION

ARTHUR J. MAY

At noon on Saturday, October 26, 1918, as World War I drew to its agonizing close, the courtyard behind stately Independence Hall in Philadelphia witnessed one of the dramatic episodes of its long and colorful history. From a platform Professor Thomas G. Masaryk, soon to be president-designate of Czechoslovakia, read out a "Declaration of Common Aims" of the newly created Mid-European Union. Flanking the venerable philosopher-statesman from Prague were representatives of European nationalities who had just signed the declaration, eminent citizens of Philadelphia, and delegates of American patriotic societies and political parties. To enliven the scene, national hymns were sung in the original tongues or performed by bands. The four-year-old daughter of a Czechoslovak immigrant unveiled a replica of the original Liberty Bell, which other children, attired in picturesque old-world costumes, tolled as each signer of the declaration eloquently expressed his gratitude to the United States and President Woodrow Wilson. "Oh, you bell! Oh, you country! Oh, you President Wilson!" declared one spokesman, "that this day should see the Uhro-Ruthenes free, free, free."

Hosts and guests then repaired to the Bellevue Stratford Hotel for a joyous dinner celebrating at once the ceremonies at Independence Hall and the impending collapse of the Central European empires. The Philadelphia merchant-prince John Wanamaker presented a handsome American flag to the Mid-European Union and said to Masaryk, "My dear friend and brother, we are here today to talk to you heart to heart. . . . What you have done today will be written in the history of the world. This country and this country's people are behind you in your signing of your Declaration of Independence."[1] Extensively publicized throughout the country, the events in Philadelphia elicited optimistic interpretations from the press. "For centuries," declared the Cleveland *Plain Dealer*, "the nations of Mid-Europe will remember the 26th of October, 1918, as the most significant day of their history. The United States and the City of Philadelphia will be regarded with admiration." "Born in Philadelphia, a Safe Mitteleuropa," proclaimed an editorial leader in the Philadelphia *Public Ledger;* the writer felt sure that the new declaration would "be heard in the echoing courts of the hoary Hapsburg Burg in Vienna." Instead of the "grandiose, imperialistic and predatory Mitteleuropa of which the two kaisers dreamed," the delegates of the Mid-European nationalities aspired to "create a new, a democratic, a benevolent Mitteleuropa."[2] Photographs of the Philadelphia exercises distributed under such captions as "Professor T. G. Masaryk . . . in Independence Hall signs the Declaration of Czechoslovakian Independence" gave rise to the legend that the Czech declaration, actually drawn up in Washington eight days earlier, had been issued in Philadelphia.

Professor Herbert A. Miller, sociologist at Oberlin College, served as master of ceremonies of the Philadelphia meeting and as director of the Mid-European Union. Of Swedish descent, educated at Dartmouth College and winner of the doctorate at Harvard with a dissertation on *Psycho-Physics and the Race Problem,* Miller had developed an ardent interest in the welfare and the future of the Czechs and to a lesser degree of other small national groupings in Central Europe.[3]

[1] Herbert A. Gibbons, *John Wanamaker,* 2 vols. (1926), II, 421-22.

[2] Cleveland *Plain Dealer,* October 28, 1918; Philadelphia *Public Ledger,* October 27, 1918.

[3] See the obituary notice by Negley K. Teeters in *American Sociological Review,* XVI (1951), 563-64. I am deeply indebted to Professor Teeters of

In 1911, inspired by Professor W. I. Thomas, who was then engaged in writing his massive monograph on the Polish peasant,[4] Miller undertook an investigation of the Czechs, or the Bohemians as he then called them, residing in Chicago and elsewhere in the United States. He was appalled by the dearth of literature available on this national grouping. For some time, among nativeborn Americans only he and Mary McDowell, director of the University of Chicago Settlement House, displayed lively and sustained interest in the Czechs. By promoting instruction in the Czech language in the high schools of Chicago, next to Prague the largest Czech-speaking community of the world, Miller established bonds of sympathy with prominent Czech-Americans, and in 1912 he accompanied a Sokol contingent to a gathering in Prague. While there he conferred at length with Masaryk on sociological and philosophical subjects and learned Masaryk's attitudes toward the tangled nationality problems of the Habsburg monarchy. Upon his return to America, Miller prepared articles setting forth the thesis that the map of Europe would have to be changed radically in order to satisfy the wishes of the nationalities; the rising forces of nationalism were threatening to explode in war, he argued, if concessions were not peacefully and quickly granted.[5]

Soon after the outbreak of the European War in 1914, Miller wrote an article, "Nationalism in Bohemia and Poland,"[6] in which he interpreted the assassination of the Archduke Francis Ferdinand at Sarajevo as "exactly in harmony

---

Temple University and Maurice Miller, son of Professor Miller, for permission to study the unpublished memoirs and other papers of Professor Miller, including the *Minutes of the Mid-European Union*, which are in their possession. These documents are cited hereafter as "Miller Papers."

   [4] William I. Thomas and Florian Znaniecki, *The Polish Peasant in Europe and America*, 2 vols. (1918).

   [5] Miller Papers; Herbert A. Miller, "What Woodrow Wilson and America meant to Czechoslovakia," in *Czechoslovakia*, ed. Robert J. Kerner (1940), 74.

   [6] *North American Review*, CC (1914), 879-86.

with the hostile spirit of the Slavs," who thoroughly detested the Vienna government. In another piece which appeared as "a prophecy of Slav domination," Miller allowed himself to be carried away by Russophilism and naively predicted Russian mastery over Europe and perhaps over the whole world. An ardent democratic idealist in his personal philosophy, he ventured to suggest that the tsarist regime would be ousted and that democratic government would be embraced by all the Slavic peoples.[7]

As a professor at Oberlin College (and subsequently at Ohio State University and Bryn Mawr), Miller pursued sociological research in nationality problems and in immigration and assimilation, publishing several books, among them *The School and the Immigrant*[8] and *Races, Nations and Classes,* his best-known work. "It is quite unnecessary to be in Europe to learn the history and results of oppression," he wrote. "One can literally learn more about Europe in a month in Pittsburgh, Cleveland or Chicago than in a year in Europe." And again, "It is as impossible that the Danube Valley should not be an economic unit as that the Mississippi Valley should be controlled by hostile sovereignties."[9] For a time Miller directed the division of immigrant heritages of the Carnegie Corporation.

As a result of his interest in immigration problems and his admiration of the Slavs and the aims of revolution in Central and Eastern Europe, Miller became the principal organizer and guiding spirit of the Mid-European Union.[10] Ties with Slavs had enabled him to participate in deliberations that eventually matured in the Bohemian National Alliance, a body with some 250 branches that furnished

[7] *New York Times,* May 23, 1915.

[8] Cleveland (1916).

[9] *Races, Nations and Classes,* Philadelphia (1924), 73, 188.

[10] The original idea of a union Miller credited to Rose Szewc of New York City, who was interested in the foreign-born; she served as secretary of the Union.

indispensable financial assistance to Masaryk and his fellow revolutionaries in the Czech emigration.[11] Miller likewise joined forces with Mary McDowell in a successful crusade to secure the release of her friend, Alice G. Masaryk, who had been cast into a Viennese prison on charges of abetting her father to escape abroad, an offense involving high treason.[12]

After the United States hesitatingly declared war on the Danube monarchy in December, 1917, Miller learned that thousands of drafted soldiers of Slav or Rumanian descent intended to withdraw from the armed forces under an order of the War Department permitting the discharge of enemy aliens. He scurried about to secure qualified speakers who, in the several native languages, explained to the draftees the aims of the United States in the struggle and how Allied victory would assure freedom and independence to their homelands. Hundreds of Slav draftees thereupon renounced the idea of quitting the army. With equal ardor, though with less success, Miller likewise fought against a military order barring immigrant soldiers who had not completed citizenship requirements from training for combat.[13]

In the meantime, Miller had been turning over in his fertile mind ways and means of fostering revolutionary sentiments among subject nationalities in Central Europe. His acquaintance with a broad range of Slav immigrant

[11] Illuminating information on these activities is available in T. G. Masaryk, *The Making of a State* (1927), 27, 84-85, 218; Eduard Beneš, *My War Memoirs* (1928), 98-102; Charles Pergler, *America in the Struggle for Czechoslovak Independence* (1926), 22-25; Emmanuel Voska and Will Irwin, *Spy and Counterspy* (1940), 26-34, 200-201; Thomas Capek, *The Czechs in America* (1920), 265-75.

[12] Miller Papers; Mary E. McDowell, "Tried in Her Father's Stead," *Survey*, XXXVI (1916), 116; "Alice Masarykova," *Survey*, LXIII (1930), 630-32. Excerpts from the letters written from prison by Miss Masaryk to her mother appeared in the *Atlantic Monthly*, CXXVI (1920), 577-87, 770-79.

[13] Herbert A. Miller, "The Lost Division," *Survey*, XL (1918), 307-309.

leaders and spokesmen of European origin, such as the Pole Ignace Jan Paderewski, stood him in good stead. On behalf of the Committee on Public Information (CPI), the official American agency for wartime propaganda, Will Irwin bestowed his blessing on an organization to fan the embers of revolt.

In the spring of 1918, the arrival of Masaryk, fresh from the Russian revolutionary scene, powerfully stimulated Miller's dreams and designs. Well known in centers of Czech and Slovak settlement by reason of his earlier visits or his wartime labors for an independent Czechoslovakia, or as the teacher in Vienna or Prague of several Slav leaders living in the United States, Masaryk was welcomed with immense enthusiasm in Chicago, New York, and other cities. Stories about the Czechoslovaks now began to appear in major metropolitan newspapers; the volume of articles increased substantially with the bold anti-Bolshevik exploits of the Czechoslovak legion in bleak, mysterious Siberia, an episode that impressed public men and the national imagination of America.[14]

Upon Masaryk's arrival in Washington, Miller learned of his strong desire for the postwar cooperation of the small states that were expected to emerge from the ruin of the Habsburg monarchy. The two men worked through the CPI and private channels to disseminate information about Central Europe in the United States. In his Oberlin study Miller had devised a map showing the distribution of several national groupings in the heart of Europe; this map together with an article, "Slavs as our Allies," he had published in the *New York Times*. He argued that the revolt of the Slav populations would hasten the end of hostilities and that recognition of Slav national councils as de facto governments

[14] Masaryk, *The Making of a State*, 218-43; *New York Times*, May 23, 26, 27, 1918.

and the formation of national army groups within the Ameri-man military forces would speed along the revolutionary cause.[15] Under the auspices of the Creel Committee, Miller arranged for exhibits at prominent locations in New York City to acquaint passersby with the national complexities of Central Europe, and especially with the Czechoslovakian problem.

While Masaryk busied himself in controversial negotiations with representatives of the Slovaks and the Ukrainians in the United States and conferred with important Americans both in and out of public office, Miller moved ahead with the plans that came to fruition in the Mid-European Union.[16] A mass demonstration in New York City was arranged for September 15, 1918. Before the meeting, speakers of the day and the committee on arrangements, eight or ten in all, conferred at a luncheon given by the CPI. In addition to Miller and Masaryk, the guests included Hinko Hinković, deputy in the Diet of Croatia, representing the Yugoslavs, Lieutenant Vasil Stoica for the Rumanians, and a Pole, Iwanowski, spokesman for Ignace Jan Paderewski. Miller proposed that a permanent association of European nationalities be organized, to which Masaryk responded, "This is what I have been looking forward to." It was agreed that delegates of the Ukrainians, the Lithuanians and the Italian irredentists should be added to the group and that Miller should convoke a meeting to set up an organization on the following day.

Since the mass meeting fell on a "gasless" Sunday, the United States Army provided cars to transport the speakers, in itself good advertising, for the streets were otherwise almost devoid of traffic. Held under the auspices of the CPI and of several New York City organizations, the

[15] *New York Times,* June 16, 1918; George Creel, *How We Advertised America* (1920), 186; Kerner, *Czechoslovakia,* 80.
[16] Masaryk, *The Making of a State,* 254.

demonstration attracted some 4,000 guests, including European soldiers in striking uniforms and girls in peasant dress —a picturesque illustration of the national diversity in Central Europe. It was advertised as "The will of the peoples of Austria-Hungary; Victory Meeting for the oppressed nationalities of central Europe," and was likened to a Congress of Oppressed Nationalities that had convened in Rome in April, 1918, and a somewhat similar assembly in May, 1918, at Prague. The press interpreted the demonstration as a pointed reply to an appeal, just released in Vienna, for a general peace. On the honorary committee were outstanding political, industrial and intellectual figures including former President W. H. Taft, Senator H. C. Lodge, Stockton Axson, brother-in-law of President Wilson, and the ambassadors of Great Britain, France, and Italy. Miller considered it a victory that Senator Gilbert M. Hitchcock, chairman of the Committee on Foreign Relations, took the chair at the meeting, for his presence showed "that the gathering had support in high places." Interspersing speeches delivered by Stoica, Hinković, Paderewski, Masaryk and others were hymns or folk melodies of the nationalities sung by choruses and soloists from the Metropolitan Opera. Each speaker demanded the dismemberment of Austria-Hungary, Hinković warning, "We have lost the war if Austria survives," while another hailed the gathering as "an episode in the Austro-Hungarian revolution." Masaryk originally intended in his speech to lay bare the realities of the situation in Central Europe, but Paderewski, who preceded him, showered the Czech statesman with such fulsome praise that Masaryk felt obliged to laud Polish art and culture as personified by the illustrious pianist. Masaryk also reiterated that the primary object of the war was the destruction of the Danube monarchy.

As the American most familiar with the tangle of nationalities in Central Europe, Miller drafted resolutions

which the meeting rapturously adopted. He called for the
dissolution of the Habsburg monarchy, the political reconstruction of the area on the principle of national selfdetermination and an independent and united Poland, and
proposed that "this present affirmation of loyal and brotherly
cooperation" be sent to President Wilson, to other political
dignitaries, and to the press. Surveying the day's events,
Miller had solid cause for satisfaction; progress had been
made toward a union of the nationalities, and the events
had been widely publicized.[17]

On September 16, the Mid-European Union was born at
a meeting of the organizational committee in the Hotel
Biltmore in New York. On nomination of Paderewski,
Masaryk, against his wish, was chosen as chairman. "If it
were known in Austria-Hungary," the Czech remarked, "that
we were sitting together in this room it would fill them with
consternation." The desirability of seeking a solution to
the conflicting territorial aspirations of the several nationalities seems to have been approved; already Masaryk and
Paderewski had exchanged views on the disposition of the
Teschen area of Silesia. "Just to be polite to one another
smooths out our differences," said Paderewski. When Masaryk proposed that Miller undertake the office of executive
director of the infant union, the American hesitated on the
ground that the post might limit his independence or prove
to be more than he could handle effectively, but he promised
to give a definite answer when the committee presented the
resolutions of the fifteenth to Wilson in the White House.[18]

Before the interview with the President, Miller revealed
what was afoot to Colonel Edward M. House, head of the
"Inquiry" Wilson had set up to accumulate information for
guidance in peacemaking. Convinced that clashing claims

---

[17] Miller Papers; *New York Times,* September 16, 1918; *Survey,* XLI
(1918), 3; Masaryk, *The Making of a State,* 250-51, 291.
[18] Miller Papers; Kerner, *Czechoslovakia,* 81.

of the nationalities would pose the most vexing problems in the peace settlement, House said nothing was more important than the adjustment in advance of as many of the differences as possible. William A. Phillips, Assistant Secretary of State, enthusiastically approved the idea of a union and urged Miller to do all in his power to smooth out moot territorial questions. When Masaryk presented the New York resolutions to Wilson on September 19, the President remarked that the Habsburg monarchy resembled an ancient structure that had long been held up by props, now about to be removed.

Miller now agreed to assume executive direction of the Union. Delegates met in the Italian Information Bureau to define the purposes of the organization, with Miller presiding. Formally appointed director and with assurances of a salary from the CPI, Miller severed his connection with the Carnegie Corporation and took a leave of absence from Oberlin. At this point, he felt that the supreme task of the Union should be to prepare the way for a Danubian federation of nations; representatives of the several nationalities should confer on mutual problems and seek to settle controversies that "inhibited effective intercommunication." And the Union, Miller believed, should combat the theory that the preservation of the Habsburg monarchy was necessary for stability in the valley of Danube. In his own words, the Union "means a solid front of free, united nations, ranged in mutually protective formation in a long sentry-line from the Baltic to the Adriatic. It means the basis of a rational and enduring peace." That vision, obviously, was the evidence of things hoped for.[19] Masaryk, on his part, wanted the Union to hammer out a program for the peace settlement in Central Europe along lines that he had set forth in contributions to the *New Europe,* a British publication

[19] Miller Papers; Herbert A. Miller, "The Bulwark of Freedom," *Survey,* XLI (1918), 5; Masaryk, *The Making of a State,* 255.

devoted particularly to the education of opinion on the eventual European settlement.

With characteristic energy, Miller worked out plans to gain nationwide publicity for the Union, in which he had the assistance of a young naval lieutenant, Lawrence Townsend, who from boyhood had been enthusiastic over freedom for the Czechs. One of their enterprises was a luncheon, on October 3, 1918, attended by members of the Union and the diplomatic corps and representatives of the State, War, and Navy Departments. Phillips was invited to make the principal speech.

The suspicions and mistrust that had dogged the Union almost from its inception now came into the open. In hot indigation the Italian ambassador, Count Macchi di Cellere, protested to the State Department that the Union was nothing but a wily Slav stratagem to deny Italy the full rewards pledged in the secret Treaty of London of 1915, and complained bitterly of the participation of an American citizen, Miller, in the work of the Union. Because of the Italian stand Phillips washed his hands of the Union; from that time Miller found himself "very much under official disapproval." The CPI cancelled its offer to defray Miller's salary and cut off official ties with the Union. Yet, out of respect to Masaryk, the State Department was represented at the luncheon by Richard Crane, and Senator Hitchcock delivered the main address. To avoid offending di Cellere, most of the European diplomats boycotted the gathering.[20]

At the luncheon Miller distributed a brochure containing a statement that he had composed on the Union. The cover carried the battlecry of the French publicist, André Cheradame, "All the racial elements necessary for the destruction of the pan-German plan exist in Central Europe;" the party

[20] Miller Papers. On di Cellere, see René Albrecht-Carrié, *Italy at the Peace Conference* (1938), 46, 79-80.

was described as a "luncheon of the Committee for the Federation of Mid-European States."[21] After the luncheon, the first regular session of the Union convened in the Italian Information Bureau with representatives of the Czecho-slovaks, Yugoslavs, Poles, Ukrainians, Italian Irredentists, Rumanians and Lithuanians present. Promising to serve in the capacity of an "honest broker," Miller took the chair and called for a full exchange of views on the agenda of the Union. Finances, including his personal remuneration and funds to rent an office, engage a press agent and a small staff, and to launch a journal, should be handled, Miller recommended, as in the Pan-American Union, each national group contributing in accordance with its resources. He wanted the Union to consider not only the guiding principles for the rehabilitation of Central Europe but the most delicate problems involving the nationalities of the area as well. Cooperation, he declared, was the price of peace. As specific objectives, Miller proposed a united front against the central empires, application of the doctrine of national selfdetermination, the dismemberment of Austria-Hungary, and a Mid-European federation of nationalities. Once a program had been hammered out, it should be given maximum publicity for the education of both native Americans and immigrants from Central Europe. The House Inquiry, he reported, looked with favor on the Union and was ready to assist its labors.[22]

[21] Miller Papers. Miller's statement also appeared in the *Survey*, XLI (1918), 5-10. To aid the common cause, Masaryk published a vigorous argument for the breakup of the Habsburg Monarchy, contending that dismemberment would not only shackle Germany but prove helpful to Russia. "The Czecho-Slavak Nation," *Nation*, CVII (1918), 386-88. Charles Pergler, "The Bohemian Question," *Annals of the American Academy of Political and Social Science*, LXXII (1917), 158-60.

[22] "Minutes of the Union," October 3, 1918, Miller Papers. The surviving records of the Union are incomplete. The minutes were so long and so detailed that "We have decided to cut them, only put in the essentials," Miller said. *Ibid.*, November 18, 1918.

Speaking for the Yugoslavs, Hinković approved the Union scheme provided the principal aims were to cooperate for victory and to inform the American public about the stakes of the war in Central Europe; once hostilities had ceased, the Union, he said, should dissolve. Controversial territorial questions should be excluded from the deliberations, since the members lacked official authority; because of the presence of north Europeans, he doubted the wisdom of calling the Union Mid-European.

Taking another tack, Masaryk endorsed Miller's proposal for candid discussion of sources of discord. Conceivably, tentative understandings could be reached inside the Union on the future of Austrian Silesia, Italian-Yugoslav rivalries and other similar problems, and this understanding would exert a powerful influence on the more nationalist-minded European leaders of the several nationalities. "We must be united against Germany," Masaryk warned, "otherwise there will be wranglings at the peace conference and the Germans will say, 'Now look, these people are fighting one another'. . . . I am in favor," he added, "of a society, club, or whatever you may call it, where there will be this inter-alliance and interdependence of these nations from the Finns to the Greeks. . . ." The name of the organization was immaterial to him—"Call it rhododendron," he jibed. In the end, after no little debate, the name "Democratic Mid-European Union" was adopted; later the word "Democratic," which grated on some ears, was dropped. Masaryk, as permanent chairman, and Miller, as director, were instructed to write a constitution and bylaws for the Union.[23] Applauding the establishment of the Union, the *New York Times* pleaded for a genuine spirit of compromise and farsightedness in dealing with matters in dispute; the creation of the Union showed,

[23] *Ibid.*

it argued, encouraging progress in "cementing the wall" against German resurgence in the future.[24]

While Miller and other Americans collaborated with Masaryk in drawing up a Czechoslovak declaration of independence, the swift surge of developments on European battlefields cast a shadow upon the work contemplated for the Union.[25] It had been suggested by an American journalist that the Czech declaration would impress Americans more profoundly if it were proclaimed from Independence Hall in Philadelphia, but arrangements for that could not be made. Eager for all the publicity possible, Miller proposed a meeting of the Union in the historic building and Masaryk, much as he disliked the fanfare essential for effective political propaganda in the United States, readily acquiesced. As a prelude to the Philadelphia meeting, a steering committee of the Union devised a tentative "declaration of common aims," which, with certain textual revisions, was ultimately approved. It was also agreed that Miller should receive a salary of $8,000 a year and an allowance of $5,000 for expenses, and he was instructed to engage an office staff including a business manager to handle the finances of the Union.[26] For the meeting at Philadelphia, Miller ordered a replica of the Liberty Bell, the funds being collected by children of Central European parents; on his initiative the bell was inscribed, "Proclaim liberty throughout all the world and unto all the inhabitants thereof."[27]

[24] October 23, 1918.
[25] Kerner, *Czechoslovakia*, 82-84; Masaryk, *The Making of a State*, 294-95; Alfred Leif, *Brandeis* (1936), 407; Robert J. Casey and Mary Borglum, *Give the Man Room* (1952), 250-51.
[26] "Minutes of the Union," October 21, 1918, Miller Papers.
[27] It was intended to display the bell in leading American and Old World cities as the symbol of a happier tomorrow for Central Europe, after which models would be cast for the capital of each participating nationality. But somehow or other Carpatho-Ukrainian-Americans got possession of the bell and shipped it to Prague.

A virulent epidemic of influenza severely limited the public audience at Philadelphia, where deliberation and debate proceeded from October 23 to 26. The press, which covered the meetings adequately, modified reports of the more acrimonious exchanges, and often alluded to the gathering as a Czechoslovak or a Slav affair, which caused no little resentment among the other participants. English served as the official language of the meeting, in itself an invitation to misunderstandings, since many delegates could not phrase their thoughts accurately in a strange tongue. Even so, a reporter felt that in "diction and rhetoric" the discussions "were equal, if not superior to the proceedings of the United States Congress."[28] In addition to the seventeen earlier participants in the Union, Carpatho-Ruthenians, Greeks, Albanians, Armenians, and Zionists were represented; an application by the "Friends of German Democracy" for admission was rejected because their credentials were suspect.

Mayor Thomas B. Smith of Philadelphia, coached by Miller, welcomed the delegates "in this cradle of the world's liberty." For the Union, Masaryk voiced appreciation that the meeting was being held "under the roof where the American Declaration of Independence was drafted and published. We shall do our work under the shadow of a great tradition." News agencies spread his words across the Republic.[29]

Seated in a chair made of wood from an elm under which William Penn had negotiated a treaty with the Indians, Masaryk presided with suavity and efficiency over deliberations which repeatedly reached turbulent dimensions. Fully aware of the explosive character of many territorial problems, Masaryk wisely suggested the appoint-

[28] Philadelphia *Record*, October 28, 1918.
[29] Philadelphia *Public Ledger*, October 23, 1918.

ment of ad hoc committees to examine specific quarrels, but nothing came of the suggestion. He also proposed that attention be focused on the conditions for setting up new states, on the contribution that the Union might make in tightening bonds of interest and esteem among the Mid-European countries, and on forestalling attempts by the Central Empires to play off one small state against another. Our "confederation will encircle the Central Empires with nations of free peoples," he explained, "so that if the Teutonic allies seek another place in the sun they will have to go straight up in the air, for there will be no place in Europe for them."[30]

Hints of the sharp antagonisms that would flare up at the Paris peace conference were plentiful at Philadelphia. For the Poles, it was galling that Myroslav Sychynski, a Ukrainian who had killed the Polish governor of Galicia, should be allowed to take part. Miller, in contrast, regarded Sychynski as "a fine fellow, and very level-headed and logical," while Masaryk described him as "an unexpectedly pleasant and sensible man."[31] From the beginning the Croat Hinković proved himself an *enfant terrible,* militant and uncompromising. Infuriated by the Miller nationality map, which allocated to Italy Adriatic areas claimed by the Yugoslavs, he dramatically tore a copy of the map to shreds. "If we lose the Adriatic," he shouted, "we lose our lungs. We will be strangled. . . . We will not tolerate any oppressor." "In a flash," a journalist commented, "it was apparent that here was the place where a world war started. Old wounds, still sore and burning, were probed with no gentle fingers."[32] Masaryk poured tranquilizing oil on the troubled waters,

[30] Philadelphia *Evening Public Ledger,* October 23, 1918.

[31] On Sychynski, see Arthur J. May, *The Hapsburg Monarchy, 1867-1914,* new ed. (1960), 341-42; Robert E. Park, *The Immigrant Press and its Control* (1922), 335-36.

[32] New York *Evening Sun,* October 25, 1918.

and to mollify Hinković it was voted that the Union would
have no official map.

Gregory I. Zatkovich said that the Carpatho-Ruthenians
preferred unfettered independence, but since President
Wilson thought such a state would be too weak to stand
alone, they would seek autonomy in either Czechoslovakia
or the Ukraine. Concerning the frontier between Ukraine
and Poland, Sychynski asked for a plebiscite and a neutral
commission to fix the final boundary.

It was generally agreed that it would be unfair to the
interests of certain nationalities if plebiscites were ordained
in districts that Germany had deliberately colonized; only
the presence of American troops would guarantee genuine
plebiscites in some areas. While Masaryk lauded national
selfdetermination in principle, he felt that local economic,
strategic, or cultural considerations would compel deviation
from that principle. Delegates unanimously agreed that
minorities in the new states would have to be protected by
the League of Nations. Because of the dissensions that
flared up at the meeting, Masaryk put aside his hopes for
some sort of a federal union for political ends; Miller, who
saw eye to eye with him on that point, concluded that
Mid-European cooperation after the peace settlement could
follow only economic and educational lines. Schools in the
new states, for instance, should inculcate respect and sympathy for neighboring nations. An American efficiency
expert, Henry L. Gantt, soberly pleaded that an economic
union of the nationalities was necessary for the welfare of
all.

At the last formal session, delegates of twelve nationalities affixed their signatures to a "declaration of the common
aims of the Independent Mid-European Nations," phrased in
prudently general language. The salient clauses affirmed the
fundamental concepts of government by consent and of

selfdetermination, repudiated secret diplomacy, promised civil rights to all citizens, pledged coordinated efforts to preserve the liberties of the new nations, and endorsed the principle of a league of nations. Signatories promised that these ideas would be incorporated in the constitutions of their respective states.[33]

There was no lack of drama in the ceremony surrounding the signing of the declaration, which took place in the room where Jefferson, Franklin, Hancock, and the other men of 1776 had put their names on the Declaration of Independence. The guard of honor on either side of the dais included a youth whose forebears had signed the Magna Carta and the American Declaration. Miller introduced each signer as he came forward.[34] Unquestionably, one objective of the Union had been achieved: knowledge of the several nationalities had been more widely spread across the United States. Although Masaryk dispatched a message to President Wilson hoping to elicit approval of what was being done, the tardy answer of the Chief Executive, voicing "deep pleasure that there should be such impressive and irresistible unanimity of principle and purpose," shot somewhat wide of the mark, since irreconcilable differences persisted inside the Union.

Reflecting upon the labors at Independence Hall, one editor felt that America was subtly building up valuable political capital for the future. "The conquests we are making," he wrote, "are of the sort that must endure through all time, above all wars and over all dissensions. They are conquests of friendship. . . . The work of unselfish idealism

[33] "Minutes of the Union," October 23-26, 1918, Miller Papers.
[34] Whirring motion-picture cameras and policemen with clubs, an observer lamented, robbed the affair of "Jeffersonian simplicity." He missed "the stateliness and dignity that might have been expected" when the new Middle-Europe Union took its place among the nations of the world." Philadelphia *Inquirer,* October 27, 1918.

that we are contributing in Middle Europe . . . will surely persist to operate in our behalf and to be like bread upon the waters that returns after many days." Another editor regretted that the delegates "did not discuss in detail the most serious difficulties in the way of cooperation." "The day of sacred egoism for any nation has passed," he confidently, if prematurely, asserted. Faith still prevailed that a confederation of Slav states, as a rampart against Germany, would somehow come into being.[35]

Before the fighting in Europe ceased, the Union convened on two occasions, once in Washington, once in New York. It was decided that the publicity campaign should be intensified, and that the Union should promote public order in Central Europe and aid in the building of democratically oriented states. Again the Union urged quiet, informal exchanges on conflicting territorial ambitions.[36] When reports of armed clashes between Poles and Ukrainians in eastern Galicia created tensions within the Union, Sychynski, acting for the Ukrainians, appealed to the Polish representatives to make use of the good offices of the Union to halt the hostilities. Instead, the Polish National Council ostentatiously resigned and could not be coaxed into reversing its decision. With daggers pointed toward the Italians, the Yugoslavs threatened to emulate the Polish example.

As soon as armistices had been signed with the central empires, the Union rapidly disintegrated. Masaryk had calculated that the Union would have six months to accomplish its purposes, but the fighting stopped much sooner than expected. He promptly made plans to return to Europe and recommended at a meeting in Washington that the

[35] Philadelphia *Evening Public Ledger*, October 28, 1918; *New York Times*, October 28, 31, 1918. See also, Simeon D. Fess, "Mid-European Union: A Bar to Germans," *New York Times*, December 1, 1918.

[36] "Minutes of the Union," October 30, November 6, 1918, Miller Papers.

Union move its activities to Paris, where it would be in a strategic position to influence the decisions of the peace conference. Miller warmly seconded not only that suggestion but also a fresh plea by Masaryk for discussion on frontiers. Sychynski delivered a detailed indictment of Polish territorial claims and requested endorsement of a Ukrainian state extending eastward from central Galicia. The boundaries of Poland, he argued, should be fixed strictly in keeping with the prescriptions of Wilson's Thirteenth Point. Problems of reconstruction in Central Europe provoked heated discussion; Masaryk reported that bankers in New York were willing to extend loans, but the Union voted to ask Henry Ford and large American industrial companies to help in rehabilitation.[37]

On the eve of Masaryk's departure for Europe, the Union decided that he should take charge of a Paris branch of the organization, while Miller acted as chairman in the United States. Once more, the subject of soliciting the cooperation of American financiers in the rehabilitation of Central Europe was explored. Extreme caution would be necessary, Miller counseled, lest cunning Wall Street financiers acquire a dominant position in Central Europe. For the future, the Union might well concentrate on shaping sentiment in America regarding reconstruction and the peace settlements, and a publicity expert should be employed for that purpose. Miller urged the Union to promote economic cooperation in Central Europe by means of an international railway network and international control of ports handling commerce for the region.[38]

On November 26, what proved to be the final meeting of the Union was convened. Claiming that the Union was not properly supporting Yugoslavia in its territorial con-

[37] *Ibid.*, November 12, 1918.
[38] *Ibid.*, November 18, 1918; *New York Times*, November 25, 1918.

tentions with Italy, Hinković withdrew. That action reflected
in part a schism within the Yugoslav contingent in America,
for Hinković was advocating a federalized Yugoslav republic,
while partisans of the Serbs wished to perpetuate the
Karageorgevich dynasty in a tightly integrated kingdom. A
prominent Serb, Professor Mihajlo F. Pupin of Columbia
University, declared that the South Slavs would rally enthusiastically behind the Union. It was agreed that members
of the Union should go to Paris, where with their American
outlook they would be in a position to exert a salutary
influence upon the peacemakers of their respective homelands. A tentative suggestion that Henry Ford might finance
the projected educational activities of the Union in return
for a monopoly on the sale of tractors in the new countries
was brushed aside. But a constitution and bylaws for the
organization, the result of weeks of hard work, were unanimously approved. The objectives of the Union were described as follows: to aid oppressed nationalities in Central
Europe and Asia Minor in winning their freedom; to
disseminate information on the just demands of these nationalities; to exert pressure at the peace conference to realize
these ends; and to ensure mutual cooperation in the tasks
of reconstruction.[39]

For all practical purposes that affirmation sounded the
knell of the Union. In midsummer of 1919, Miller wound
up the affairs of the organization and returned to the tran-
quility of Oberlin. Beyond doubt, the Union accomplished
something in arousing shortlived American interest in Central Europe and urging the dismemberment of Austria-
Hungary; yet almost from the beginning clashing territorial
aspirations thwarted the exalted objectives that Masaryk and
Miller cherished so devoutly. Someone has well said, "The

[39] "Minutes of the Union," November 26, 1918, Miller Papers.

story of the Mid-European Union shows not only Masaryk's wisdom and foresight. It reveals the fact that the New Europe which he had in mind refused to be born."[40]

[40] Herbert A. Miller, "Statement concerning the history and present prospects of the Mid-European Union" (undated, but apparently written in the summer of 1919), Miller Papers; J. B. Kozak, "The Legacy of T. G. Masaryk," *Czechoslovak Government Press Bureau*, April 20, 1945.

THE POLES

Louis L. Gerson

The entrance of the United States into the First World War
had a significant effect on the liberation of East Central
European peoples and the rebirth of their nations. The
diplomatic and military involvement of America in the affairs
of Europe introduced the idea that every nation should be
free to govern itself and that such freedom is an essential
condition of a lasting peace. In accordance with this principle there arose, at the end of the war, a new political order
in the large region of Europe between Germany and the
newly established communist state of Soviet Russia. Poland
was one of the states reborn as a result of the war.

The First World War did not start as an ideological
crusade. In 1914, none of the belligerent nations was in
favor of liberating oppressed nationalities or extending
democracy.[1] There were two powerful deterrents to any
formulation of a policy of liberation. One stemmed from
the alliance of the Western Powers with Tsarist Russia; the
other resulted from the unwillingness of the Entente Powers
and the United States to dismember the Habsburg Empire.
Then too, as long as there was a hope of separating Austria-
Hungary from Germany, the Allies—particularly the United
States—did not want to alienate the Habsburg empire by an
outright policy of liberation.[2] By 1917, however, the belligerent nations were exhausted and near moral and physical
collapse. To win sympathy and to maintain the morale of
their suffering peoples, governments resorted to ideological
appeals. Psychological warfare, as it was called in the
Second World War, became a vital weapon from the time
of American intervention and the Russian revolution.

The Bolshevik Revolution of 1917, and especially the negotiations at Brest-Litovsk, forced the United States and the Allies to present to the world a complete outline of their war and peace aims. A program had to be devised which, among other things, could induce national or political groups in the enemy countries to support the Allies. Soviet propaganda from Brest-Litovsk, which promised independence to Poland and other nationalities, had to be countered. By proclaiming the principle of liberation of nationalities, Lenin threatened to capture full control of the psychological offensive.

To Lenin, selfdetermination was primarily a tactical device for exploitation in the struggle for power. Like all democratic phrases, selfdetermination did not mean the same thing for him as for the West. The fundamental view on the nationality question that guided Lenin until the end of his life was that the primary task of his party was to "assist the self-determination, not of peoples or of nations, but of the proletariat of every nationality." At all times, his support of nationalities depended on the interest of the proletariat.[3]

Nevertheless, Bolshevik policy toward nationalities was misunderstood by the West as well as by many leaders of nationality groups in Europe. To many, the Soviet revolution transformed the war into a crusade for the liberation of oppressed nationalities. The democratic phraseology of the Bolsheviks inspired confidence and hope in the hearts of some patriots, labor leaders, and liberals, while conservatives were aghast at the consequences of the collapse of Tsarist Russia. The former cheered the change; the latter, believing communism to be a temporary aberration, attempted to

[1] Georges Clemenceau, *Grandeur and Misery of Victory* (1930), 180.
[2] Victor S. Mamatey, *The United States and East Central Europe, 1914-1918* (1957), 269.
[3] V. I. Lenin, *Sochineniia*, 3rd ed. (1935), 337-39.

restore the empire in the hope that it would continue to play a vital role in the European balance of power. Neither way held out any real hope for the liberation of oppressed nationalities.

It was natural that Woodrow Wilson should become the champion and apostle of selfdetermination in the first months of 1918. The Bolshevik bid for leadership in the nationalist movement menaced not only the Allied cause but also the future character and composition of the states created out of the crumbling empires of Russia, Germany, and Austria-Hungary. Communist propaganda, which appealed to the hungry, tired, and disillusioned, had to be countered and Wilson took up the challenge to compete with Lenin for the minds of men.[4] A clear statement of the peace objectives of the United States, Wilson believed, would inspire liberal and socialist elements everywhere to support a peace settlement based on justice. Moreover, it might also convince the Bolsheviks themselves not to withdraw from the war. On January 8, 1918, Wilson proclaimed his Fourteen Points, which became the signpost for a new liberal world. It attracted whole nationalities to the Allied side; it held out hope for defeated Germany; and it promised a new international order.

In justice to Wilson, it is important to note that he was the first President, indeed the first Western leader, to respond to the Soviet communist challenge. Neither in the experience of the American people nor in their traditions could Wilson find an easy rationalization, a simple justification, or guiding principles sanctioned by usage or custom, to answer not only the Soviet challenge but also the demands, hopes, and aspirations of the peoples in war-torn Europe.

Wilson saw the need of adapting the historic principle

[4] Stephen Gwyn, ed., *The Letters and Friendships of Sir Cecil Spring Rice* (1929), II, 423.

of noninvolvement in European affairs to the changing conditions of his time. To accomplish this, he sought in selfdetermination the bridge between isolationism and internationalism. Wilson's championship of selfdetermination was rooted in realism and idealism. Although before 1914 the President had not been deeply interested in the fate of East Central Europe, by 1918 this area confronted him with problems of great magnitude, which demanded both action and an ideological response. Unhesitatingly and with enthusiasm, he formed his foreign policy on the principles of the "new freedom" which he sought to apply at home—faith in morality as the basis of action; belief in the capacity of people to govern themselves; and the conviction that the mission of the United States was to broaden the area of world peace and prosperity. Furthermore, American tradition, he believed, was on the side of selfdetermination. Had not the English freemen in colonial America revolted against the empire in the name of selfdetermination?

In 1918, the political reality in East Central Europe seemed to be in accord with Wilson's ideas. Then he could say with evident sincerity and conviction, as he did on February 11, "Self-determination is not a mere phrase. It is an imperative principle of action which statesmen will henceforth ignore at their peril." Selfdetermination thus became a keystone of his foreign policy.

In his Fourteen Points Wilson did not commit himself fully to the idea of selfdetermination; the time was not yet propitious. The President was aware of the danger of advocating a principle which, if narrowly and specifically defined, could easily have defeated his whole peace program. Points X, XI, and XII testify that Wilson was not prepared to advocate full application of the principle. "The peoples of Austria-Hungary," Point X states cautiously, "whose place among the nations we wish to see safe-guarded and assured, should be accorded the great opportunity of autonomous development."[5] Point XI, dealing with Rumania, Serbia, and Montenegro, merely asks that "relations of the several Balkan states to one another should be determined by friendly counsel along historically established lines of allegiance and nationality." Point XII, which concerns itself with the liquidation of the Ottoman Empire, pleads that the non-Turkish nationalities should be "assured . . . an absolutely unmolested opportunity of autonomous development."

The outright and unqualified commitment to an independent Poland in the thirteenth point highlights the ambiguous application of the principle of selfdetermination in the three preceding points. More than that, it demonstrates the uniqueness of the Polish cause in the Wilsonian program. Poland was the only nation in East Central Europe that was accorded individual attention. It should be further noted that the President and his advisers were aware that the nationality and religious conflicts that would accompany the rebirth of Poland would in no way be less intense and chaotic than those that would follow the breakup of the Dual Monarchy.

The thirteenth point was a result of the existence of a large Polish-American community in the United States and the extraordinarily skillful propaganda with which its spokesman, Ignace Jan Paderewski, swayed Colonel House. In 1914 Polish immigrants outnumbered those of any other nationality of the East Central European area; they were almost three times as numerous as the Czechs and Slovaks. The very number of American Poles made them important in American life. Moreover, they enjoyed special advantages. One was the pro-Polish tradition which had grown out of American attitudes toward Thaddeus Kosciuszko and Casimir Pulaski, Poles who had fought for American independence during the Revolution. Another was the sympathy

---

[5] Mamatey, *The United States and East Central Europe*, 179.

which Americans have always felt for oppressed peoples. Literate Americans were well aware of the injustices that Poland had suffered as a result of the eighteenth-century partitions and the later heroic but unsuccessful revolutions of 1830, 1848, and 1863.[6]

The outbreak of the First World War increased the patriotic ambitions of immigrant groups in the United States. The Polish-American community was no exception. This natural interest in the fate of the old country did not escape the notice of American party strategists. Politicians in charge of winning elections began to appeal to the deeply ingrained cultural traditions, attitudes, and experience of Polish-Americans. Seizing on such issues as the literacy tests required of immigrants to the United States, promises of relief to the war-ravaged Polish population, and the American debt to Kosciuszko and Pulaski, they were able to reach and bring to the surface the emotional attachments to Poland. More than that, they openly encouraged American Poles, who had not hitherto been politically organized, to unite into effective, closely knit political units. Once this was accomplished, Polish-American leaders were able to make their demands felt by the American government—often with telling results.

Democratic party regulars had little difficulty convincing Wilson of the importance of the Polish-American vote. In the 1916 election campaign an allout effort was made to capture their allegiance. Soon after his renomination, Wilson took a firm stand against requiring literacy tests of immigrants. This was followed by strong appeals to the Central Powers for the relief of starvation in Poland. Wilson's humanitarianism and ethical considerations for war sufferers merged with his political ambition. They also laid the foundation for sympathy for the Polish demands for unity,

[6] Louis L. Gerson, *Woodrow Wilson and the Rebirth of Poland* (1953).

and for some kind of independence for the nation. Polish-American organizations were quick to sense the significance of Wilson's new attitude. Letters from prominent Polish-American leaders endorsing Wilson's action and praising him for having "solidified the great Polish-American vote" began to pour into the White House.[7]

The climax of Wilson's attempt to capture the Polish-American vote came on October 26, 1916, when he delicately reminded the Poles abroad and the Polish-Americans that they were "unorganized." In the same speech, the President invited Americans of foreign birth to come to the White House to interpret for him and for the American people the problems and issues of Europe at war. "I venture to say," Wilson continued, "that America is the only country that understands the other countries of the world. Men of our own citizenship can interpret for us all of the countries of the world. . . ."[8] Wilson, no doubt influenced by his political advisers, wanted to organize Polish-Americans for his reelection. In so doing, the President furthered Paderewski's political ends as well. Wilson was to profit, but it was Paderewski who profited most.

A short time after Wilson's suggestion for Polish-American unity in backing his campaign, he allowed Colonel House and Paderewski to persuade him that the latter was the spokesman of Polish-Americans. Recognizing Paderewski as head of the Poles in the United States was to be a way of keeping Wilson at the head of those same voters. Under the leadership of Paderewski, Polish-Americans kept alive the ideal of Polish independence and offered financial support and political pressure at critical moments. It mattered

[7] Roman L. Modra to Wilson, August 24, 1916, Wilson Papers, Library of Congress.

[8] Cincinnati *Enquirer*, October 27, 1916. Wilson undoubtedly believed that Americans of foreign origin could and should interpret European events for him and suggest policies.

not whether they really voted as a bloc, or whether all of them were really united behind Paderewski.[9] What mattered was the conviction held by the political strategists that American Poles voted or could be made to vote on the basis of their national origin, and—what is perhaps more important —the fact that Wilson was convinced that Paderewski represented all Polish-Americans as well as all the Poles in Europe.

Paderewski had come to the United States in 1915 as the representative of the Polish National Committee headed by Roman Dmowski. The United States was of the utmost importance to the Polish cause. In no other country outside Poland were there so many Poles. No other country could supply so much money to relieve Poland's devastation, and to help the political activities of the committee. Moreover, the voice of the United States carried authority.

The famous pianist was the best person the Poles could have found to present their case to the American people and their leaders. When Paderewski arrived, he lost no time in cultivating prominent Americans. On November 12, 1915, he met the right person in Colonel Edward M. House, Woodrow Wilson's confidant.[10]

It was House who did his best to keep the President in

[9] House Diary, August 5, 1918, House Papers, Yale University Library.

[10] On June 27, 1925, Paderewski told House how the meeting had come about. In his diary, House recorded: "We dined with the Paderewskis last night at the Carlton Hotel. . . . He told us . . . when he conceived the idea that the United States was the key to Polish freedom he came to New York in order to start a system of propaganda. He was much depressed at first because he did not have a proper avenue of approach to Wilson. One Sunday morning he saw a full page sketch in the New York Times about me, written by Charles Willis Thompson. He realized then he had found the key if he could reach me. Unhappily, none of his friends knew me. . . . He then forgot the German but in about two months he came to him one day and said 'I have got the man who will take you to Colonel House. It is Mr. R. W. Woolley, Director of the Mint.' And that, Paderewski said, was the beginning of our friendship and of the campaign we waged for Polish freedom."

line for the Polish cause during the war and the peace conference. Paderewski's brilliant propaganda was enormously advanced by the support of House, this "providential man," as the pianist-politician called the enigmatic Texan. "It was solely through Paderewski," House recorded, "that I became so deeply interested in the cause of Poland, and repeatedly passed upon the President Paderewski's views which I had made my own. That was the real influence that counted. . . ."[11]

The first dramatic instance of House's influence in behalf of a free Poland occurred on January 8, 1917, when House asked Paderewski to prepare for him a detailed memorandum on the Polish problem which he wished to submit to the President. On January 22, Wilson, in his famous "peace without victory" address, endorsed the movement for Polish independence, while still postulating the continued existence of Austria-Hungary: "No peace can last, or ought to last, which does not recognize and accept the principle that governments derive all their just powers from the consent of the governed, and that no right anywhere exists to hand peoples about from sovereignty to sovereignty as if they were property." As a "single example" he cited that "there should be a united, independent, and autonomous Poland."[12]

A year later, in the Fourteen Points, Wilson again called for complete independence of the Poles, but only for autonomy of the other Austria-Hungarian nationalities. This was a most remarkable commitment, particularly since Wilson, in the case of Poland, did not rely exclusively and fully on the Inquiry's recommendations, as he had done for the others. The Inquiry, a committee of prominent American specialists charged with preparing proposals for peace, had

---

[11] House to Orlowski, January 15, 1931, House Papers.
[12] Gerson, *The Rebirth of Poland*, 70-72.

noted in December, 1917, that the problem of Poland was "by far the most complex of all problems to be considered."[13] While it suggested the establishment of an independent and democratic Poland, the Inquiry counseled, "The form of Poland's government . . . should be left to the determination of the people of Poland acting through their chosen representatives."[14] The committee gave attention to the difficulties of drawing effective boundaries because ethnically determined lines did not conform with those desirable from an economic standpoint. "Potentially explosive" internal friction among the several minority groups within Poland was also noted. Early in January, 1918, the Inquiry further recommended:

> In our opinion the best solution of the Polish question, both economically and politically, would consist in the inclusion of Poland as a federal state in democratic Russia. The second best solution would probably be the unification of Russian and Austrian Poland as an autonomous state within the Austro-Hungarian monarchy. It is believed that the effect of the inclusion of so large a number of independent Slavs might do more than any other thing to upset the existing German Magyar ascendancy, might release the Czechs and south Slavs, might result in a reorganization of the Dual Monarchy on the federal principle with Slav preponderance, and might consequently break the ascendancy of Berlin over Vienna.[15]

Despite the grave complexities of the Polish problem, in his final consideration Wilson invoked the doctrine of self-determination. Point Thirteen read: "An independent Polish

[13] Lawrence E. Gelfand, *The Inquiry: American Preparations for Peace, 1917-1919* (1963), 146-47.
[14] Gerson, *The Rebirth of Poland*, 83.
[15] Gelfand, *The Inquiry*, 148.

state should be erected which should include the territories inhabited by indisputably Polish populations, which should be assured a free and secure access to the sea, and whose political and economic independence and territorial integrity should be guaranteed by international covenant." The thirteenth point, too, was a consequence of Paderewski's influence on House. The final drafting was guided by the Polish division of the Inquiry, headed by Robert H. Lord, and two Polish collaborators, Professors Arctowski and Zwierzchowski (Zowski), as well as by a memorandum the Polish National Committee in Paris had sent to House. The thirteenth point as House and Wilson finally wrote it came, House wrote in his diary, as near to Paderewski's committee's memorandum "as we felt was wise and expedient."[16] It was House, more than anyone else, who swung the idealism of the President behind Paderewski's efforts to bring about a large, independent, free, and united Poland, and who safeguarded it during its first formative years.

It was to be expected that Polish boundaries would pose difficulties for the statesmen in Paris. The Inquiry had recognized earlier obstacles to the application of the principle of selfdetermination. Altogether, it had drawn up forty-two reports on Polish questions, and despite Point XIII, in which Wilson had declared himself fully in favor of an independent Poland, the Inquiry was prepared to recommend alternatives such as Polish trialism within a refurbished Austrian empire. It was concerned about Polish claims to regions inhabited by large numbers of Russians and Germans, and about the consequences of establishing a Polish corridor through German territory to the Baltic Sea.

Fortunately for the Polish cause, Arctowski and Zowski saw nothing wrong in supplying Paderewski and Dmowski with information about the Inquiry's activities relating to

[16] Gerson, *The Rebirth of Poland*, 83, note.

the Polish question. During September, 1918, the Polish nationalist representatives in the United States learned from them that the Polish division had not received instructions to assemble data concerning a Polish corridor. Knowing this, the Polish leaders asked the Polish National Council of Chicago to mount a campaign of pressure on Wilson to favor not only the creation of a corridor but the absorption of the Baltic provinces, including the port of Danzig, into a reborn Poland.

By the time of the Peace Conference, January, 1919, Wilson and the Inquiry had gone through a remarkable metamorphosis. The President's pro-Polish feeling had begun to cool considerably; the Inquiry had lost its inhibitions and uncertainties about the Polish nationalists' territorial claims and strongly supported them. Illustratively, the Inquiry urged incorporation of Lithuania and the Duchy of Teschen in the Polish state; it recommended that Eastern Galicia, with twice as many Ukrainians as Poles, be assigned to Poland "only if the Ukraine is in its present state of chaos," its autonomy to be watched over by the League of Nations; and it supported Polish claims in the Baltic coastal region, including those for a Polish corridor that would sever East Prussia from Germany and the incorporation of Danzig, a predominantly German-inhabited city, in Poland.

Wilson, despite pressures from the Inquiry, set aside the pro-Polish recommendations: Danzig was made a free city; Lithuania became an independent state; other recommendations, with the notable exception of that for a Polish corridor, were modified in favor of Poland's neighbors. Wilson became aware, at the Peace Conference, of the inapplicability of his principle of selfdetermination in the face of European nationalistic ambitions. By then, too, he was increasingly apprehensive of the consequences of political pressure from Polish-Americans under the ostensible leadership of Paderewski and the certainty of embarrassment over championing one ethnic group in a country that abounded in hyphenates.

Wilson's espousal of a free and independent Poland, like his advocacy of selfdetermination, was a blend of realism and idealism. In a sense, it is true that in 1918 it required no particular boldness to advocate the recreation of Poland. The political process that led to the revival of the Polish state began with rival concessions to Polish nationalism on the part of three belligerents, Russia, Germany, and Austria-Hungary, when the immediate exigencies of the war compelled them. It must be remembered, however, that by "Poland" Germany and Austria-Hungary meant the Russian part of Poland "in union with them;" Russia meant the Poland under her tutelage. After the collapse of Tsarist Russia, the Russian provisional government came out in favor of a free Poland which was to be "in a free military union" with Russia and whose boundaries were to be settled by the Russian Constituent Assembly. Even the Bolshevik Revolution with its espousal of selfdetermination brought no promise of a free, reunited, and independent Poland. In part then, the thirteenth point was a reiteration of promises, albeit dubious, already made. It was only when the United States entered the conflict that Poland had, for the first time, a wholly disinterested force at work on her side—one whose commitment to selfdetermination for Poland had no strings or reservations. "Without the powerful support of President Wilson whose heart has been won to our cause by our best friend, Colonel House," Paderewski acknowledged in his last speech before the Polish Parliament, "Poland would undoubtedly still remain an internal question of Germany and Russia. . . ."[17]

[17] *Ibid.*, 96-97.

Paderewski's statement is significant for what it contains, but perhaps more significant for what it omits. To be sure, it was motivated by deep respect and appreciation of Wilson's role in the restoration of Poland. But over and above that, it was calculated to strengthen what Paderewski believed to be his right to lead the resurrected Polish state. By extolling Wilson, Paderewski acclaimed himself the founder of the reborn nation. In so doing, he minimized the revolutionary role of patriots in partitioned Poland—men like Jozef Pilsudski, the hero who had led Polish legions against the three partitioning powers, Russia, Austria, and Germany. While he was in the United States, Paderewski was able to win the undisputed right to speak for Poland, with the concomitant understanding that once Poland were free he would head its government. Both Wilson and House expected that and were willing to make it happen.[18] Though in the United States Paderewski's contributions to the cause of Polish freedom had overshadowed Pilsudski's, it was not so in Poland. At the end of the war Pilsudski gained control of the new government despite the efforts of Paderewski—with the help of the United States—to supplant him. In December, 1919, Paderewski voluntarily exiled himself from his native country for whose freedom he had labored with great conviction.

Wilson's greatness lay in his ability to project American political tradition into a liberal international faith. He did so eloquently. It has been said that the main weakness of Wilson's international order lay in the generality of his principles, particularly that of selfdetermination. Robert Lansing and other critics have pointed out its contradictory nature and its impracticality as a universal tenet. Yet, for all its weakness, it became a foundation upon which the new,

[18] House Diary, June 4, 1919, House Papers.

reborn, and transformed states in East Central Europe were built. With more insight into the realities of European politics and more good will on the part of the European allies, as well as the succession states, Wilson's program could have been better adapted to historic forces.

THE JEWS

Morton Tenzer

In August, 1914, European tensions exploded into a general war. Everything that had been would be changed. The war was greeted with shock, horror, and enthusiasm; outbursts of hysteria and patriotism encouraged the men in the first military offensives that began the mass slaughter. In America, aside from slight incredulity in educated circles, the outbreak of the European war was generally received with indifference. In the Middle West and on the Pacific Coast there was almost no concern at all with the subject. Only certain interested parties were immediately forced to action. The government adopted a policy of strict neutrality; armament manufacturers planned expansion of their facilities; foreign traders were cautious; and editors dispatched correspondents abroad; but at least one local branch of an international organization felt the situation so desperate for its own interests that it convened on August 30, within weeks of the European mobilizations, an extraordinary conference of its membership to take account of the drastic impact of the war on the organization's operations, and to formulate policies to meet the problem. These were the American Zionists.

The Zionist movement in America had been weak until that time, but the war was the occasion for its rapid growth in influence and prestige in the American Jewish community. Zionism became, during the war, a dominating force in American Jewry and an important influence on United States foreign policy. The Zionists were determined that what they thought were the interests of the Jews should be given due consideration in the making of the peace. The Zionist con-

ception of Jewish interest was outlined at the first World
Zionist Congress held in 1897 in Basle, Switzerland, under
the leadership of Theodore Herzl. The Basle program speci-
fied: "The aim of Zionism is to create for the Jewish people
a home in Palestine secured by public law."

Most non-Zionist American Jews thought that Jewish
interests could best be achieved by securing civil, political,
and cultural rights for Jews in countries that had previously
denied these rights. Still other Jews felt there were no
special Jewish interests in the outcome of the war, since
they believed that Jews shared the political interests of the
countries in which they lived, or the interests of the social
classes to which they belonged. By the time the peace was
to be made, however, the Zionist definition of Jewish interest
(which included concern for Jewish rights in Europe) had
become the dominant interpretation among American Jews
and among the world's statesmen, including President Wilson.

How did that small group of men in New York who
founded the Provisional Executive Committee for General
Zionist Affairs in August, 1914, expand their influence so
decisively among their fellow Jews and in connection with
government policy? Part of the answer to this question lies
in the history, structure, and motivation of American Jewry,
which was essentially divided into two ethnic stocks, about a
half million German Jews most of whom had come to the
United States before 1880 and two and a half million East
European Jews who had immigrated primarily in the two
decades before the outbreak of the war. The Germans were
relatively well assimilated into the American society and
culture and, by the decade before the war, had achieved a
fair measure of economic prosperity. While many were concentrated in the large eastern seaboard cities, there were
centers of German-Jewish life in the Ohio valley in Cincin-

nati and in Louisville. Politically, the Germans were by and large Republicans after the Civil War.[1] They had brought from Germany and developed in America a tendency toward Reform Judaism, which departed radically from the customs and rituals of the Orthodox faith. They created a host of philanthropic and charitable institutions, and such families as the Belmonts, Seligmans, Loebs, Strauses, Kahns, Schiffs, Rosenwalds, Untermeyers, Guggenheims, Flexners, Adlers, Pulitzers, Ochses, Sulzbergers, and Morgenthaus reached prominence in American finance, commerce, industry, journalism, law, medicine, and public service. The bourgeois elite of American Jewry, they were for the most part decidedly hostile to Zionism.

The flood of East European Jews differed markedly from the Germans economically, politically, and in religious belief. They crowded into the slums of large urban centers (in New York City lived 1,500,000, the largest concentration of Jews in the world, comprising about half the Jewish population in the United States, and one tenth of the whole of world Jewry). They were desperately poor, and provided the factories and shops, especially in the garment industry, with cheap labor. They spoke Yiddish, and came from the fiercely orthodox religious background of the East European ghetto. A small number of them were radical intellectuals who spread socialist ideas among their brethren working in the infamous sweat shops of the garment trade. A sprinkling were Zionists. The East European Jews, freed from the restrictions of the ghetto, experienced a rare creative outburst in the new world. They developed fully for the first time their own literature, art, theater, and press. Although the German Jews dominated financially and socially, the East Europeans, outnumbering them by far, gave

[1] Lawrence H. Fuchs, *The Political Behavior of American Jews* (1956), 43-47.

the American Jewish community the qualities which have, for better or worse, served to define the Jews as a group in American society.

Both elements of American Jewry shared a powerful tendency toward assimilation, the Germans openly and directly, the East Europeans more ambivalently. Loyalty to the old country and concern with the problems and politics of their native lands retarded the Americanization of other immigrant groups. Hierarchical church organizations that were experienced in resisting alienating cultural pressures in Ireland or Poland also may have retarded their acculturation. Among the Jews no such distracting patriotisms existed; on the contrary, most Jews had been denied citizenship and civil rights in their native lands, and had never identified themselves as Polish, Russian, Hungarian, or Rumanian, but always as Jewish.[2] They were deaf to sentimental appeals about the problems of their native lands (but not to the difficulties of Jews still there) and they threw themselves with vivid determination into an effort to become Americanized. Many German Jews did, however, have a sentimental attachment to Germany and especially to German culture. The Jewish religion in America with its congregational basis and theological liberalism encouraged assimilation by enabling a Jew to remain within his faith while shrugging off the traditional patterns of the sacred observances of orthodoxy which in Eastern Europe had permeated all Jewish social life. The immigrant Jews were rapidly assimilated, flooding the available educational facilities. (The proportion of Jews in City College of New York in 1916 was estimated at 85 percent.)[3] Another powerful factor encouraging Americanization was the Yiddish press, which served to introduce the immigrant to his new country. By

[2] Robert E. Park and Herbert H. Miller, *Old World Traits Transplanted* (1921).

[3] *The American Jewish Yearbook*, XIX (1917-1918), 407.

1916, the circulation of the Yiddish daily press in the New York area was a staggering 532,787 copies. These papers featured popular articles on science and American history, grammar lessons, essays, short stories, and serialized novels. They helped transform the ignorant "greenhorn" from rural Eastern Europe into an alert, albeit sketchily informed, urban participant in American life.[4]

The Jews had come to America to stay. They brought their families with them, and 94.8 percent remained in the United States, while among other pre-World-War-I immigrants as many as two in three returned to their homelands. Nearly half (45.8 percent) of Jewish immigrants between 1900 and 1925 were women; among all other immigrant groups in this period, only 32.9 percent were women.[5] The German and East European Jews shared not only a common drive toward assimilation but a sense of common identity. The Germans acknowledged this bond in generous philanthropies for their less advantaged brethren at the same time that they kept their social, political, and religious distances and distinctions.[6] Zionism served as a bridge through which this sense of identity could be given political expression.

The leadership of the American Jewish community in 1914 was still in the hands of those of German descent. Men like Louis Marshall, Simon Wolf, Cyrus Adler, Oscar S. Straus, Julius Rosenwald, and Jacob H. Schiff were op-

[4] Mordecai Soltes, *The Yiddish Press: An Americanizing Agency* (1923). On pages 182-86 is listed political affiliations and circulation of the Yiddish press in this period.

[5] See the table, "The Remigration of Various Peoples from the United States (1908-1925)," in Jacob Lestschinsky, "Jewish Migrations, 1840-1946," in Louis Finkelstein, ed., *The Jews: Their History, Culture, and Religion* (1949), IV, 1227, 1228. The remigration rate of the Rumanians is given as 67 percent, of the Magyars, 64.2 percent, of the Italians, 55.8 percent. The Jewish rate was 5.2 percent. The next lowest rate was the Germans' 15.3 percent.

[6] Zosa Szajkowski, "The Attitudes of American Jews to East European Jewish Immigration (1881-1893)," *Publications of the American Jewish Historical Society*, XL (1951), 221-80.

posed to Zionism not only because of its national and political orientation but also on religious grounds, since Zionism contradicted the Reform view that the Jews were a religious and not a national or racial community. This wealthy, politically conservative, and theologically liberal point of view was promoted by the American Jewish Committee, an organization led and financed by lawyer Marshall, banker Schiff, and other figures in the German Jewish group. The committee, founded by these men in 1906 in the aftermath of Russian anti-Semitic outrages, attempted to act as spokesman for the Jewish point of view in American life, and to extend assistance to victims of anti-Jewish persecution around the world. To displace the American Jewish Committee was a major tactical aim of the Zionists in this period.[7]

The shift from Zionist weakness to strength can be illustrated briefly and dramatically. At the outbreak of the war, there were 14,000 Shekel payers (members) in the loose grouping that was known as The Federation of American Zionists. In June, 1914, the annual convention of the federation adopted a budget amounting to only $12,150.[8] It did not even have a full-time president; Henry Friedenwald, a Baltimore dentist, was the honorary president, succeeding Professor Richard Gottheil of Columbia University, and the organization was run by a young man named Louis Lipsky, the chairman of its executive committee. There was no one of broad national distinction on either the administrative or the executive committee.

The well organized Zionist Organization of America, which claimed a total membership of 144,820, had by 1919

[7] Nathan Schachner, *The Price of Liberty: A History of the American Jewish Committee* (1948) is an uncritical authorized history of the organization. I have been permitted to read the executive committee's minutes and its correspondence covering this period in the archives of the American Jewish Committee.

[8] *American Jewish Yearbook*, XV (1913-1914), 137.

replaced the decentralized and impoverished Federation. From a small group the Zionists grew into a mass movement with numerous subsidiary organizations and publications. Millions of dollars were raised for war relief, Palestine development, and internal organization. Among the officers were such nationally prominent men as Supreme Court Justice Louis D. Brandeis (its honorary president), Judge Julian Mack of the United States Circuit Court, and Rabbi Stephen S. Wise. On the executive committee were Felix Frankfurter, Horace Kallen, Lincoln Kirstein, Nathan Straus, and Eugene Meyer, Jr. Perhaps most important, the Zionist movement developed from a small fringe group to one with the best political connections of any Zionist party in the world. Men like Brandeis, Frankfurter, and Wise had easy personal and official access to the leaders of the Wilson administration and to Colonel Edward M. House and President Wilson himself. The Zionists grew to dominance through the mechanism of the American Jewish Congress, which they used to legitimize a pro-Palestine posture among the American Jewry. The Zionists created and organized the Congress to replace the American Jewish Committee as the spokesman for the American Jews on general Jewish questions; adherents of the Congress assailed the Committee as undemocratic and elitist, and claimed that they were representative of Jewish opinion. The only issue really dividing the Congress and Committee groups before 1917 was the question of Palestine, and whether or not demands should be made at the end of the war concerning Palestine's future. The Congress supported such (Zionist) demands; the Committee opposed them; the demands were eventually presented to the Peace Conference, in 1919.[9]

[9] Joseph Rappaport, "Jewish Immigrants and World War I: a Study of American Jewish Press Reactions," unpublished doctoral dissertation, Columbia University, 1951, 53, 123, 212. A good summary of the Committee-Congress dispute can be found here.

A combination of fortuitous circumstances and Zionist exertions brought the weak Zionist movement to a position of strength in both Jewish and non-Jewish American circles. First and foremost, the war itself provided the opportunity for the enlistment of large numbers in the cause. The great powers had imperialist ambitions that were at least in part congruent with Zionist aims (the fragmentation of the Turkish Empire), and in this context Zionist goals became for the first time really feasible. The war also excited nationalist tensions within the United States to an unprecedented peak. Not only the Jewish nationalists, the Zionists, but the Czechs, Poles, Irish, Italians, Germans, and many other hyphenate group organizations in America grew in size and influence in the war period. The melting-pot psychology was replaced, perhaps temporarily, by an emphasis on differences. Many of these immigrants, paradoxically, took an interest in their old countries in order to be better accepted in American life. Such interests were expected of them, and among the Jews the Zionists were the custodians of a legitimizing nationalism that allowed the Jewish immigrant to emphasize his own interests while behaving like everyone else.

Another factor of decisive advantage to the Zionists was the assumption of the leadership of the movement by Louis D. Brandeis in August, 1914. His energy, acumen, national prestige, and organizational ability provided the Zionists with a generating center, an ideological rationale, a tactical flexibility, and an American "legitimization" they had previously lacked. Although Brandeis' leadership in American and world Zionism during the Wilson period has not been widely recognized, his powerful impact on American jurisprudence both as a lawyer and Associate Justice of the Supreme Court has long been acknowledged. In recent years historians have raised him to retrospective eminence in both the Wilson and New Deal eras. Wilson's most authoritative biographer call Brandeis "the chief architect of the New Freedom," and the latest volume of Arthur Schlesinger's biography of Franklin D. Roosevelt presents an account of the victory of the Brandeis adherents over their opponents in the inner circle around the President.[10] Brandeis has emerged as one of the major figures of American political life in the first half of the twentieth century. His activities in Zionist matters have been obscured partly because he carried them on while a Supreme Court Justice, ostensibly removed from the pull and passion of politics, and partly because he severed his connections with the Zionist movement in 1921 and spent the last twenty years of his life dissociated from it. In the summer of 1916, after his controversial nomination to the Supreme Court had been approved by the Senate, he publicly resigned his official Zionist positions, but privately continued to run the Zionist movement in America. Daily reports, including a statement of the movement's financial situation, were sent to him in Washington from Zionist headquarters in New York, and he replied with a stream of directions, exhortations, and advice. Although he operated behind the scenes, Brandeis was an extremely active organizational leader and was referred to as "the Chief" by the top echelon of the Zionist movement. The leaders of European Zionism addressed their communications to him as the American leader, and they consulted him regarding the broad strategy of the world movement. In the spring of 1917, when Arthur Balfour, the British Foreign Minister, led a mission to the United States to coordinate the war effort, he had private meetings with the Supreme Court Justice to discuss the future of Palestine. These discussions laid part of the

[10] Arthur S. Link, *Wilson: The Road to the White House*, I (1947); Arthur Schlesinger, Jr., *The Age of Roosevelt: The Politics of Upheaval*, III (1960).

groundwork for the issuance of the Balfour Declaration that autumn.[11]

Brandeis brought other men of high caliber into leadership positions in Zionist affairs, and his personal relationship with President Wilson helped influence both the government and non-Zionist Jews in favor of Zionist policies. His other friendships with men in politics, labor, and law, his long association with progressive leaders, and his reputation for liberalism and probity helped rally the general American public, the Congress, and the press to the Zionist cause. Brandeis gave speeches and interviews, wrote on Zionist subjects, and inspired favorable articles by his old acquaintances in the press.[12]

Superior organization was another important element in the rise of the Zionists to dominance. Even before Brandeis, they were committed to the idea of a mass organization. Their opponents, the leaders of the wealthier German Jewish element, limited themselves, until too late, to the elite American Jewish Committee, whose members were co-opted rather than recruited. Brandeis profoundly improved the regularization and centralization of procedures and the financial aspects of the Zionist organization. He constantly called for more men and money, a prerequisite for building a movement with political strength and efficacy.

"Organization, thorough and complete, can alone develop

[11] The Louis D. Brandeis Papers deposited at the University of Louisville, of which I have read microfilm facsimiles, are a rich source for the study of Brandeis' role in the Zionist movement.

[12] See Brandeis' correspondence with his friend Norman Hapgood, the editor of *Harper's Weekly*, in the Brandeis Papers. No fewer than five articles favoring Zionism were written by Hapgood and published in 1915 in *Harper's Weekly*, then a significant journal of opinion. See also such articles as "Brandeis as a Jew," *Literary Digest*, LII (1916); "Zionism and the Struggle towards Democracy," *Nation*, CI (1915); "Palestine Redeemed," *New Republic*, XVI (1918). Other favorable publicity appeared in *Atlantic Monthly, Public, Outlook, Survey, Review of Reviews, Independent*, and other journals of the period. Brandeis himself contributed pro-Zionist articles to *Outlook* and *Independent* before his elevation to the bench.

. . . leaders and the necessary support. Organize, Organize, Organize,—until every Jew in America must stand up and be counted—counted with us—or prove himself, wittingly or unwittingly, one of the few who are against their own people."[13] Brandeis not only argued powerfully for organization, he labored mightily to achieve it. He personally cultivated potential converts to Zionism among the wealthier German Jewish elements, and he sponsored youth and university Zionist groups. If such a comparison is not misunderstood, it may be helpful to say that if Theodore Herzl was the Marx of the Zionist movement, providing its theoretical base, then Brandeis was its Lenin, who created its operational form.

The Zionists possessed other advantages in their struggle for influence on American foreign policy. Their ideology gave them a sense of direction, an objective to which they could bend all their efforts. The non-Zionist and anti-Zionist Jews could only respond to Zionist maneuvers and propaganda negatively, without positive alternative policies. The Zionists knew what they wanted, and their aims appealed to the Wilsonians both because they sounded echoes of the religious basis shared by Jew and Gentile in the Old Testament, and because they seemed to be a part of the worldwide movement for the selfdetermination of peoples for which the United States was, in part, fighting the war.

Zionism combined the two major thrusts of American Jewish life—assimilation (Americanism) and self-identity (ethnocentrism). Zionism under Brandeis combined both American patriotism and Jewish nationalism in a form acceptable to the broader American society, just as Irish-American, Czech-American, Polish-American, and other ethnic patriotisms had arisen and been accepted in American life. Brandeis wrote:

[13] Louis D. Brandeis, *The Jewish Problem: How to Solve It* (1915), 16.

> Let no American imagine that Zionism is inconsistent with Patriotism. Multiple loyalties are objectionable only if they are inconsistent. A man is a better citizen of the United States for being also a loyal citizen of his state, and of his city. . . . Every Irish-American who contributed towards advancing home rule was a better man and a better American for the sacrifice he made. Every American Jew who aids in advancing the Jewish settlement in Palestine, though he feels that neither he nor his descendants will ever live there, will likewise be a better man and a better American for doing so. . . .
>
> There is no inconsistency between loyalty to America and loyalty to Jewry. . . . Indeed, loyalty to America demands rather that each American Jew become a Zionist. . . .[14]

The apparently contradictory drive toward assimilation and the impulse toward retention of roots, the Jewish identity, were happily fused and transformed for puzzled Jews in the Zionist movement. Ethnic patriotism, rallies, meetings, fund-raising drives, etc., were an American phenomenon. The immigrant Jews would not have dreamed of such activities back in the old country *shtetl;* yet these activities maintained, if they did not increase, the emphasis on Jewish identity. The two basic drives were also transformed: Zionism restrained the Jew from further assimilation and shifted the terms by which Jewishness was defined from religious beliefs and ritual practices to a concept of nationality that was cultural, political, and self-consciously historical in nature.

The Zionists, too, had the strategic advantage of being part of an international organization that kept them informed on relevant developments abroad, both public and clandestine. This allowed them to outmaneuver their Jewish op-

14 *Ibid.,* 12.

ponents in America—and even, in the notable instance of the Morgenthau Mission, the United States government itself. When President Wilson and Secretary Lansing decided to send Ambassador Henry Morgenthau to the Near East in June, 1917, to see if it was possible to secure for the Allies a separate peace with Turkey, the Zionists were able to head off the mission in Gibraltar and persuade Morgenthau to abandon his task.[15] (A separate peace for Turkey was against Zionist interests because the achievement of an independent Jewish Palestine required the dismemberment of the Turkish empire, of which Palestine was then a province.)

American Zionists were in communication indirectly with Berlin and Constantinople throughout the war. Sympathetic figures in the British government passed along useful information concerning political developments relating to Zionist aims in the Middle East. As early as 1915, by an extremely circuitous route, Brandeis received reports on British views toward Palestine. Alfred Zimmern in London, after interviewing Lord Percy, wrote to Horace Kallen in Madison, Wisconsin. Kallen then relayed the information to Brandeis in Boston. Later Lewis B. Namier also served as an informant for the American Zionists, and Percy, who shared a house in Washington with Felix Frankfurter, Brandeis' chief disciple, was won over completely to the Zionist cause. Zimmern, Namier, and Percy were all officials in the British Foreign Office during World War I.[16] Despite the difficulties and interruptions in wartime communications, the American Zionists were far better informed on matters in which they were interested than the State Department

[15] William Yale, "Ambassador Henry Morgenthau's Special Mission of 1917," *World Politics*, I (1949), 308-20. See also Harlan B. Phillips, ed., *Felix Frankfurter Reminisces* (1960), 145-53, for a different view.

[16] Horace Kallen to Brandeis, May 14, 1915, Brandeis Papers; Phillips, *Felix Frankfurter*, 105-106.

which frequently turned over to the Zionists information relating to Palestine or Jewish matters.

Also contributing to the emergence of Zionism in this period was the alignment of the Brandeis group with the cause of the Allies (although, of course, it remained formally neutral until 1917); among their Jewish opponents were some of the most prominent pro-Germans in America during the First World War, notably Jacob Schiff, the head of Kuhn, Loeb & Co., one of the most important private bankers in the country. The fact that anti-Zionist leaders were mostly Republicans, while the Zionist leaders were Progressives and Democrats, helped give the Zionists access to the Wilson administration, and the administration, by responding favorably to the Zionists, helped them in their struggle for dominance in American Jewish life. There is no reason to believe that Wilson or his administration consistently and consciously helped the Zionists in order to secure an electoral advantage among the mass of Jewish voters, although occasionally such considerations seem to have arisen. It is rather that the Zionists had prior access to the Wilson administration. In non-Zionist matters they were its supporters, its familiars; indeed, of some of them, it could be said they were members of the administration (Frankfurter, Meyer, etc.). Satisfying their Zionist requests was a congenial task, and hardly an electoral tactic.

When groups are struggling for leadership (the role of representative) within a social or ethnic grouping, the government can play a key, but paradoxical role in favoring one or another among the competitors. Wilson, by a series of actions intentional or not, "legitimized" the Zionist movement. He appointed Zionist leader Brandeis to the Supreme Court. The State Department did many petty favors for the Zionists in connection with attempts to aid war sufferers in Palestine. After some hesitation Wilson encouraged the American Jewish Congress and discouraged its opponents. Above all, Wilson gave his approval to the Balfour Declaration, placing the weight of the government behind its specific support of Zionist aims. Wilson's benevolent patronage of the Zionists allowed them to shatter the hold of the American Jewish Committee and its German Jewish leadership on American Jewish affairs, and it helped create a swelling Zionist movement in America whose demands, even if the government had been disposed against them, would have been hard to resist. By 1917, the Zionists had established a Washington office headed by Irving Peyser, with full responsibility for liaison with the government. The activities of this office, however, mainly concerned minor matters under the jurisdiction of the Shipping Board, the State Department, etc. High political matters were broached directly by the Zionist leaders with Wilson and House.

What use did the Zionists make of their position of influence with the Wilson administration in the period of peacemaking? Their primary object was to secure a homeland in Palestine for the Jewish people. As early as 1914 Brandeis had discussed Zionism with Wilson, and in December, 1916, Rabbi Stephen S. Wise, Brandeis' successor as chairman of the Provisional Executive Committee for General Zionist Affairs, called on Colonel House to enlist the latter's sympathy for the restoration of Palestine to the Jews under British suzerainty.[17] The next month, Wise submitted a memorandum on the subject to House, to which House responded favorably as he had to their conversation. These developments occurred even before the United States had entered the war.

The influential position of the American Zionists also affected Great Britain's calculations and policies in the Near

[17] Alpheus T. Mason, *Brandeis: A Free Man's Life* (1946), 451; House Diary, IX (December 16, 1916), 317.

East. By the spring of 1917, the British government was
seriously considering the possibility of issuing a declaration
of sympathy with Zionist aims. The British, sympathetic to
the Zionists, had offered them Uganda at the turn of the
century. Balfour, then running unsuccessfully for reelection
as Prime Minister, met Chaim Weizmann, leader of the
English Zionists, in 1906. It was not until ten years later,
however, that the Zionist cause was again well received in
higher British policy-making circles.[18] Not the least influential factor in the British government's decisions concerning
Palestine was its perception of the American government's
attitude. Brandeis' advocacy of Zionism to Balfour in April
and May of 1917 carried all the weight of his forceful per-
sonality plus the dignity and official influence of his position
as Justice of the Supreme Court and of his friendship with
Wilson. Brandeis also spoke to Wilson at this time and
reassured himself of Wilson's sympathy for Zionism. In
April, Nahum Sokolow, Weizmann's associate, received
assurances from the French government of its favorable
view of the Zionist aim. He went to Rome in May for an
audience with the Pope to receive assurance from that
quarter and from the Italian government that no opposition
to a Zionist proclamation would be forthcoming.[19] Brandeis
was kept informed by Weizmann of the success of Sokolow's
negotiations.

On June 29, 1917, President Wilson received Rabbi Wise,
who had succeeded Brandeis as formal chairman of the
Zionist committee. The conference, arranged at Brandeis'
suggestion, primarily concerned Wilson's wavering attitude
toward the American Jewish Congress movement, and Wise
elicited a statement from Wilson indicating sympathy for the
Congress. Wise then took up the question of a presidential

[18] Blanche E. Dugdale, *Arthur James Balfour,* II (1937), 167.
[19] Nahum Sokolow, *History of Zionism,* II (1919), 52-53.

statement on Palestine, indicating that he and Brandeis would not press for it since the United States was not at war with Turkey and such a statement would cause embarrassment in American relations with the Sublime Porte. Wilson expressed appreciation for Brandeis' and Wise's sensitivity to his problems and said to Wise, "You know of my deep interest in Zionism. . . . Whenever the time comes and you and Justice Brandeis feel that the time is ripe for me to speak and act I shall be ready."[20]

In England by the end of June, the final phase of the negotiations preceding the Balfour Declaration began. Public opinion was mobilized in favor of a statement by the government of a pro-Zionist policy. Weizmann and Lord Rothschild submitted a draft of the proposed declaration to Balfour, and a good part of the summer passed in a struggle over the measure within the cabinet, since Edmond Montagu, head of the Indian Ministry, was an ardently anti-Zionist Jew. On September 4, Lord Cecil, Balfour's assistant, cabled House to have him ascertain unofficially whether Wilson favored a British declaration of sympathy with Zionism. House, who had expressed his sympathies for Zionism to Wise earlier in the year, advised Wilson against endorsing the proposal, saying he thought there were many dangers in it, and that if he were the British he would be very chary about it.[21] House wired Cecil on September 11 that the President thought the time was not opportune for any definite statement beyond an expression of sympathy that implied no definite commitment. Wilson allowed House's caution to prevail, and the British government interpreted

[20] See the memorandum, "Two Conferences with the President; the former June 29, 1917; the latter Tuesday, August 27, 1918," in the Stephen S. Wise Papers in the custody of Rabbi Wise's daughter, Justice Justine W. Polier, New York City.

[21] Ray Stannard Baker, *Woodrow Wilson: Life and Letters*, 8 vols. (1938), VII, 256.

House's cable as a virtual veto of the proposal. This development was a severe setback to the expectations of the English Zionists. In desperation, they sent Justice Brandeis the tentative text of the declaration on September 19 to see if he could use his influence to reverse the American position. Brandeis and Rabbi Wise visited House on September 23 with the text, and House, reading it through, said that it conformed with the suggestion cabled to Cecil on September 11. He arranged for Brandeis to assure Weizmann that Wilson was in "entire sympathy" with the declaration.[22] Upon receiving this contradictory information, the British government again cabled House on October 6, this time including the proposed formula. Now Wilson concurred in it when House left it with him to examine. House dutifully relayed Wilson's approval to the British, and two weeks later on November 2, 1917, the first public pronouncement of a great power favoring Zionism was issued. Weizmann considered the House cable, giving Wilson's assent to the Balfour Declaration, a crucial weapon in the final overriding of the Montagu opposition in the war cabinet.[23]

Wilson's reversal has puzzled scholars.[24] Examination of the House diary, however, reveals that no veto was originally intended, and that the final text of the declaration, which the British and Zionists considered binding, was viewed by House and Wilson as conforming to their desire to avoid a definite commitment.[25] Wilson's responses to the inquiries

[22] See House Diary, II (September 23, 1917), 290-91.
[23] Chaim Weizmann, *Trial and Error* (1949), 261.
[24] Leopold Stein, *The Balfour Declaration* (1961), 529.
[25] The final text of the Balfour Declaration reads: "His Majesty's Government view with favour the establishment in Palestine of a national home for the Jewish people, and will use their best endeavours to facilitate the achievement of this object, it being clearly understood that nothing shall be done which may prejudice the civil and religious rights of existing non-Jewish communities in Palestine, or the rights and political status enjoyed by Jews in any other country."

about a pro-Zionist declaration were the reactions of an
extremely busy man, not terribly interested in the subject,
and ignorant of basic facts relating to the Jewish question.
House relates in his diary that one evening in February,
1918, after dinner, he and President and Mrs. Wilson
discussed "how ubiquitous Jews were." House said it was
surprising since there were so few of them in the world.
This brought on an argument about the number of Jews.
House thought about fifteen million. Mrs. Wilson guessed
fifty million, and President Wilson one hundred million.
House was right.[26]

Wilson's decision to give prior approval of the Balfour
Declaration had entirely bypassed Secretary Lansing and the
State Department. After learning of the declaration, Lansing
wired Ambassador Walter Hines Page in London on December 15: "Investigate discreetly and report fully and promptly
to the Department reasons for Balfour's recent statement
relative to the Jewish state in Palestine."[27]

Lansing had openly expressed himself against Zionism to
Wilson. On December 13, he wrote to the President:

> There is being brought considerable pressure for
> the issuance of a declaration in regard to this Gov-
> ernment's attitude as to the disposition to be made
> of Palestine. This emanates naturally from the
> Zionist element of the Jews.
> My judgment is that we should go very slowly
> in announcing a policy for three reasons. First, we
> are not at war with Turkey and therefore should
> avoid any appearance of favoring taking territory
> from that Empire by force. Second, the Jews are
> by no means united in the desire to reestablish
> their race as an independent people; to favor one
> or the other faction seems unwise. Third, many

26 House Diary, XIII (Feb. 28, 1918), 80.
27 *Foreign Relations of the United States, 1917: Supplement 2*, I, 317.

Christian sects and individuals would undoubtedly resent turning the Holy Land over to the absolute control of the race credited with the death of Christ.[28]

Whether Lansing's opposition modified Wilson's position is difficult to determine. In his famous Fourteen Points speech to Congress on January 8, 1918, the President made no direct reference to Palestine, but in the twelfth point he assured the Turkish parts of Turkey their secure sovereignty, and said that the other nationalities under Turkish rule should be offered "an absolutely unmolested opportunity of autonomous development." Although this was interpreted by many Jews as signifying the President's sympathetic attitude toward Zionism, it fell short of being a clear public endorsement of the Balfour Declaration and Zionist aims.

The Balfour Declaration gave great impetus to the Zionist forces in America. Even the staunchly socialist newspaper *Forward,* which had been put on the Post Office's list of subversive periodicals because of its intransigent pacifism, gave its tacit support to the Zionist cause. The Zionist press hailed the Balfour Declaration as the Magna Charta of the Jews.[29]

The President continued to support Zionism although he delayed making a specific public statement expressing his position. On February 27 the Zionists wrote Lansing requesting passports for representatives of the Provisional Executive Committee to accompany the Weizmann Commission being sent to Palestine under sanction of the British. They also asked recognition from the State Department for an American Zionist Medical Unit, which would proceed to Palestine to give assistance to the population there. Lansing opposed

[28] *Foreign Relations of the United States: Lansing Papers,* II, 71.
[29] Rappaport, "Jewish Immigrants and World War I," 330, 342.

the requests, but appeals by Rabbi Wise to Wilson and House led to approval by the State Department within a month.[30]

In February, 1918, two young Zionist refugees from Turkey, David Ben-Gurion and Isaac Ben Zvi, who were to become the first Prime Minister and second President of the State of Israel, but who were then agitating in America for Zionism, sent word to London that permission had been secured to begin recruiting for the Jewish Legion to fight in Palestine. Although only Jews who were not naturalized could be recruited, over two thousand volunteers from America arrived in Palestine in July-December, 1918, to join the last push against the Turks in Syria.[31]

In the summer of 1918, as the war drew toward its end, the Zionists in America were in the last stages of the preparations, which had been going on for two years, for the December meeting of the American Jewish Congress in Philadelphia. They wanted the President's public commitment to their policies as a ratification of their legitimacy and leadership, and for its value at the peace conference. Having hesitated for almost a year to give his indisputable public sanction to Zionism, Wilson finally rejected Lansing's views and on August 27 was persuaded by Rabbi Wise to make a pronouncement. Wise had made an appointment ostensibly to see the President about the Russian situation. He decided (after discussion with Brandeis) to take the opportunity to press Wilson to speak out on Zionism. Wilson greeted Wise heartily and Wise began the conversation by telling him of the wide support and confidence the President enjoyed in the country. Wise submitted the draft of a letter he and Brandeis had prepared for Wilson, and the President, after

[30] *Lansing Papers*, II, 107-109, and the House Diary, XIII (March 8, 1918), 87.

[31] Vladmir Jabotinsky, *The Story of the Jewish Legion* (1945), 109.

revising a few words, sent him the following text for release on August 31, 1918, the eve of the Jewish New Year:

> I have watched with deep and sincere interest the reconstructive work which the Weizmann Commission has done in Palestine at the instance of the British Government, and I welcome an opportunity to express the satisfaction I have felt in the progress of the Zionist Movement in the United States and in the Allied countries since the Declaration by Mr. Balfour on behalf of the British Government of Great Britain's approval of the establishment in Palestine of a National Home for the Jewish people, and his promise that the British Government would use its best endeavors to facilitate the achievement of that object, with the understanding that nothing would be done to prejudice the civil and religious rights of non-Jewish people in Palestine or the rights and political status enjoyed by Jews in other countries.
>
> I think that all Americans will be deeply moved by the report that even in this time of stress, the Weizmann Commission has been able to lay the foundation of the Hebrew University at Jerusalem with the promise that that bears of spiritual rebirth.[32]

Wilson committed himself carefully and deliberately to the Zionist cause, even though the United States had never gone to war with Turkey. But the war was nearing its conclusion, and the Turks were hardly in any position to do much damage to American interests. The congressional elections of 1918 were approaching, and support for Zionism at this time would maximize the political returns of such an action. There is no evidence, however, that Wilson calcu-

[32] See the memorandum already cited in the Wise Papers. The original draft of the letter with Wilson's handwritten corrections is in the Wilson Papers, Library of Congress, File VI, no. 618.

lated the possible electoral advantage before issuing the letter. The Zionists had thus gained public adherence from the United States as well as the Allies. All that remained was to join with the European Zionists at the peace conference to see that the statesmen of the world kept their promises.

A little over a month after the armistice, representatives of most of the Jewish national organizations in America met in Philadelphia to form a solid front for their demands at the peace conference. This meeting, the long-awaited American Jewish Congress, pledged its representatives to work for minority rights in European countries as well as to support the Zionist aim. The Congress appointed a Zionist-dominated delegation to go to Paris but also included the anti-Zionist leader, Marshall. Judge Mack, Rabbi Wise, and Frankfurter were among the Zionists who went to Paris; Justice Brandeis stayed in America, directing the delegation from afar until June, 1919, when he too appeared briefly in Paris.

Colonel House preceded President Wilson to Europe in the fall of 1918 to lay the groundwork for the peace conference. A memorandum prepared by Frank Cobb and Walter Lippmann, two of his advisers, served as the official American commentary on each of the Fourteen Points. On the twelfth point, concerning the Turkish Empire, it commented, "Britain is clearly the best mandatory for Palestine." When Wilson received the memorandum from House on October 29, 1918, he replied by cable that the commentary was "a satisfactory interpretation of the principles involved."[33]

Christian missionary interests and Arabs, uniting with a few diehard anti-Zionist Jews, tried to upset Zionist plans at the Peace Conference, but their chances for success were

[33] See David Hunter Miller, *My Diary at the Peace Conference* (1924), II, 79; Charles Seymour, ed., *The Intimate Papers of Colonel House* (1928), IV, 153.

never great. There is no doubt that President Wilson was prepared to violate his cherished principle of selfdetermination to exclude Palestine from the application of its majority rule yardstick. Wilson apparently never perceived the contradiction between selfdetermination in Palestine and Zionist claims to the area. In an "Outline of the Tentative Report and Recommendations" prepared by the group of experts called the Inquiry, the American position which had been maturing through 1918 was presented to the President and his plenipotentiaries. The recommendations, which Wilson accepted in January, 1919, as the basis for negotiations, were, in the sections relevant to Palestine, the fulfillment of Zionist dreams.

The Inquiry's thinking on Palestine was influenced by the current of support for Zionism by the public and among statesmen and experts. Four main points were made in the report. First, an independent state in Palestine should be established, its separation from Syria being justified on the grounds of "the religious experience of mankind." Second, this state should be placed under Great Britain as a mandatory of the League, because British administration would bring the necessary experience, wisdom, and stability to a traditionally fanatical area. Third, the Jews should be invited to return to Palestine and settle there, being assured by the conference that the policy of the League of Nations would be to recognize Palestine as a Jewish state as soon as it was one in fact. Recognizing that the Jews were in so great a minority, the report again urged a mandate, and offered as a reason for favoring Zionism the Jewish "right" to it as the cradle of their race. Finally, the Inquiry recommended that the holy places be protected by the League.[34]

The report is significant because, although the Zionist cause at the Peace Conference was to be threatened from

[34] Miller Diary, IV, 263-64. Miller gives the text of this report.

March through the summer of 1919, the final result was close to what the American intelligence section, the Inquiry, advocated in January.

January and February, 1919, were halcyon months for the American Zionists in Paris. The Arabs were friendly because they hoped to benefit from what they thought was the extensive influence of the Zionists at the Peace Conference, and the American government's pro-Zionist policy seemed settled. The American Zionists' plans for Palestine, the socalled Pittsburgh Program developed under the influence of Brandeis, emphasized an economy based on public ownership and control that was displeasing to the conservative European, and especially the bourgeois Russian, leaders of Zionism. The conflict that would force Brandeis from leadership in the summer of 1921, although it was only faintly stirring in the early months of 1919, is evidenced by the fact that the American Zionists, who undoubtedly had closer access to the statesmen of their country than Zionists anywhere in the world at that time, were not represented in the delegation that presented the Zionist program to the Peace Conference on February 27.

When the Zionists appeared before the Council of Ten, they made clear that the essence of their demands was a prerogative position in Palestine for the Jews.[35] Sokolow spoke on behalf of the Jewish community in Palestine. Weizmann spoke for world Jewry. Zionist proposals, Weizmann argued, were practical. His thesis was that there was room for another four or five million people in Palestine. To facilitate the Zionist program Weizmann urged that a mandatory power promote Jewish immigration and close land settlement, accept the cooperation of a Jewish council in charge of education, and give the council priority in any concessions for the development of the country.

[35] See *Foreign Relations of the United States: Peace Conference*, IV, 161-70, for the transcript of the Zionist appearance at the Council.

The quarrels between Lloyd George and Clemenceau over the interpretation and modification of the secret agreements made during the war concerning the division of the Turkish spoils, which took place in Wilson's presence, prompted him to give serious thought to the possibility of sending a commission to the area to investigate actual conditions and the wishes of the peoples whose lands were being cut up on the map. Although Wilson thought that justice might be done the Syrians if their attitudes were surveyed by an impartial commission, he left Paris, for a month in America, without making a decision. He did, however, instruct the American delegation in their discussions to ignore the secret agreements unless, by chance, they happened to contain provisions in accord with the Wilsonian principles.

Wilson had given little inkling of his consideration of an investigating commission, and while he was in America the Zionists in Paris proceeded with their plans. Frankfurter, who was Brandeis' intermediary in Paris, wrote and rewrote drafts of the proposed mandate for Palestine, integrating in his texts the Balfour Declaration and the suggestions of the Zionists to the Council of Ten.[36] On March 2, back in America, Wilson made Frankfurter's efforts seem modest when he issued a statement exceeding the scope of the Balfour Declaration's mild proposal of a "homeland for the Jews in Palestine." To Judge Mack, Zionist president of the American Jewish Congress, Wilson affirmed the support of the government and people of the United States for a Jewish commonwealth in Palestine.[37]

Returned to Paris, Wilson again confronted the struggle

[36] The Miller Diary, II, 369-75, contains Frankfurter's draft and memorandum submitted to the American delegation. See also Phillips, *Felix Frankfurter*, 154-64.

[37] Frank Manuel, *Realities of American-Palestine Relations* (1949), 233-34. He says Wilson was "casual" in making the statement.

between England and France over the Turkish booty. On March 20, he abruptly halted the wrangling with the announcement that the United States was not bound by any of the secret agreements negotiated during the war, and that he thought them an improper method for settling such questions. The only "scientific basis possible for a settlement," he said, was an interallied commission sent to determine the desires of the people in the area.[38] The Jewish commonwealth of two weeks earlier was evidently forgotten, for it should have been obvious to him that a canvass of the populations in the Near East would not find a majority favoring Zionism. Within a few days Henry C. King, the president of Oberlin College, who had been doing religious work with the American Expeditionary Force in France, and Charles R. Crane, a millionaire dabbler in progressive politics, world traveler, financial supporter of Wilson's electoral campaigns, and amateur orientalist, had been chosen to head the American section of the investigating commission.

The Zionists viewed the commission with great apprehension as a threat to their hard-won position of favor in the eyes of the statesmen gathered at Paris. King was friendly with the missionary Protestants who opposed Zionism, and Crane, who had once been close to Brandeis, was a sympathizer of the Arabs, whose Prince Feisal had become disaffected with Zionist and British promises. In great anxiety, Frankfurter wrote President Wilson on May 8 imploring him not to send the commission, which had been busying itself in Paris for a month studying the Near Eastern situation. Wilson's cool reply brought forth a despairing appeal from Frankfurter, which evidently moved Wilson deeply. Although the Council of Four authorized Wilson on May 15 to send King and Crane alone to the Near East, since neither

[38] *Peace Conference*, V, 1-14.

the British nor French would send representatives of their own, and on May 16 Wilson gave Frankfurter renewed assurance of his adherence to the Balfour Declaration, Wilson wrote that he had found no one seriously opposing it, and that there were no grounds for Zionist discouragement.[39] Brandeis was, of course, notified of the exchange of letters, as were the British. Wilson had effectively drawn the teeth of the King-Crane Commission, as far as Zionism was concerned, before it had even left Paris.

Justice Brandeis himself arrived in Paris in June on his way to an inspection tour of Palestine that would coincide with the King-Crane Commission's investigations. He consulted with Wilson, House, Balfour, members of the French cabinet, and the Italian ambassador.[40] His long conversation with Balfour on June 24 enabled him to elicit from the British statesman the promise that he would support Brandeis' ideas concerning the future of Palestine. Balfour asked Brandeis how Wilson would reconcile his adherence to Zionism with his doctrine of selfdetermination. Brandeis assured Balfour that Wilson would take the "dynamic" view, realizing that Zionism dealt with a "definite building up for the future . . . and not merely with the disposition of an existing community."[41]

Brandeis left Paris with the assurances he had come to seek. The King-Crane report's criticism of Zionism had been nullified in advance by the smoothly functioning Zionist organization. Although the King-Crane Commission went vigorously about its task all summer in the Near East, listened to representatives of hundreds of villages, and received over a thousand petitions, its report was not delivered to the White House until September 27, 1919, while

[39] *Documents on British Foreign Policy, 1919-1939, First Series* (1952), VI, 261-62.

[40] Mason, *Brandeis,* 456.

[41] *Documents on British Foreign Policy,* VI, 1276-78.

Wilson was on his illfated trip across the United States appealing for support of the League of Nations. It is doubtful whether he ever read it.[42]

The American Zionists were able to rouse the ailing Wilson significantly on their behalf once more before his term of office expired. Frankfurter's draft of the mandate was the basis of the negotiations in London between the Zionists and the British Foreign Office. Brandeis, stopping off in London on his way back to America in August, 1919, had amended the draft. By December 1, agreement was reached on the final form. Herbert Samuel, an English Zionist who was later appointed High Commissioner for Palestine, notified Frankfurter that negotiations would soon begin on the question of boundaries. The Zionists were satisfied with the British thinking on the northern boundaries, but the proposed southern boundary of Syria caused the French to balk.[43]

The American Zionists took the hint; Brandeis wrote Wilson, who was then confined to bed, and on February 10, 1920, Wilson sent a message to the British and French urging that Palestine should have rational boundaries and supporting the Zionist view. Then, getting in a dig at an old annoyance, he expressed his hope that the French and British governments were not carrying out the secret agreements to the detriment of the Balfour Declaration.[44] It appears, however, that John W. Davis, the American ambassador in London, delivered the President's views with less than enthusiasm.[45] In May at San Remo, the British received

[42] *Peace Conference*, XII, 751-863; Harry N. Howard, "An American Experiment in Peace Making: The King-Crane Commission," *Moslem World*, XXXII (1942).

[43] *Documents on British Foreign Policy*, VI, 428, 571, 605.

[44] *Ibid.*, 634.

[45] John W. Davis to Frank L. Polk (then Acting Secretary of State), March 5, 1920, in the Polk Papers, House Collection, Sterling Library, Yale University.

the Palestine mandate with a compromise border. Wilson's role in Palestinian affairs was over.

One major focus of Jewish activity at the Peace Conference has been slighted in this account. The Jewish-Americans devoted at least as much energy to the problem of securing the minority rights of Jews in the treaties with East European countries as to the Palestine problem. Complex negotiations among the Jews led to a consensus on what was desirable. Then, working primarily through the United States delegation, and with the encouragement of President Wilson, they succeeded in having minority rights clauses written into the treaties. All Jewish activities at the Peace Conference in this matter were coordinated by the Committee of Jewish Delegations under the leadership, in the critical months of March through June, 1919, of two Americans, the Zionist Judge Mack and the anti-Zionist Marshall. The disparate elements of world Jewry worked well together, since they were in agreement that the Jews in Europe should be given specific minority rights. Treaties or provisions for minority rights were included in the settlements with Poland, Czechoslovakia, Rumania, Yugoslavia, Greece, Austria, Hungary, Bulgaria, and Turkey. To many, these treaties seemed of infinitely greater significance than the activities of the Zionists relating to Palestine, because half the world's Jews lived in these areas. Jewish leaders at Paris felt that the minorities treaties had "at last absolved the Jews of Eastern Europe from the serious disabilities from which they have so long suffered and will forever end the grave abuses of the past. They will enable the Jews as well as all other minorities to live their own lives and develop their own culture."[46] If ever agreements turned out to be mere scraps of paper, however, it was these minorities treaties. The abuses

[46] Oscar I. Janowsky, *The Jews and Minority Rights (1898-1919)* (1933), 389. This is still the standard work on the subject.

they were designed to end were transcended in enormity by the mass slaughter of the Jews, less than twenty-five years later.

This analysis of the growth and development of the Zionist movement in America during President Wilson's administration has attempted to demonstrate how the Zionists utilized their organizational skill and personal access to top governmental leaders to achieve their policy objectives. Of all the immigrant ethnic groups in America, the Jews were probably the most staunch supporters of the Versailles settlement. Both Zionist and non-Zionist Jews saw in the peace designed by Wilson the fulfillment of their most deeply felt political desires: minority rights for Jews in Europe and the opportunity to rebuild Palestine. The struggles, sacrifices, and sufferings of the war years had not been in vain, or so it then appeared. No adherents of Wilson in the struggle to ratify the League of Nations in 1919 and 1920 were more loyal than the Jews. Wilson's consistent support of Jewish interests was widely publicized, and Jewish leaders, both Zionist and non-Zionist, urged the value of the League on their brethren and the general public. But the League failed of passage, and the settlements of 1919, which seemed so worthy of the exertions that had preceded them, soon lost their attractiveness to the Jews. Antisemitism grew stronger than ever in Europe. Arab hostility, British indifference, and Jewish apathy retarded the development of Palestine. The Brandeis-Wise-Frankfurter group was forced out of the leadership of American Zionism, and a period of disunity, drift, and disorganization ensued in the American Jewish community which ended only in the face of even graver crises in the 1930s.

INDEX

322 INDEX